W9-AKB-610

WANG HUI is a Professor of Chinese Language and Literature at Tsinghua University in Beijing and the former editor of *Dushu*, China's most influential literary journal. He participated in the Tiananmen protest of 1989 and is the author of *The Rise of Modern Chinese Thought*.

THE END OF THE REVOLUTION

China and the Limits of Modernity

WANG HUI

VERSO

London • New York

First published by Verso 2009
This paperback edition first published by Verso 2011
The collection © Verso 2011
Translation © the translators 2009

All rights reserved

The moral rights of the author have been asserted

1 3 5 7 9 10 8 6 4 2

Verso
UK: 6 Meard Street, London W1F 0EG
US: 20 Jay Street, Suite 1010, Brooklyn, NY 11201
www.versobooks.com

Verso is the imprint of New Left Books

ISBN-13: 978-1-84467-379-7

British Library Cataloguing in Publication Data
A catalogue record for this book is available from the British Library

Library of Congress Cataloging-in-Publication Data
A catalog record for this book is available from the Library of Congress

Typeset in Fournier by Hewer Text UK Ltd, Edinburgh
Printed in the US by Maple Vail

Contents

Foreword to the English Edition by Rebecca Karl

In the mid 1990s, a book entitled *Gaobie Geming* (*Farewell to Revolution*) was published in Hong Kong. It was received in China with great acclaim. Written by a well-known philosopher, Li Zehou, and a famous literary critic, Liu Zaifu, the farewell to which the book's title points represents a deliberate turn away from the revolutionary twentieth century towards an indefinite but, to them, more promising new horizon.[1] Yet the book was not merely the announcement of a personal turn. Rather, it explicitly called for the abandonment of revolutionary understandings of history and philosophy in favor of an alternative and less radical critical approach to the historico-philosophical problems of modern China. A condemnation of twentieth-century Chinese intellectual and political history for its supposed fetishizing of revolutionary solutions to crises, the book quickly became a standard-bearer in the intellectual and political world in China and in Chinese Studies circles globally for its call to completely de-radicalize thought, practice and political-social ambition. In this sense, *Farewell to Revolution* both summed up an ongoing trend and gave sanction to its further entrenchment and development in the intellectual and political worlds of China's 1990s. It was a book of the *zeitgeist*.

Wang Hui's *End of the Revolution* is an entirely different type of critical consideration. Instead of a willful call to abandon revolution—after all, revolution was a central aspect of China's and the global modern experience—Wang's collection of essays and interviews presents a sober and yet impassioned historical accounting for China's 1980s and beyond, as seen from the vantage of its many twentieth-century revolutionary encounters and experiences. In this perspective, the contemporary era does indeed mark the end to what French philosopher Alain Badiou calls the twentieth century's historical sequence, as this was a sequence dominated, shaped and irrevocably characterized in China by the problem and practice of revolution. Wang Hui identifies the end of this historical sequence not as an end to history, nor as a willed ideological farewell, and nor even as the end to the relevance of revolutionary politics altogether, but rather as the end of the possibility for twentieth-century solutions to contemporary problems. It is to *this* type of ending (and the new beginning heralded by such an end) that the opening lines of the second essay in the book refer: "One could almost say that the twentieth century was summed up a little early, in 1989, even as history since then has proceeded apace."[2]

The difference between the farewell of the first type and Wang's consideration turns on the different interpretive weights given to revolution as a historical form of social politics in the context of a global economy. For Wang Hui, revolution is and was intimately intertwined with the century-long debate and struggle in China and globally over the relationship between modernization and democracy. That is, if we understand modernization and democracy as two important poles of political and intellectual struggle of the twentieth century, revolutionary politics can be seen as the solution chosen in China's twentieth century to help resolve the contradiction between them. In this understanding, Wang Hui's intellectual and academic approach is deeply embedded in the historical problem presented to and in China by the arrival in the late nineteenth century of the most undemocratic form of global modernizationism: the form known as capitalist-imperialism. This is the problem that Wang Hui names modernity. It is from this historical premise that his analysis of the contemporary moment begins. In this sense, according to Wang, from the late nineteenth century onwards, the multiple Chinese debates about China in the world were inextricably connected to global debates about economic development and socio-political forms, including prominently the debates over socialism as a form of anti-capitalist modernity and democracy. Indeed, these are debates that underpin the core content of modern global and Chinese intellectual and political explorations over the past century.

However, the past two decades—from the post-1989 era through to the recent celebration of the sixtieth anniversary of the Chinese Communist Party's accession to power (October 1, 2009)—has seen the absolute triumph of modernization—now defined exclusively as economic developmentalism—over democracy, understood as a potentially broad social politics. The historical struggle between them appears to have been abandoned, and along with it the attempt to think and practice politics as a form of broad social democracy. This is what Wang despairingly calls the "depoliticization of politics." Indeed, for Wang's critics in China and elsewhere, revolution is and always has been about mob rule—or uncontrolled radical social and political excess—a form of "politics" leading to extended periods during which both modernization and social order suffered. According to these critics, then, it is best to abandon aspirations towards broad social democracy, to tame the mob through consumerist modernization (economic developmentalism) and nationalist patriotism, the two poles of social participation now identified as the only possible forms of mass political practice.

Broadly speaking, this narrowing of political and imaginative horizons is the target of much of Wang Hui's work, as seen in this collection of essays and interviews. Yet Wang's is no nostalgia for revolution—far from it. Nevertheless, as the pieces collected here make clear, Wang insists on engaging with the failed potential of revolution as a democratic form that transcends and is more substantive than the market and its neoliberal nostrums calling for individual responsibility. He is unwilling to give up on the prospects of democracy by handing its discourse and practice over to the uneven and unequal workings of the contemporary Chinese market-state-intellectual complex.

The combination of sober critical assessment of the present and the continuing hope for a more democratic future lends Wang's work— here and elsewhere—potent force and a lightning-rod quality for his intellectual and political opponents in China. For, mild-mannered and fair-tongued as Wang Hui is as an individual, and as full of honesty and integrity as he is in his intellectual and personal practice, his insistence that history matters and that the problem of modernity *is* the problem of mass democracy (in its many potential forms) and not merely of economic development seems to irk his critics in unusual ways. The sharpness of the attacks on him reflect the felt threat he poses to the desired hegemony of the market-state-intellectual complex, which would rather dehistoricize the present by erasing the possibilities presented in the past, and thereby pretend that the present and future offer only one solution: *their* solution. Wang Hui's conviction, that a "pressing issue of our time is ... how to link a critical internationalism to political struggles within the nation-state framework,"[3] strikes these many creators and conservators of the contemporary Chinese and global order as a rabble-rousing call to the mob to overthrow the hard-won system of privilege and profit established since the early 1990s in China. It is against such a position that Wang Hui, in his public as well as in his denser academic writings, struggles to find an historical ground of logic and analysis that could point to a more socially democratic way forward.

This collection, ranging over a number of topics and a decade or more of intellectual output, represents well Wang's multisided and impassioned engagement with the contemporary world. Translated by a number of scholars in the academy (including myself), these essays can provide for many in the English-speaking world—including students, concerned global citizens, and others—a vantage on China rarely seen in journalism or much technical academic work. These essays are accessible and serious-minded critical inquiries into the problems of the present; their hard-headedness will satisfy the desires of any concerned historian or engaged social commentator. For Wang Hui proves himself to be both.

Rebecca E. Karl
New York City
October 8, 2009

Preface to the Chinese Edition

The way ahead is so long and far, yet I will search far and wide.

Qu Yuan

The era of the 1990s continues on, born through the global transformations that began in the period from 1989 to 1991 and extending beyond the usual markers with which we keep time. In my own terminology, "the Nineties" doesn't overlap completely with the Nineties: the former denotes a course of events that progressed from the late 1980s into the present, and is characterized by the forging of the market era and the complex and significant changes that occurred as a result; the latter denotes merely a fixed period of time. As for the vicissitudes of thought, it was only in the mid Nineties that Chinese scholars recovered from the previous shock and shifted their thinking from considerations of the past to the unfamiliar age that constitutes our present. Having emerged prematurely from the upheaval of 1989, they were forced to think through the violent social reorganization. Perhaps the ending will look just like the endings to countless other eras, and for this the ending to "the Nineties" would require an event to decisively mark its close. But it is also possible that no strict division will separate this prefatory stage from the main narrative to come. Its symbol will then be its ambiguous continuity.

My basic view is that "the Eighties" were the final act of a revolutionary century, an era formally launched by socialism's self-reform and whose inspiration actually stemmed from those past eras it had criticized (all the trademark theoretical issues of the Eighties—practice as the sole criterion for discerning truth, the law of value, consumer economies, humanism, and the problem of difference—emerged from the history of socialism through the Fifties, Sixties and Seventies). "The Nineties" were actually the opening act to the end of a revolutionary century, from which would emerge a new play of events. The meanings behind the economy, politics, culture, and even the military were fundamentally changed during this period, so that without redefining them and the familiar categories of "political parties," "the nation," and "the people," there can be no way to analyze this era. Thus, although there are countless different connections between the two epochs, the latter period is in no way the natural extension of the former. During "the Nineties," the forceful confrontation between the different schools of thought and neoliberalism constituted an important intellectual event. The rise of the New Left, the vicissitudes of postmodernism, the spread of conservatism, the ebb and flow of nationalism, and the popularity of liberalism were all fraught with ambiguous tendencies so that, without placing them and reading them in terms of the rise, fall and transformation of neoliberal globalization, we cannot possibly clarify their true directions. By examining the intellectual confrontations and the media scuffles, we not only discover a whole series of concrete social, legal, political and cultural issues that reveal themselves in the form of public debate. We also discover that all the disputes regarding contemporary issues inevitably involved reevaluations of the historical traditions of twentieth-century China. The other striking symbols of "the Nineties" are the profound crises experienced by value systems and past perspectives on history, not to mention the values of the revolutionary era and of socialist history, which were of little concern in the aforementioned theses of the Eighties. When we inquire into the meaning of "the Nineties," we cannot help but wonder whether the "twentieth century" was simply a part of the "long nineteenth century," or whether its revolutions ushered in expediently the spirit of the twenty-first century.

The overlap between the birth of "the Nineties" and the disintegration of the twentieth century looks even stranger since "the Nineties" appears to have stronger affinities with the "long nineteenth century" than with the "twentieth century." The latter seems much more remote. On the one hand, the "twentieth century" was marked by rapid economic growth, great technological strides, the deepening of the globalization process, the rapid rise of China's status within the global economy, and the crisis of American hegemony that revealed itself more with each day. At the same time, it was also characterized by imperialist wars, military containment strategies and "counter-terrorist" military alliances; the widespread crisis faced by farmers, farming villages and agriculture; and the disintegration of the traditional working class, accompanied by the formation of a new working class (with peasant labor as its main component). During this period of monumental change, we witnessed how market society converted its professors, doctors, lawyers, poets, scholars, artists, and journalists into "wage-laborers" (to use Marx's words). We saw how the various social elements that socialism had sought in practice to constrain finally broke free to become the foundation for the new order. As the curtain closed on the twentieth century, those characteristic social relations that constituted the nineteenth century reappeared on stage, as if the shocks and the transformations of the revolutionary epoch had never occurred. On this reading, "the Nineties" is less an "end to history" than "history beginning again."

History (particularly in the nineteenth-century sense of the word) continues in the form of repetition; yet repetitions are nonetheless always clearly different. That the end of the Cold War overlaps with the end of the revolution signifies that this era is not simply the extension of the nineteenth century, straddled across time. Yet it also means that we cannot simply transfer and apply the political models of the twentieth century to solve the problems we now face. The monumental transformations of the nineteenth century bred internal enemies for the capitalist age—such as the proletariat and the new socialist movements—and finally developed into a system that was fundamentally a socialist party-state system in form, one fully external to Western capitalism. Yet the fall of these systems exterior to capitalism was adopted as the symbol of the huge transformations that occurred at the end of the twentieth century, including not only the disintegration of socialist systems but also the large-scale decline of class struggles, national struggles, and party politics that constituted traditional politics. In exploring this new state of affairs, a series of symbolic theses began to appear within the sphere of Chinese thought—such as marketization, globalization, nationalism, the "clash of civilizations," "humanism," post-colonialism, system innovation (*zhidu chuangxing*), state capacity (*guojia nengli*), urbanization, and peasant labor; neoclassical liberalism or neoliberalism, financial crisis, the crisis in the management of agriculture, peasants and rural community (*sannong*, or the Three Rural Issues), health-care system crisis, housing system crisis, and labor rights crisis; postmodernism, cultural conservatism, a rethinking of modernity, humanistic education, university reform, and so on. Even if we can find traces of these theses in the scholarly research and cultural discussions of "the Eighties," the topics, methods, fields of vision and scope of "the Nineties" will already be clearly separated from the former period. To clarify the distinct characteristics of this era, we must at least provide answers to the following questions: Why does the end of the Cold War overlap with the end of the revolution? Why were "the Nineties" not the end of the "short twentieth century," but rather an extension of the "long nineteenth century"?

All the essays collected in this volume were written during "the Nineties," ranging in publication date from 1994 to 2007. The publication of each essay incited different scales and levels of discussion, though I have never had the chance to formulate systematic responses to any of them. In order to grasp better this period of upheaval, I had to pursue several different paths simultaneously, both tracking short-term leads and making long-term observations, reflecting on what had happened at a theoretical level as well as becoming concretely involved. My explorations are far from complete; yet, in editing this anthology of texts written in a different time and responding to a different set of questions, I accidentally discovered intrinsic connections and continuities between the essays—connections that were more significant than I had ever expected. Perhaps the publication of this collection will help me to achieve a better understanding of the rolling continuities that exist between the various arguments contained in the essays, and to explain more effectively how the problems I elaborated during this period are all mutually interrelated (such as anti-modern modernity, the historical roots of neoliberalism, depoliticized politics, and so on).

Today, the journey of "the Nineties" is reaching its end, soon to become a distant memory. There are various ways of exploring the thought of one's own time—yet, to select one method is also to give up many others. The period of time in which I wrote these essays overlapped with that in which I was editing the journal *Xueren* ("The Scholar") and, more importantly, *Dushu*, and to this day the people, stories, cataclysms, and landscapes that were part of my life are still very clear in my mind. But even in this short span of ten years, there have been many goodbyes and departures, along with many moments of missing and forgetting.

"The Nineties" still appears to me now as a period of great ambiguity, one whose journey and whose logic we can only hope to understand from the positions of both history and present-day realities, as well as both theory and practice. Only in this way might we truly grasp its shifting sentiments and its transforming values. With the completion of *The Rise of Modern Chinese Thought*, my research interests shifted once more toward the "short twentieth century," with both my new focus and the shift itself constituting an extension of my last research project. I like to think of my new projects as having been propelled by the questions posed in this collection.

HQY Residence, Tsinghua University
March 11, 2008

Preface to the English Edition

Perry Anderson passed through Hong Kong as it was returning to China in 1997. At the time, I happened to be a visiting fellow at the Chinese University of Hong Kong and had the opportunity to converse with him about various issues regarding China and the contemporary world. His erudition, insight, boundless curiosity and endless discussions were an immense encouragement for me to explore the question of the modern (*dangdai*). About three years ago, Perry suggested that I edit a collection to be published by Verso. This book before you is the result.

Each of the chapters was written in the 1990s, which is a different time from today. The People's Republic of China had its sixtieth anniversary on the eve of this book's publication. At around the same time, Perry came to Beijing once more, and the question he asked when we met this time was: how can we explain China's growth? Most Left intellectuals maintain a critical view toward growth. Professor Hui Pokeung and I coedited an anthology entitled *Fazhan de Huanxiang* (*Illusions of Development*) that was published in 1999, which was just such a critique of the rising trends of neoliberalism and developmentalism. But even critical intellectuals must confront the question of China's unprecedented economic growth. Only by simultaneously presenting an analysis of growth that differs from the neoliberal one can their critiques be truly persuasive. China's economic development has broken many predictions—a seemingly endless string of theories that China would collapse began to appear after 1989, but then it wasn't China that collapsed but those theories themselves. In the discussions surrounding the sixtieth anniversary of the People's Republic and the founding of the nation, the universal issue of concern among Chinese intellectuals was how to view the road China has taken over the past sixty years. Given the continuing urgency of this question, I wish to briefly highlight several of these views below.

Self-reliance (duli zizhu) and its political connotations

In discussing the Chinese model, many scholars are in the habit of comparing China's development to the disintegration of the Soviet and Eastern European system, emphasizing China's stability while forgetting conveniently that the general crisis that broke out in 1989 began in China. Its traces can still be found in different spheres in China today. Like the recent financial crisis, what happened in 1989 was part of a larger global phenomenon, but although it also occurred in the context of an economic crisis it appeared to be political in form. Why did China not collapse along with the other Communist Party–led countries in the Soviet Union and Eastern Europe? What factors helped to maintain China's stability and created the conditions for rapid growth? Having undergone thirty years of reform, how have these conditions now been transformed? This is the first question to which we must respond.

The collapse of the Soviet and Eastern European system involved many deep and complex historical factors, including the conflict between the bureaucratic system and the people, Cold War political absolutism and the mass poverty brought on by shortage economies. By comparison, a more widespread consciousness of self-renewal existed within the Chinese system. Under the Cultural Revolution, middle- and senior-level bureaucrats in the Party and state were sent by Mao Zedong to work and live in factories, farms and within other basic units of society. When they returned to positions of authority in the late 1970s, an unexpected consequence was that the state was better able to respond to the needs of the lower strata of society, which was a significant difference from the rigid bureaucratic systems of the Soviet and Eastern European countries. Space limitations do not permit me to elaborate on these issues and the stories surrounding them in greater detail, only to concentrate on the distinguishing characteristic that sets the Chinese system apart from the Soviet system—namely, its independent search for its own path of social development, and the unique sovereign status it achieved as a result.

In his memoirs, the last general secretary of Eastern Germany's former Communist Party, Egon Krenz, explained the reasons for the collapse of his entire country after 1989. He mentioned many aspects, but the most important of these was the transition that had occurred in the Soviet Union and the transformations this produced within the Soviet–Eastern European bloc. During the Cold War, Western politicians often referred to the Brezhnev Doctrine as a way of ridiculing the Eastern European countries for their condition of "incomplete sovereignty." Under the Warsaw Pact system, Eastern European countries were not completely sovereign and were limited by Soviet control, so that once problems began to appear in the Soviet Union, the entire Soviet–Eastern European system collapsed as a result. After World War II, the system of sovereign nation-states was established formally, but from a global perspective, very few countries actually achieved real independence and autonomy (*duli zizhu*). Which countries in the Soviet Union and Eastern Europe, or even among the Western European allies, were truly independent? In Asia, the positioning of Japan and Korea within the Cold War structure meant that their sovereignty was limited by US global strategy, and as a result they were incompletely sovereign countries as well. Both camps in the Cold War were systems of allied nations, so that transitions and policy changes in the hegemonic countries of each side profoundly affected all the other countries.

In the early years of its founding, China was part of the socialist camp within this polarized system, and during the war to resist US aggression and to aid Korea in the early 1950s, China entered into armed conflict with the US and its allies. In this era—particularly during the first Five-Year Plan—China's industrial development, post-war recovery and international standing were greatly aided by the efforts of the Soviet Union, making it dependent upon the Soviet Union in some ways and to some degree. But China began supporting non-aligned movements in the mid-1950s and later engaged in open debates with the Soviet Communist Party, gradually shedding its "suzerain" relationship with the Soviet Union in the spheres of politics, economics and the military, and establishing its own socialist system and achieving independent status on the international scene. Although the Taiwan Strait still represents a line of division, the Chinese state is now sovereign and self-reliant in its political character. The national economic and industrial systems that were constructed under this political climate are also highly self-reliant as a result. Absent this condition of self-reliance, it would be very difficult to picture how China's path of reform and opening up would have looked, and it would be very difficult to imagine what China's fate might have been after 1989. When the period of reform and opening up began, China already had a self-reliant national economic system, which laid out the conditions for reform. China's reform was self-directed and had an internal logic—it was an active and not a passive process, differing from the various and complex "color revolutions" of Eastern Europe and Central Asia. It also differed from the dependent economies of Latin America and their related crises, as well as the dependent development of Japan, Korea and Taiwan under the Cold War structure (i.e. their dependence upon the US-led regional political structure and war economies (Korean and Vietnam Wars) were the critical junctures in their early development). In this way, mainland China's development has followed an entirely different path.

China's relatively independent and complete level of sovereignty was achieved through Party practices, which was one of its most prominent characteristics in the twentieth century. Regardless of how many mistakes the Chinese Communist Party (CCP) committed in either theory or practice, its anti-imperialism and, later, its disputes with the Soviet Union provided important historical foundations for Chinese sovereignty and independence. Its open debates with the Soviet Communist Party helped the CCP to break its suzerain relation with its Soviet counterpart, and only once this occurred could the Chinese state extract itself from its corresponding suzerain relation with the Soviet Union, producing a new model of independence. In other words, the roots of China's sovereignty are political, and this political independence, which developed through party relations, came to be manifested in the state and economic spheres. In effect, China's sustained critique and struggle with the polarized Cold War structure was connected to its gradual disintegration. In the economic, political and cultural spheres, China's explorations and attempts at reforming the socialist path produced various deviations, problems and even tragic results, but in the fifties, sixties and seventies, the policies of the Chinese state and party were continuously being adjusted. These modifications were in essence self-modifications, carried out in response to the demands and problems of reality, rather than having been driven by external force or guidance. Because the Communist Party lacked democratic mechanisms, line struggles often turned into violent power struggles, but these factors should not conceal the historical importance of those factional and theoretical debates. From this perspective, it is necessary to rethink our conventional wisdom on reform, for instance that there are no ready-made models of reform or policies, making the notion of "crossing the river by feeling for the stones" correct. But in fact the lack of ready-made models has been a characteristic of the Chinese revolution as a whole. Without any basic value orientations, who knows where "crossing the river by feeling for the stones" will lead us? The theoretical origins of reform and the concept of a socialist commodity economy emerged through theoretical discussions on commodities, commodity economies, the law of value and bourgeois rights; they were also constituted through socialist practice. Discussions surrounding the problem of the law of value originated in China in the 1950s against the background of the Sino-Soviet split and Mao Zedong's analysis of contradictions in Chinese society. This problem became the central topic of inter-party debate once more in the mid-1970s. Absent such a theoretical debate, it would be extremely difficult to imagine how subsequent Chinese reform would follow a developmental logic from the law of value, the division of labor and a socialist commodity economy up to the present socialist market economy. From this perspective, the economic reforms begun in the late 1970s contained an intrinsic theoretical vein.

The role of the peasantry and its transformations

The Chinese revolution occurred within a traditional agricultural society in which the peasantry became the revolutionary subject. Whether in the early stages of revolution or war, or during the era of social reconstruction and reform, the sacrifices and contributions of the agricultural class were always significant, and their expressions of active spirit and creativity left a profound impression on people's minds. Through the entire twentieth century, the mobilization of China's rural society and the transformations of rural social organizations could be described as earth-shattering and wholly unprecedented. The agricultural class achieved a strong sense of political consciousness through the land revolution and a transition in the rural social order; in the Eastern European countries and even the Soviet Union, such prolonged armed struggle and agrarian revolutions were rarely seen. Absent such a background, it would have been impossible for the transformation of land relations to become the central aspect of a prolonged rural mobilization.

This is also a premise for understanding radical politics in China in the first half of the twentieth century. The CCP was established as a result of the international communist movement, but the central task of China's socialist party was to mobilize peasants and to construct a new politics and society through a rural movement. Through thirty years of armed revolt and social struggle, the party finally became the foundational core of the social movement and was a party of the rural and worker's movements in particular. Its grassroots nature and capacity for organization and mobilization set it far apart from the parties of the socialist Eastern European countries. China's observers tend overwhelmingly to attribute the successes and failures of the Chinese revolution to individual leading figures without discussing this process itself to its full extent. In the reflections on the Chinese revolution, the focus on its violence has also resulted in the neglect and even the denial of the new social subjectivities created through this process. In a socialist revolution carried out in a society where peasants are the primary subjects, the subjective initiatives and will of the leaders are certainly important, yet they alone are not the key to understanding its history.

The new land relations created through the Chinese revolution and their subsequent reconstruction created the conditions for China's reform, which was something Lenin had already recognized in his appraisal of Sun Yatsen. After the revolution in 1911, Lenin pointed out in his commentary on Sun Yatsen's *Jianguo Dawang* (*Program for Construction of the Republic*) that the agrarian program of the Chinese revolution and socialist-leaning national plan provided the preconditions for the development of agricultural capitalism. It is difficult to imagine how traditional farmers and their village organizations would have displayed such enthusiastic spirit of initiative if these social transformations had not occurred. On this point, we need only look at the situation of peasants in other farming societies and market conditions, including those in Asia—and particularly South Asia—or Latin America to see clearly how profound this was in China: these other societies have yet to initiate any significant land reforms, so that farmers remain largely bound in landlord or plantation economies and are unable to develop a strong consciousness of their own autonomy. The process of land reform has been closely connected to the popularization of village education, the rise in literacy, the capacity for self-organization and an increase in technical abilities.

Under conditions of market reform, these early inheritances became the preconditions for a more mature labor market in China.

Compared with many socialist and post-socialist countries, the value of equality in China may have taken root to a greater degree in the popular consciousness than in other societies. But under conditions of marketization and globalization, discussions concerning the equal standing of peasants and migrant workers today will nonetheless differ drastically in content from discussions concerning how the standing of farmers changed in the early twentieth century. At the end of the last century, the questions of agriculture, peasants and rural community (*sannong*) and of migrant workers became key topics in contemporary China once more, surrounded by the issues of how to resolve urban-rural relations under market conditions and how to resolve the land issue in China. The strong dependence of the rural economy upon the urban economy and the impacts it has felt as a result of urbanization have led peasants to migrate on mass scales, transforming them into a new urban working class. These peasants, who have experienced the process of rural land reform, are now being transformed into a cheap labor force in the coastal and urban industries. This process is closely related to the contemporary rural crisis. Most importantly, peasants as political subjects are currently undergoing a transformation into a free labor force, thanks to the definitions and categories of property rights.

The position of the state

Another key element to understanding China's period of reform is the explanation of the nature and evolution of the Chinese state. In *Adam Smith in Beijing*, Giovanni Arrighi writes: "National markets are no more a Western invention than national states and interstate systems ... through the eighteenth century by far the largest national market was to be found not in Europe but in China."[1] He even goes one step further to analyze the factors behind the development of the contemporary Chinese economy, looking in particular at its attraction for foreign investors. He writes: "Contrary to widespread belief, the main attraction of the PRC for foreign capital has not been its huge and low-priced reserves of labor as such ... The main attraction, we shall argue, has been the high quality of those reserves—in terms of health, education, and capacity for self-management—in combination with the rapid expansion of the supply and demand conditions."[2] Peking University economist Yao Yang offers a similar perspective in his overview of the conditions for China's economic development, identifying a neutral government or neutral state as the condition for the success of Chinese reform.

The question of national resources in reform is an important one. I have two supplementary points to make regarding Arrighi and Yao Yang's discussions. Arrighi, for one, establishes his narrative of the Chinese and Asian national markets within a long national tradition, but without the Chinese revolution or its reorganization of social relations, it would be difficult to imagine how the traditional "national market" would transform into a new national market on its own. Through national efforts during the late Qing to construct a military and commercial system, as well as the Agrarian Revolution that continued after the Xinhai Revolution (1911), a new form of internal-external relations was created that differed from that under the traditional national market. In discussing the state character of modern China, it is impossible to leave aside the transformations in land relations and rural identities that occurred as a result of the Chinese revolution. For instance, critiques are often carried out of the people's commune experiments, but very rarely do these discuss the fact that this experiment resulted from the continuous transformations in land relations in modern China. On the one hand, the small-scale peasant economy that takes the family household as its basic unit no longer exists, but on the other hand, household, family and geographical relations have been restructured under conditions of reform and through other means to fit within the new social configurations. Rural reform was a reform of the commune system, yet at the same time it was also built upon social relations that were transformed through these experiments. The initial period of rural reform was driven by the state and was a reform movement that had at its core the management and adjustment of agricultural prices through different methods. The grand development from the rural industries of the 1960s through to the rural enterprises of the 1990s has brought with it a vastly different context of political and economic management, but this sequence obviously cannot be explained using the logic of neoliberalism.

As for Yao Yang's perspective, the political preconditions behind the initiation of modern revolutions and socialist histories by neutral states were not neutral. Chinese socialism in practice strove to establish a state that would represent the masses and the universal interests of the overwhelming majority, and this led to a break between the state or government and special interests. At the level of theory, the state practice of socialism was a revision of early-Marxist class theory, with Mao Zedong's works, including *On the Ten Major Relationships* and *On the Correct Handling of Contradictions Among the People* providing the foundations for this new state theory. Because the main objective of the socialist state is to represent the interests of the overwhelming majority, under market conditions its connection to special interest groups is looser than under other state forms. But only in this way can we describe it as a "neutral" state. The success of the early years of reform can largely be attributed to this, and it was a source of legitimacy for reform, without which it would have been very difficult for members of the different social strata to believe that the state-led reforms represented their own interests. But the real meaning of "neutralization" is often concealed in the use of the term, which is that the universality of interests represented by the state was established upon Chinese revolution values and socialist practices. At least in the early years, the legitimacy of the reforms derived from the universality of interests represented by the socialist state.

But it is very difficult to determine China's state character if we only look at one of its standard points of origin, for the state itself contains different traditions. In the reform process, people often use the concepts of "reform" and "counter-reform," "progress" and "conservation" to describe the contradictions and struggles between these traditions, but from a dynamic historical perspective, the ways these traditions come into harmony with one another, check and balance one another, and contradict one another are also useful in significant ways. In the socialist era, we saw how the strength of the two or many social forces fluctuated in concert with one another, and how the "far left" and "far right" were overcome; but as marketization reforms become the predominant trend, the absence of checks and balances from socialist forces between the inner workings of the state, the inner workings of the party and the entire social sphere will quickly shorten the distance between the state and special interest groups. The social resources accumulated during the socialist era have been transformed under these relations to become limitations on socialist policy. The state's "neutrality" was achieved through non-neutral forces and the reciprocal relationship between the two.

Chinese reform has yielded many experiences worth overviewing, for instance the implementation of a talent strategy, education reform and other economic policies, but I think that the few elements listed above are the most fundamental and also the most frequently neglected. These points also represent some of twentieth-century China's most unique experiences.

Shifts in the sovereignty structure

Under the new conditions of globalization, localization and market-ization, the conditions mentioned above are being significantly challenged: the foundations of social relations, economic life and political subjectivities are undergoing change. If we are unable to grasp these new historical conditions and the direction of their change, it will be very difficult to construct structurally new and effective mechanisms and policies. To understand these transformations, I wish to point out some of the new tendencies in the contemporary world.

First, the traditional form of sovereignty is undergoing significant transformation under globalization. The current process of globalization appears to be moving primarily in two directions. The first is the transnational movement of capital and thereby transnational production, consumption and circulation; large-scale immigration and a market dependence that has arisen through trade and investment; and the globalization of various risks as well. The second is the creation of international regulatory mechanisms to manage and respond to this transnational movement of capital and to control risk. These include the WTO and the European Union, alongside other international and regional organizations. The former is something like an anarchical force, while the latter is a mechanism for harmonizing and controlling it. These two forces came into effect simultaneously.

The shape of national sovereignty will also inevitably change alongside these other important transformations. With the first trend just mentioned, and particularly after the late 1980s had passed, China gradually began to take on the form of an export-led economy. The transnationalization of production made China into the "industrial workshop of the world," and this configuration differed completely from the forms of labor force and resource deployment of the past, forging a new relationship between the coastal and inland areas, and between urban and rural regions as well. With the gradual liberalization of the financial system, China's foreign exchange reserves shot up to become the largest in the world, and its economic development became highly dependent upon international markets, and especially the American market. The concept of "Chimerica," which describes the symbiotic relationship between the Chinese and American economies, is perhaps a little exaggerated, but in light of the transformations of these relatively independent national economies into dependent economies of varying degrees, this concept also has very strong implications.

As for the second trend, China has joined the WTO and other international treaties and agreements and actively participates in other regional organizations, such that it is now difficult to describe China's structure of sovereignty in the traditional sense. The current financial crisis has shown that crises arise precisely from shifts in the autonomy of societies, so that a crisis elsewhere can quickly become China's own crisis, and these crises cannot be overcome simply by reasserting old ideals of sovereignty. International cooperation cannot be avoided. Thus, under conditions of globalization and the open global networks involved, the question of how to achieve new forms of autonomy must be asked with reference to history alongside new explorations of the situation.

Next, the role of the state is undergoing transformation not only within the realm of global relations but in domestic relations as well. Simple descriptions of the role of the Chinese state as "totalitarian" often confuse the positive with the negative aspects of the role of the state. China did not undergo "shock therapy" in its period of reform, as did Russia, but was significantly more skilled at economic regulation than the latter country. That the Chinese financial system has shown itself to be relatively stable is due to the fact that China has not entirely pursued the neoliberal path, and this is the product of conscious policy planning rather than the limitations imposed by social movements, social contradictions and the socialist tradition. Land has not been privatized in China (although it can be exchanged relatively freely to adapt to the demands of market conditions), which has not only been essential for China's low-cost rural social security system but also enables the state to utilize land resources for organization and development, and for increasing the possibility of undertaking land profit-sharing reforms. The large tax revenues from China's state-owned enterprises have also provided essential resources for the government's regulative capacity under crisis conditions. These aspects are certainly connected to state capacity and will. But the Chinese state should also step up on those spheres it is responsible for, such as resolving the rural crisis in a positive way, reconstructing the social security system, protecting the environment, increasing investment in education and initiating educational reform. The Chinese government will correspondingly be required to shift from a development-oriented government to a social services oriented one, which will also transform the Chinese economy from being reliant on exports to being led by domestic needs. The real issue is that this is not a question of will but of social forces and the games they play.

Whether these positive social policies can be implemented is not purely dependent on state will. After thirty years of reform, in which it has acted as the driving force behind marketization reforms, state apparatuses are now deeply embedded in market activities. The various state departments within the current state cannot appropriately be described using the concept of neutral states. The state is not isolated but rather interwoven within the social structure and relations of social interest. The present issue of corruption not only involves individual corrupted officials but also the question of the relationship between social policy, economic policy and special interests. The development of the hydrocarbon industry and energy projects, for instance, are often impeded or led by individual special interest groups. The influence of these special interest groups in the area of public policy has primarily limited public discussion, social protection movements and the different traditions emanating from the state and within the party. In the recent past, the large-scale discussions in the late 1990s on the *sannong* question resulted in the modification of state rural policy; the debates on the medical insurance system that were initiated in 2003 by the SARS crisis facilitated a change in the direction of health reform; the large-scale labor movement and the debates on the restructuring of state enterprises that began in 2005 led to the appearance of related policies; and calls from the people to do something about corruption and for strict party discipline provided internal strength for China's anti-corruption movement. But domestic and international special interest relations have now seeped into state mechanisms and even the process of legislation to an unprecedented degree. Under these conditions, the question of how the state can represent the so-called "universal interest" has already become extremely tenuous.

The paradox of the statification of the party

Discussions of the state are directly related to questions about the formation of democratic mechanisms. There is one basic paradox one must face, which is that, on the one hand, China's ability to govern effectively has been widely acknowledged in comparison with the governments of many other countries, from its disaster relief mobilization after the May 12 Wenchuan earthquake to its rapid response in initiating a bailout plan after the financial meltdown, and from its successful management of the Olympic Games to the efficacy of its various local governments in organizational development and controlling the crisis. But on the other hand, contradictions have appeared between officials and the people in certain areas, and have become sharp at certain times, with the administrative abilities and levels of honesty of different levels of government having come into question. The key issue is that such contradictions are often blown up into large-scale and widely debated legitimacy crises. By observing the situation in other countries, we can see that an institutional political crisis may not result even if the capacity of the state declines, the government accomplishes nothing, the economy is in recession and social policies remain unimplemented. This issue is closely connected with democracy as the source of political legitimacy.

In the 1980s, the democratic question was fairly simple. The wave of democratization had been building over twenty years, and on the one hand, democracy remained the most important source of political legitimacy. But on the other hand, the method of simply imitating Western democracy had lost the attraction it had possessed in Asia in the 1980s. In the wake of the crises in the emerging democracies and the fading of the "color revolutions" after 1989, the tendency toward democratization began to decline in Eastern Europe, Central Asia and other regions. At the same time, the formation of a democratic cavity in the democratic nations of Western society and in the Third World (for instance India) is creating a universal democratic crisis, one closely connected to the conditions of marketization and globalization. For one, the dominant forms of the post-war political democracies were multi-party or two-party parliamentary systems, but under market conditions, political parties are becoming less representative each day than they were in the early days of democracy. In the drive to attract votes, the political values of the parties are gradually becoming obscured, so that the representative system of democracy exists now in name only. Second, the connection between democracy and states is also being threatened under the condition of globalization: as economic relations gradually exceed the traditional categorizations of national economies, and as its related activities become difficult to balance within the confines of a single country, the political plans of any country are forced to adjust to the international system. Third, in some countries, the shift toward oligarchical forms and the consolidation of special interests in political parties has resulted in the gradual disconnection of democracy as a political structure from the basic units of society. The interests and needs of the lower strata find no expression within the political sphere. As a result, they resort to a self-defensive anarchy (i.e. the rise of Maoism in India). Fourth, the reliance of the election process on large amounts of money and financial resources has resulted in the existence of both legal and illegal forms of election fraud in many democratic countries, thus destroying public confidence in the election process. This is not to say that democratic values are dead. The real question is what kind of democracy do we need and what form should it take. How do we make democracy something more than an empty form, into something with substantive meaning?

The Chinese political system has also undergone significant transformations, including a change in the role of the party. In the 1980s, the primary goal of political reform was the separation of the party from the state, but after the 1990s, this grew out of favor as a popular slogan, so that the government and party intersected more frequently in concrete practice and institutional arrangements. I interpret this phenomenon to be part of the shift toward party stratification, and it is worth analyzing why this tendency arose. According to traditional political theories, the party represents the will of the people—through parliamentary struggles and debates, or through procedural democracy—to become state and public will, and even the expression of sovereignty. In China, the multiparty cooperation system, under which eight other democratic parties are led by the ruling Communist Party and are also involved in state affairs, is built upon multi-party representation. But under market society conditions, state apparatuses are directly involved in economic activity, and the various branches of the state become entangled with special interests. This infiltration of the state by the party is not a new phenomenon—the primary issue faced during Mao Zedong's time was not simply the bureaucratization of the state but also the bureaucratization of the party—but its intense permeation of the state under market society conditions is new. What was called the "neutral state" in the early years of reform is now undergoing a transformation. Because the party remains relatively disconnected from economic activity, it is able to express the will of society with relative independence and "neutrality." The weeding out of corruption, for instance, is largely reliant upon effective implementation by party mechanisms. After the 1990s, the will of the state was presented primarily through the goals and slogans of the party, including the "Three Represents," the "Harmonious Society" and the "Scientific Outlook on Development,"[3] but these were no longer direct and special expressions of the party but instead directly invoked the interests of the entire people. In this sense, the party has become the core of public sovereignty.

However, the statification of the party also involves a dual challenge. For one, if the division between the party and the state vanishes entirely, then what forces or mechanisms can prevent the party from becoming trapped within the relations of interest of market society, as the state has? Second, the universal representation of the traditional party (and the "neutrality" of the early socialist state) was built on its clear political values. The statification of the party will mean a weakening and transformation of the party's political values, so that if the achievement of a "neutral state" is closely connected to the political values of the party, then what apparatuses can enable China to maintain its broad representation of interests under these new conditions? What force can the party rely upon for self renewal, and how might the voices of the common people find expression in the public sphere? What is required to initiate change in the basic lines and policies of the state and party, through true freedom of speech, venues of negotiation and continuous interaction between officials and the people? How can we attract and consolidate international and domestic forces on a wide scale to achieve the most widespread democracy? These questions cannot be avoided in discussing the self-renewal of the party.

These are also questions we need to consider in thinking about China's political transformation, alongside the question of China's democratic road. Specifically, I think there are at least three aspects we need to consider. First, China experienced a long and profound revolution in the twentieth century, so that Chinese society retains an acute sensitivity toward the demands of fairness and social equality. How should these historical and political traditions be translated into democratic demands under contemporary conditions? In other words, what is the mass line or the popular democracy of this new era? Second, the Chinese Communist Party is massive and has experienced significant changes, becoming more entangled with state apparatuses with each day. How can this party system become more democratic, and how can the state's ability to represent the universal interest be preserved while the role of the party is being transformed? Third, how can a new political form be constructed upon the social base, granting greater political capacity to mass society and thereby overcoming the condition of "depoliticization" created through neoliberalism's marketization? These questions have bred further important, theoretical lines of inquiry, including: under conditions of globalization of marketization, in what political direction will the PRC move towards? How can a dialectic of increased self-reliance and increased opening up be forged in Chinese society? This "self-reliance" does not refer to nationalistic or ethnocentric tendencies but rather the reestablishment of values and politics along different lines—if anything, it is a new internationalism. The global significance of this exploration should be obvious given the universal crisis of democracy and market.

The 1990s are over. This post-1989 process has shown signs in the past few years that it has already reached its end, but the year 2008 has provided the clearest signs of all. Globally, neoliberalism's economic path has been hit by a massive crisis, while in China this became evident through a series of events: from the March 14 Tibet Incident to the Wenchuan earthquake, from the Beijing Olympics to the financial crisis, Chinese society has come to understand its own global position in a different way. In Western societies, discussions regarding China's rise have been conducted for quite some time, but amid the crisis, people suddenly realized that China was an economy to be reckoned with, second only to the US. Its rise has occurred more quickly than had been predicted, expressed in a corresponding level of self-confidence. This change was dramatic and some of its elements were coincidental, though not accidental. The issue may be that China is still scrambling to adjust to its new international identity. The contradictions that have accumulated in Chinese society during the process of marketization and the dangers it now faces as a result of globalization are both unprecedented. Whether we are talking about the so-called "end of the 90s" or analyzing the "end of the revolution," the real goal is to clarify the situation we face, and to question and to formulate a new politics, a new path in a new direction. This "end" is not an end in the Hegelian sense but rather the will to break with the past and the desire to construct a new politics. It is from here that we must look back upon the revolutionary inheritance of the twentieth century.

For the publication of this book, I give my heartfelt thanks to each of my friends that have provided help in various ways. First, I wish to thank the journals that have supported me: *New Left Review, Positions, Inter-Asia Cultural Studies, boundary 2, Kaifang Shidai (Open Society), Taiwan Shehuiyanjiu Jikan (Taiwan: A Radical Quarterly in Social Studies)* and *Tianya*. I thank Perry Anderson, Susan Watkins, Tani Barlow, Wu Zhongqing, Chen Kuanhsing and Li Shaojun for their efforts in editing and publishing the individual papers, and I thank Audrea Lim for her efforts in this book's publication. I also want to express my particular gratitude to Perry Anderson, Wang Chaohua, Sechin Yeong-Shyang Chien, Chao Kang, Chu Wanwen, Li Tuo, Wang Xiaoming, Cui Zhiyuan, Wang Shaoguang, Gao Jin, Han Shaogong, Lin Chun, Lindsay Waters, Zhang Xudong, Wang Ban, Gan Yang, Andrew Jones, Wang Mingming, Yang Lihua, Lu Xinyu, Alessandro Russo, Claudia Pozzana, Viren Murthy, Theodore Huters, Christopher Connery and Rebecca Karl for their valuable suggestions during my writing and revision process; and especially to the last three of these friends who made considerable efforts in translating my essays and works. Rebecca Karl also wrote a preface for this book. I would also like to thank my former colleagues at *Dushu* with whom I edited that journal over the course of more than eleven long years. And I would like to give special thanks to Xiao Liangzhong, who passed away a few years ago—we once strove together for the future of the Jinsha River—and all the workers at the Jiangsu Textile Corporation in Yangzhou (and especially Xu Zhiming and Yin Zhihong) for their help in my investigations of the restructuring process at their factory. My report of that investigation didn't make it into this book, but like my exploration of the Jinsha River region, this project provided very important foundations in my thinking on the question of contemporary China.

October 23, 2009

HISTORICAL CONTEXTS

1

Depoliticized Politics: From East to West

Chinese commentators have been curiously absent from international discussions about the Sixties, despite the fact that the Cultural Revolution was so central to that tumultuous decade. This silence, I would argue, represents not merely a rejection of the radical thought and practice of the Cultural Revolution but a negation of China's whole "revolutionary century"—the era stretching from the Xinhai Revolution in 1911, which ended the monarchic rule, to around 1976. The century's prologue was the period running from the failure of the *wuxu* or Hundred-Day Reform in 1898, initiated by the Guangxu Emperor and his supporters, to the 1911 Wuchang uprising, the triggering event for the Republican Revolution; its epilogue was the decade from the late 1970s through to 1989. During this whole epoch the French and Russian Revolutions were central models for China, and orientations toward them defined the political divisions of the time. The New Culture movement of the May Fourth period (roughly 1915–1921), which rejected Confucian values in favor of a new Chinese culture based in deomcratic and scientific principles of the West, championed the French Revolution and its values of liberty, equality and fraternity; first-generation Communist Party members took the Russian Revolution as a model, criticizing the bourgeois character of 1789. Following the crisis of socialism and the rise of reform in the 1980s, the aura of the Russian Revolution diminished and the ideals of the French Revolution reappeared. But with the final curtain-fall on China's revolutionary century, the radicalism of both the French and the Russian experiences had become a target of criticism. The Chinese rejection of the Sixties is thus not an isolated historical incident, but an organic component of a continuing and totalizing de-revolutionary process.

Why do the Sixties seem to be more of a Western than an Asian topic today? First, although the Western and the Asian Sixties were connected, there were also very important differences. In Europe and America, the rise of the Sixties protest movements saw an interrogation of capitalism's political institutions and a far-reaching critique of its culture. The Western Sixties targeted the post-war state, ruthlessly criticizing its domestic and foreign policies. By contrast, in Southeast Asia (particularly Indochina) and other regions, the uprisings of the Sixties took the form of armed struggles against Western imperialist domination and social oppression. Revolutionary political movements fought to transform the nation-state, to create their own sovereign space for economic development and social transformation. In today's context, the armed revolutions of the Sixties seem to have vanished from memory as well as thought; the problems of capitalist critique remain.

A second point concerns the particular character of the Chinese Sixties. Beginning in the 1950s, the People's Republic of China (PRC) was unfailingly supportive of Third World liberation movements and the non-aligned movement generally, to the point of clashing with the world's greatest military power, the United States, in Korea and Vietnam. When European radicals developed a left critique of Stalinism in the Sixties, they discovered that China had already developed a far-reaching critical analysis of the orthodox Soviet line. Yet, as China's wholly new form of party-state was being established, the corrosion of depoliticization was already beginning to set in. Its most important manifestations were bureaucratization and internal power struggles within the party-state, which in turn led to the suppression of discursive freedom. In launching the Cultural Revolution, Mao and others sought a range of tactics to combat these tendencies, yet the end result was always that these struggles became implicated in the very processes—of "depoliticizing" faction fights and bureaucratization—that they were designed to combat, leading to renewed political repression and the rigidification of the party-state.

Even before 1976, the Sixties had lost their luster in the eyes of many Chinese because of the continuous factional struggles and political persecutions that had occurred during the Cultural Revolution. Following the death of Mao and the restoration to power of Deng Xiaoping and others, the Chinese state undertook a "thorough negation" of the Cultural Revolution from the late Seventies. Combined with popular feelings of doubt and disappointment, this led to a fundamental change in attitudes that has lasted to the present day. Over the past thirty years, China has transformed itself from a planned economy to a market society, from a headquarters of world revolution to a thriving center of capitalist activity, from a Third World anti-imperialist nation to one of imperialism's "strategic partners." Today, the most powerful counter to any attempts at critical analysis of China's problems—the crisis in agricultural society, the widening gap between rural and urban sectors, institutionalized corruption—is: "So, do you want to return to the days of the Cultural Revolution?" The eclipse of the Sixties is a product of this depoliticization; the process of "radical negation" has diminished the possibility for any real political criticism of current historical trends.

Revolutionary endings

How then should we understand the politicization of the earlier post-war era? The outcome of the two World Wars had served to dismantle the Eurocentric inter-state system; with the onset of the Cold War, the world order was defined above all by the antagonistic division between the US and Soviet blocs. One prodigious accomplishment of the Sixties was to break this bipolar order. From the Bandung conference in 1955 to the victory of the Vietnamese Revolution in 1975, the social movements and armed struggles in Asia, Africa and Latin America took the form of a "politicization process" that forced an opening in the Cold War order. Mao's "Three Worlds Theory" was a response to this new historical configuration. As the national liberation movements broke the grip of Western imperialism, the rupturing of the Communist bloc that began with the Sino-Soviet split also created a space for renewed debate on the future of socialism. Theoretical and political struggles led to challenges to the structure of power, which had grown ever more ossified within the socialist camp. This too can be viewed as a politicization process.

Yet the Chinese Sixties also contained a self-contradictory "depoliticizing tendency," with the anti-bureaucratization struggles becoming subsumed in faction fights—and, above all, in the violence that came to accompany them at the end of the Sixties. In his important essay, "How to Translate 'Cultural Revolution'," the Italian sociologist Alessandro Russo argues that these violent factional struggles created a crisis in the political culture that had developed in the early years of the Cultural Revolution, centered upon open debate and multiple forms of organization.[1] This crisis provided the opening for the reentry of the party-state. In this sense, the final stages of the Cultural Revolution unfolded within a process of depoliticization.

The hollowing of Western democracy

Russo's reflections on the Cultural Revolution are set against his analysis of the decline in the parliamentary-democratic systems of the West over the last thirty years. The cornerstones of these parliamentary democracies, he argues, were the political parties. A multi-party system presupposes that each party has a specific representative character and political values, for which it will fight against its rivals within the parliamentary-institutional framework. However, as the character and values of the parties become increasingly indeterminate within a broad macroeconomic consensus, real democratic politics disappears. Under these conditions, parliament is transformed from a public sphere into an apparatus for ensuring national stability.

At the heart of the contemporary crisis of democracy, then, is the decline of the political party. In the context of a weakened party system, nation-states become depoliticized. From this perspective, there would appear to be an internal dynamic common to both the single-party and the multi-party systems. Over the past thirty years, their structural, internal and historical differences notwithstanding, both China and the West have been caught within a current of depoliticization. In contemporary China the space for political debate has largely been eliminated. The party is no longer an organization with specific political values, but a mechanism of power. Even within the party it is not easy to carry on real debate; divisions are cast as technical differences on the path to modernization, so they can only be resolved within the power structures. Since the mid Seventies the CCP has conducted no public debates about political values or strategy. An outstanding characteristic of twentieth-century China's revolutionary transformations, however, had been the continuous and intimate connection between theoretical debate and political practice.

A key instance of this process was the disappearance of the concept of "line struggle" after the Cultural Revolution. If this was the terminology used by the victors of the factional conflicts, it also illustrated a central element of the CCP's history: that every great political battle was inextricably linked to serious theoretical considerations and policy debate. From the conflicting analyses of the question of revolutionary defeat following the catastrophe of 1927, when Chiang Kaishek ordered the violent large-scale purge of Communists from the Kuomingtang nationalist party, to the theoretical disputes of the early 1930s on the social character of the Chinese revolution; from the discussions of national and international politics in the Central Soviet (1931–1937) and Yan'an periods (1935–1947) to the debates on the notion of contradiction during the Cultural Revolution, we can trace a series of important theoretical divisions arising from differing analyses of social conditions, and with divergent implications for party strategy. In my view, it is precisely these theoretical battles that maintain a party's internal vitality and ensure that it does not become a depoliticized political organization. Subjecting theory and practice to the "line struggle" also functions as a corrective mechanism, enabling the party to recognize and repair its errors.

Due to the absence of functioning mechanisms for inner-party democracy, these debates and differences often found their "resolution" through faction fights. After the Cultural Revolution, many of those who had suffered in the process came first to detest and then to repudiate the "line struggle" concept. On regaining power in the late Seventies they sought only to suppress this type of argument in the name of party unity, rather than to analyze the conditions whereby "line struggle" had degenerated into mere power play. This not only resulted in a thoroughgoing suppression of the political life of the party, but also destroyed the possibility of exploring the relationship between the party and democracy. Rather, it laid the foundation for the statification—i.e. depoliticization—of the party.

During the Sixties, China had developed a wide-ranging theoretical agenda, revolving around such questions as the dynamics of history, the market economy, the means of production, class struggle, bourgeois right, the nature of Chinese society, and the status of world revolution. There were heated exchanges between different political blocs on all these questions; the link between theory and political culture epitomized the period. In the context of its subsequent trajectory, we can see that China's depoliticization process has had two key characteristics: firstly, the "de-theorization" of the ideological sphere; secondly, making economic reform the sole focus of party work.

In terms of de-theorization, the turning-point came in the Seventies, when the mutual interconnection of theory and practice was replaced by the notion of cautiously "crossing the river by feeling for the stones." Nevertheless, the figure of "feeling for the stones" does not accurately describe the reform process, for several reasons. First, in the mid Seventies the CCP did engage in quite lively theoretical discussions about the market, labor compensation, civil rights and other questions, thus touching on many of the fundamental issues facing the country. Without these debates, it is difficult to imagine how the course of reform and the development of a market economy would have come about. Subsequently, from the end of the Seventies, there were a series of discussions about the problem of socialism, humanism, alienation, the market economy and the question of ownership, both within the CCP and Chinese society as a whole—the two discussions, inside and outside the party, constituting a single continuous process. These, then, were countervailing trends to the general "de-theorization."

The second characteristic of the depoliticization process has been to set economic reform at the center of all party work. Formally speaking, this has involved the substitution of "construction" for the former "two-line" goal of "revolution and construction." These political choices—understandably—met with wide approval at the end of the Seventies, appearing as a response to the factional struggles and chaotic character of politics during the latter years of the Cultural Revolution. Yet, by this stage, the tension between party and politics that had characterized the early years of the Cultural Revolution had been thoroughly eliminated. The unification of politics and the state—the party-state system—diminished the earlier political culture.

From party-state to state-party?

The concept of the "party-state" was, of course, a derogatory Cold War term applied by the West to the Communist countries. Today all the world's nations have become party-states or—to extend the term—parties-states. Historically, the development of modern political systems from the preceding monarchical forms was a highly uneven process; by the mid twentieth century, parties had still not been completely subsumed within the parameters of national politics in China. The creation of a new form of party-state system was a fundamental development of the post-war period.

As the party, through the process of exercising power, became the subject of the state order, it increasingly changed into a depoliticized apparatus, a bureaucratic machine, and no longer functioned as a stimulant for ideas and practice. For this reason, I would characterize the dominant contemporary form as having undergone a transformation from a party-state to a state-party or "state-multiparty" system. This implies that the party no longer conforms to its past political role, but becomes a component of the state apparatus. What I want to emphasize here is the change in the party's identity: no longer possessing its own distinctive evaluative standpoint or social goals, it can only have a structural-functionalist relationship to the state apparatus. If the state-party system is the result of a crisis transformation of the party-state, contemporary China is the embodiment of this trend. Yet the Chinese case should also be seen as a symptom of the worldwide dynamic toward depoliticization. Those analyses which, avoiding recognition of the generalized crisis in party politics, attempt to prescribe the best means of reforming the Chinese system—including setting Western-style multi-party representative democracy as the goal of Chinese political reform—are themselves only extensions of this depoliticization.

The Great Proletarian Cultural Revolution was possibly the last stage of the political sequence wherein the party-state recognized that it faced a crisis and attempted to carry out a self-renewal. The political debates in the early stages of the Cultural Revolution included currents that hoped to smash the absolute authority of the party and the state, in order to further the goal of progress toward genuine popular sovereignty. The Cultural Revolution was a reaction against an early stage in the statification of the party; in order to change course, it was thought necessary to re-examine the party's political values. Efforts at social remobilization and stimulation of political life outside the party-state context were crucial characteristics of this early period. In these years, factories across China were reorganized along the lines of the Paris Commune, and schools and other units engaged in social experimentation. Due to the forceful reassertion of the party-state system, most of these innovations were short-lived, and the extra-state processes of political activism were quickly suppressed. Yet traces of these early experiments remained in later state and party reorganizations—for example, the policy of admitting worker, peasant and army representatives into leadership positions, or the requirement that every level of state and party send their members to do social work in rural villages or factories, and so on. These practices, tainted with the character of the bureaucratized system and thus unable to unleash creative energies, became, at the end of the Seventies, prime targets of the government's drive to "clean up the mess" and "return to normal."

Today, workers and peasants have wholly disappeared not only from the leadership bodies of party and state, but also from the National People's Congress, the sole legislative house in the PRC today. Following the failure of the Cultural Revolution and the development of a market society, depoliticization has become the main current of the age. At its core has been the growing convergence of politics and the party-state, and the emergence of the state-party system.

Concepts of class

The consolidation of the state-party system in the Chinese context is directly connected to the concept of class. The representative character of the Communist parties had inevitably become increasingly problematic with the establishment of Communist-led states. Following the Sino-Soviet split in the late Fifties and early Sixties, Mao emphasized the concept of class to stimulate a renewal of the party's political culture. His target was the Soviet notion of the "party of the whole people," which not only indicated confusion about the representative character of the Communist Party of the Soviet Union, but marked the depoliticization of the party-state system. While there is not room here to evaluate the classical Marxist theory of class, what needs to be emphasized is that, in Chinese political practice, class is not merely a structural category centered on the nature of property ownership or relation to the means of production; it is rather a political concept based on the revolutionary party's appeal for mobilization and self-renewal. Similarly, within the party, the concept was used to stimulate debate and struggle, in order to avoid depoliticization under the conditions of the party's administration of power. The concept denoted the attitudes of social or political forces toward revolutionary politics, rather than the structural situation of social class.

However, this highly subjective concept of class contained internal contradictions and dangers. Once crystallized into a structural, immutable notion—i.e. a depoliticized concept of class—its political dynamism vanished. As an essentialized discourse of class identity, it proved incapable of stimulating political transformation. Rather, it became the most oppressive kind of power logic, the basis for the merciless character of subsequent faction fights. The increasing predominance of discourses of identitarianism, "family origin" or "blood lineage" was a negation and betrayal of the subjectivist and activist outlook that was the core of the Chinese Revolution, whose central task was the dismantling of class relations formed through a history of violence and unequal property relations.

The tragedy of the Cultural Revolution was not a product of its politicization—signified by debate, theoretical investigation, autonomous social organization, as well as the spontaneity and vitality of political and discursive space. The tragedy was a result of depoliticization—polarized factional struggles that eliminated the possibility for autonomous social spheres, transforming political debate into a mere means of power struggle, and class into an essentialized identitarian concept. The only way to overcome the tragedy of this period is through understanding its dimensions of repoliticization. If we take 1989 as the final end-point of the Sixties—the consolidation of depoliticization—this must imply that it could also have marked the beginning of the long road toward repoliticization.

Defeats and depoliticization

Explaining the phenomenon of depoliticization is a complicated task; clearly its dynamics cannot be analyzed within the confines of China alone. Considered in historical perspective, it could be argued that broad currents of depoliticization arose in the wake of virtually every defeated revolutionary upheaval: after the French Revolution and the crushing of the 1848 uprisings; after the European and Asian Sixties; after 1989. Carl Schmitt's analysis of what he called "neutralization" offers a further insight into this process.[2] For Schmitt, the central political problem of the 1920s was the containment of the rising power of the working class. The unsystematic interpenetration of the political and the economic during the period was, from this perspective, a mistake and a danger. He sought a new form of relationship between the political and the economic, neither laissez-faire nor social-democratic. Schmitt's concept of neutralization, although specifically situated within the context of Western intellectual and political history, is clearly open to broader application.

Historically, the development of the capitalist system was based upon the hypothetical separation of economy and politics, through the nascent bourgeoisie's challenge to the feudal aristocracy's monopoly over both. Schumpeter used the concept of "political exchange" to describe the process through which this took place. Without the substantive protection of some aristocratic elements, the bourgeoisie would have been unable to further its own class interests. Political exchange already implies a certain separation between the political and economic spheres, without which there could be no such trade-offs. From this perspective, the separation of politics and economics is not a naturally existing phenomenon, but the product of capital's drive to realize an ever-greater share of power. Over the long nineteenth century, this objective was gradually achieved in the national and supranational structuring of the market economy. Contemporary capitalism attempts to create a self-enclosed market-economic sphere and a depoliticized political order, in which the key concept is that of the neutral state.

Classically, once the bourgeoisie had asserted its rule against the power of the monarchy and aristocracy, a kind of depoliticized politics replaced the multiple political structures of the revolutionary period— the product of political exchange, through the unification of capitalist and non-capitalist elements in the ruling stratum. This depoliticization process involved, for example, the legitimation through constitutional means of the nouveau-riche expropriation of social and national assets. As a result, the meaning of democracy shifted from popular to representative forms, the nation-state was transformed from a political space to an institutionalized structure of rule, and party politics from a struggle for representation into a power-distribution mechanism.

The era of finance capital has involved a further institutionalization and legalization of the concept of the spontaneously self-ordering market—the central nostrum of neoclassical economics, under which all non-capitalist institutions and forms of labor allocation are disparaged as "political interference." The unlimited expansion of the market economy into the political, cultural, domestic and other spheres is seen as an apolitical, "natural" process. In this sense, the neoclassical and neoliberal concept of the market is an aggressively positivistic, depoliticized political ideology. The retreat of the state championed by these forces is a fundamentally depoliticizing proposition.

China's party-class exchange

China's current depoliticization encompasses yet another kind of political exchange, characterized by the party elite's effort to transform itself into the representative of special interests while still holding onto political power. In this instance it is transnational capital that must pass through a depoliticizing exchange process in order to gain the support of the power apparatus. Since marketization takes place under the aegis of the state, many aspects of the state apparatus are imbricated in the economic sphere. (In a state-party system, this must include the party apparatus as well.) The "reform" of property rights, which has led to large-scale expropriations, has been a conspicuous example of this depoliticizing exchange, which uses the law to depoliticize the property-right transfer. In the contemporary Chinese context, notions such as modernization, globalization and growth can be seen as key concepts of a depoliticized or anti-political political ideology, whose widespread usage militates against a popular political understanding of the social and economic shifts at stake in marketization. Against this background, the critique of corruption is also a critique of much deeper levels of inequality and injustice involved in the asset-transfer process.

Three factors underpin the current stage of China's depoliticization:

- In the marketization process, the boundary between the political elite and the owners of capital grows gradually more indistinct. The political party is thus changing its class basis.
- Under conditions of globalization, some of the economic functions of the nation-state are ceded to supranational market organizations (such as the WTO), so that a globalized, depoliticized legal order is consolidated.
- As both market and state are gradually neutralized or depoliticized, divisions over questions of development become technical disputes about market-adjustment mechanisms. Political divisions between labor and capital, left and right, are made to disappear.

If these developments began at the end of the Seventies and flourished in the Eighties, they have achieved worldwide predominance in the era of neoliberal globalization.

State and ideology

The contemporary depoliticization process is a product of this historical transformation, under which a new social inequality has been naturalized. The critique of this inequality must realize a repoliticization as the precondition for its own success. At the heart of this repoliticization is the destruction, in theory and practice, of the "natural," neutral state. De-naturalization must be used to combat depoliticization.

How should we conceptualize the contemporary state? In the realm of Marxist theory, the emergence of the "neutral" state led some authors to posit a separation between state power and the state apparatus, and to limit the objectives of political struggle to the question of state power. In fact, as Althusser pointed out, "in their political practice, the Marxist classics treated the state as a more complex reality" than in the definition provided by their theory.[3] This definition, he argued, lacked an objective description of the "ideological state apparatuses." In contradistinction to the "repressive state apparatus," the ISAs include religion, education, the family, law, labor unions, political parties, the media, the cultural sphere. While there is only one, unified, repressive state apparatus, there exists "a plurality of ideological state apparatuses." And whereas the RSA belongs in the public domain, the larger part of the ISAs are in the private sphere. Under the pre-capitalist state, "there was one dominant Ideological State Apparatus—the Church," while under capitalism the dominant ISAs shifted to the School-Family couple. Victory in the political struggle for state power, then, also depended on engaging in struggle within the sphere of the ideological apparatuses.

The central ISA system in socialist-era China comprised the Ministries of Propaganda, Culture and Education. This system combined the functions of ISAs and RSA, but the ISA was foremost. In contemporary China, although this apparatus still strives to perform an ideological function, it faces insurmountable obstacles. It has therefore largely turned into a repressive one; its control of media and other spheres is not primarily ideological, but rather is based on the need to preserve stability. Yet, because all state apparatuses penetrate deeply into the institutions of daily life, the fundamental existential character of the state itself assumes a kind of depoliticized political form. Increasingly, this is now supplemented by the ideological hegemony of the market.

Three components of hegemony

To confront the logic of depoliticized politics, we must therefore analyze the forms of contemporary hegemony. I will argue that there are three components of this hegemony, with complex historical interrelationships. First, as clarified in Gramsci's concept of hegemony and Althusser's "ideological state apparatuses," hegemony and the sovereign state's monopoly of violence are mutually implicated. Gramsci identified two modes of the operation of hegemony: dominative power, and intellectual and moral leadership. Dominative power operates in the realm of coercion, while leadership refers to the ruling group's strategy of proposing solutions to common problems, which at the same time allocate exceptional powers to itself. According to the *Prison Notebooks*, the state is a particular form of collective structure whose aim is to create the most advantageous conditions for the expansion and development of its total capability.

Second, the concept of hegemony has been closely connected to interstate relations. Western scholarship has tended to distinguish Gramsci's approach from the critique of the international hegemon within Chinese political thought. My concern here is to attempt to reconstruct the theoretical and historical links between the two. Mao's concept of the hegemon was always deployed within the sphere of global relations. The "Three Worlds" theory did not only posit the Third World as a political subject which, through links and breaks with elements of the Second World, would oppose the two hegemonic powers, the US and USSR, and form a new kind of international relations. It also sought, through theoretical investigation, political debate and moral appeal, to break the ideological power and prestige of the American and Soviet systems. The practice of counter-hegemony implied a contestation of *cultural* authority. The ancient Chinese classics, *The Spring and Autumn Annals* and *Master Zuo's Commentary*, use the concepts of ducal authority (control by force) and hegemonic authority (domination through rites and rituals) to differentiate the two types of power in the ancient states of Qi, Jin, Chu and Qin. Although the concept of hegemony in the Chinese-speaking world normally refers to political, economic or military domination and control, it also involves the question of ideology.

Gramsci's concept of hegemony and Machiavelli's concept of power are explicitly combined in Giovanni Arrighi's *The Long Twentieth Century*, where the sphere of national ideological hegemony is linked to international political relations. In Machiavelli, power links consent and force: power implies the use or the threat of armed force; consent implies moral authority. By virtue of its hegemonic power, the US has become a model of depoliticization, and likewise one for modernization, marketization, globalization; it has thus established its own global ideological authority. American hegemony rests on the multiple foundations of a monopoly of violence, economic dominance, and ideological "soft power." But, just as the process of depoliticization has national and international dimensions, the possibility of breaking this depoliticized political settlement also exists within these two dimensions. The debacle of America's military expansionism since 2001 may unite an increasing number of global forces in "de-Americanization."

Thirdly, hegemony not only relates to national or international relations, but is intimately connected to transnational and supranational capitalism; it must also be analyzed within the sphere of globalized market relations. Classical political economists emphasized that the process of reproduction was an inexhaustible and unending global process; something that has never been clearer than today, when market ideology constitutes a type of hegemony. Neoclassical economics is itself a textbook case of globalized ideological hegemony—its principles permeate the rules and regulations of the major transnational trade and financial institutions. All of these function as "ideological global apparatuses," though of course they also have the power of economic coercion. The most direct expressions of the market-ideological apparatus are the media, advertising, the "world of shopping," and so forth. These mechanisms are not only commercial, but ideological. Their greatest power is in their appeal to the "common-sense," ordinary needs which turn people into consumers, voluntarily following market logic in their daily lives. Market-ideological apparatuses have a strongly depoliticizing character.

The three components of hegemony discussed above do not operate in abstraction from each other but form mutually entangled networks of power. They are internal to contemporary social mechanisms and institutions, internal to human activity and beliefs. Depoliticized politics is structured like this network of hegemony—an essential point for understanding China's current situation. Contemporary hegemony commonly uses internal contradictions to expand its operationality. For example, China's economic policy and developmental trajectory are locked into the process of capitalist globalization, whose outcomes have included successive financial crises and growing social tensions and inequalities. Yet in China, capitalist globalization is never viewed as a factor in the contradictions and conflicts of interest at the national level.

De-statification?

The more open climate in China during the Seventies and Eighties permitted definitions of autonomy and liberalization that challenged the ideological state apparatuses. However, this "de-statification process," as it was known within critical intellectual circles, did not result in repoliticization. Rather, occurring just as the sovereign authority of the nation-state was beginning to be challenged by new forces of capitalist globalization, the processes of autonomy and liberalization of the period were reincorporated into the dynamic of depoliticization and the consolidation of international ideological hegemony.

In fact, "de-statification" denotes the outcome of fierce conflict between two different national political systems, two ideologies. The "state" to be "de-statified" is understood to refer only to the socialist nation. De-statification, therefore, is simply the process of identification with a different hegemonic form. In contemporary China, anti-socialist ideology uses the image of anti-statism to cover up its inner connection to this new national form. But the above analysis of the multiple dimensions of hegemony demonstrates that this new form of state ideology has a supranational dimension as well, which often expresses itself as an attack on the state from the supranational position.

This de-statification process was accompanied by an ideological depoliticization, incorporated into the new form of hegemony that privileged modernization, globalization and the market. "De-nationalization" presumes the erosion of any distinction between state power and the state apparatuses. Once this distinction has been obliterated, the space for political struggle is diminished, and political problems are turned into a "non-political" process of de-nationalization or de-statification. Indeed many of today's social movements (including most NGOs) are themselves a part of the depoliticization process. They are either absorbed by the state apparatus, or constrained by the logic of national or international foundations. Not only are they unable to offer different understandings of development, democracy or popular participation; they actually function as cogs of the depoliticized global mechanisms. A pressing issue of our time is thus how to overcome the social movements' self-imposed depoliticization, and how to link a critical internationalism to political struggles within the nation-state framework.

Today, any challenge to the fundamental logic of depoliticized politics will require us to identify the fissures within the three forms of hegemony; to dismantle the totalizing quality of these spheres and find within them new spaces for political struggle. Contemporary globalization and its institutions encourage the transnationalization of finance, production and consumption, but at the same time strive to limit immigration to the framework of state regulation, thus creating regional rivalries between workers. Our response should not be to retreat into nationalist mode, but rather to redevelop a critical internationalism in order to expose the inner contradictions of globalization. In China, because of the huge conflicts between the practice of reform and socialist values, there remain internal contradictions between the reform movement and the ISAs. As a result, the ISAs are mutating into repressive state apparatuses, relying on force or administrative authority to impose a system of control. In this respect, the Chinese ISAs operate according to a logic of de-ideologization and depoliticization, even though they make their appeal in the language of ideology.

Based primarily on the requirements of legitimization, the Chinese Communist Party, while thoroughly repudiating the Cultural Revolution, did not repudiate either the Chinese Revolution or socialist values, nor the summation of Mao Zedong thought. This has created a twofold effect. First, the socialist tradition has functioned to a certain extent as an internal restraint on state reforms. Every time the state-party system made a major policy shift, it had to be conducted in dialogue with this tradition. At minimum, it had to couch its announcement in a particular language designed to harmonize the policy transformation with its proclaimed social goals. Secondly, the socialist tradition gave workers, peasants and other social collectivities some legitimate means to contest or negotiate the state's corrupt or inegalitarian marketization procedures.

Thus, within the historical process of the negation of the Cultural Revolution, a reactivation of China's legacy also provides an opening for the development of a future politics. This opening is not a simple doorway back to the twentieth century, but a starting point in the search for a means to break the hold of depoliticized political ideology after the end of the revolutionary era. In a situation where all earlier forms of political subjectivity—party, class, nation—face the crisis of depoliticization, the search for new forms must be accompanied by a redefinition of the boundaries of politics itself.

2

The Year 1989 and the Historical Roots of Neoliberalism in China

One could almost say that the twentieth century was summed up a little early, in 1989, even as history since then has proceeded apace. In that year the events in Beijing became a spark for the breakup of the Soviet Union and of Eastern Europe, which in turn marked the beginning of the global domination of neoliberalism in economic and political structures. China did not undergo the same process of breakup as did the Soviet Union and Eastern Europe, and as a result, transformations in its social structure appear rather as a continuation of the events of 1989. If we characterized this process simply (bearing in mind that it is not yet complete), we might say that, upon the premise of a continuity of its political system, China has promoted radical marketization; in addition, under the guidance of state policy, China has become one of the most enthusiastic participants in the global economy. This continuity and discontinuity has lent a special character to Chinese neoliberalism. Indeed, Chinese neoliberalism has at times expressed its contradictions with the state in an anti-political (or anti-historical, or even anti-socialist—in its traditional sense) way. But these oppositions seem incapable of really concealing neoliberalism's intimate connections with state-directed economic policy. For neoliberalism, in truth, relies upon the strength of transnational and national policies and economies, and it depends upon a theory and discourse of economic formalism to establish its own hegemonic discourse. Its extrapolitical and anti-state character is thus utterly dependent upon its inherent links to the state. That is, in the absence of such a policy/state premise, neoliberalism would be incapable of concealing unemployment, the decline of social security, and the widening gap between rich and poor using the mystifications of a "transitional period": indeed, "transition" is one of the most important unarticulated premises of all discussions of Chinese society, and the failure to articulate it better preempts any discussion of the connection between contemporary inequality and some ultimate future ideal and goal. For this reason, using the existence of state interference in the economy to prove—as some have done—that there is no neoliberal hegemony in China is really beside the point, as the hegemonic position of neoliberalism in China was established precisely from within a domestic process during which the state's crisis of legitimacy was overcome through economic reform itself. At the level of theory, then, such national modernizationist and historical narratives as "neo-authoritarianism," "neoconservatism," and "classical conservatism" that appeared one after another prior to 1989 (and this includes the various democracy narratives that were closest to modernization theories) all have an intimate link of one sort or another to the establishment of neoliberal ideology. These nominally mutually exclusive (and even mutually contradictory) theories, however, also reflected structural transformations in power within China and globally.

Neoliberalism is a coercive discursive formation and ideology; while it is incapable of describing actual social and economic relations, it is not unconnected to actual social and economic relations. Ubiquitously deployed tropes such as "transition" and "development"—seen in the media, as well as in ideological trends within intellectual thought and practice—have completely infiltrated national policy, all the while concealing their own contradictions. For this reason, to expose the limits of the contradictory methods of neoliberalism requires an examination of the historical links its discourse (free markets, development, globalization, common prosperity, private property rights, etc.) has established with the real progress of society. This would explain the confused relationship between neoliberal articulations and reality. What is most clear is that, in the different regions and arenas of the contemporary world—North America, Western Europe, Russia, and China—neoliberalism has its own origins and social effectivity. Differences in historical conditions have determined that, at its most abstract level, the characteristic theories of neoliberalism are unable to lead to any persuasive conclusions, and that neoliberalism's real content is difficult to glean from its own general theoretical narrative.

One goal of this essay is to explore, through historical analysis, how the discursive hegemony of Chinese neoliberalism has been articulated within and established upon particular domestic and international conditions, as well as what its policy foundations and its ideological, domestic, and international contexts and debates are. This essay will also analyze Chinese neoliberalism's various guises and internal contradictions, in addition to the various theories and critiques that have surrounded it and evolved from problems it has posed. Those theories and experiences that have been aimed against neoliberalism have included mutually contradictory—simultaneously radical, moderate, and conservative—elements. In my opinion, the most important task of progressives today is to prevent these critiques from developing in the direction of conservatism (including the tendency to re-establish the old system) and to attempt to transform these elements into forces for achieving real and broad democracy and freedom in China and the world today.

What needs to be clarified first, then, is that the economic transformations that took place between 1978 and 1989 were broad processes; using the term "revolutionary" to characterize the depth of these transformations is thus not unwarranted. The space of this short essay is sufficient neither to make a complete inventory of the successes and urgent internal crises of the Chinese reforms, nor to give a detailed narrative of the social movement of 1989; these would require the efforts and investigations of many experts and scholars. What I intend to do here—and this I must say in advance—is simply to begin this larger effort with a brief consideration of the causes of the 1989 social movement, in order to specify anew the field of activity in contemporary China.

The 1989 social movement was an event of far-reaching significance not only for China, but also for the world. Whether in China or abroad, whether in the official media and propaganda or in the proliferation of memoirs and analyses after the fact, the vast majority of discussions have centered on the student and intellectual movement; even analysis of the so-called public sphere has concentrated mainly on the role of such economic entities as the Sitong Company in the process. Yet the 1989 social movement mobilized a broader array of social elements than what could be directly mobilized through the strength of student organization, as demonstrated by its spontaneity and scope. To be sure, old ideologies had already been undermined by the trends of intellectual liberation and enlightenment and the opposing theories and ideas they provided no doubt played an important role. But as a social group, intellectuals were nevertheless unable to propose social goals that could be realistically implemented; indeed, they did not even comprehend the full depth of the social mobilization. This is because, as an intellectual trend that sought primarily to oppose the practices of the socialist state, social thought in the 1980s was unable to perceive and understand the special characteristics of new social contradictions; it was unable to grasp that socialist leanings were deeply inherent in the social mobilization; and it was unable to overcome the ideological framework of the Cold War. It is thus necessary first to distinguish two types of socialism: one is the "socialism" of old state ideology, who is characterized by the system of state monopoly; the other is the "socialism" of movements for social security and social democracy and against monopoly, under conditions of state monopoly and market expansion. In the post-Cold War global context, and in the context of reevaluating socialist practice, the 1989 movement for social security—with its deeply concealed internal social contradictions, its opposition to monopoly and special privileges, and its intention to promote democracy—remains poorly understood. My interpretation of the movement thus takes the following issues as points of departure.

Firstly, from the mid 1980s through 1989, there were several student movements in mainland China (including the late-1986 student movement that forced Hu Yaobang from office); but their scope was small, and they did not spark broad social mobilization. The question thus becomes: Why did the death of Hu Yaobang in 1989, which was the spark for the student movement, touch off a huge mobilization and the participation of every level of society all over the country? Why, from May 1989, did the organs of the national media—such as the Central TV Station, *People's Daily*, the Xinhua News Agency, *Guangming Daily*, and others—begin to cover the movement so broadly, to the point where, for the first time in modern Chinese history, something approaching "a period of press freedom" seemed to emerge, which provided motivation and the conditions for the mobilization of the whole nation and society?

Secondly, what differences were there between the appeals made by the students and those made by other social groups? The reason for this question is that the 1989 movement was not merely a student movement; it was a broad social movement that involved workers, individual entrepreneurs, state cadres, teachers, and other social elements. Even members of the Central Party Committee, various Ministries of State

Affairs, the National People's Congress, various organs of the Chinese People's Consultative Congress (including such "mouthpieces" as the *People's Daily*, the *Guangming Daily*, and the Xinhua News Agency) participated. We could say that, apart from peasants, who did not directly participate, people from every other social class—and particularly those in large and medium-sized cities—were drawn into the movement. The reasons that workers, intellectuals, and other social groups participated are not that difficult to fathom, but why did conflicts begin to appear within the state as well? More accurately, why did the state begin to behave in contradictory ways? Were the power struggles, clash of interests or differences in values intrinsic to the state as a unified whole or did they arise between different organs of the state?

Thirdly, given wide social support for the process of reform, why did critiques of the reform process itself appear? Who or what social conditions were the target of critique? What constituted the ideology of social mobilization, and what elements were it constructed upon?

If one wants to respond clearly to the above questions, one needs briefly to review the progress of reform from 1978 onward. The social reforms of 1978–89 can be divided into two major phases: the 1978–84 rural reform phase, and the urban reform phase from 1984 onward. The successes of the reforms of 1978–84 or 1985 were concentrated in the area of rural issues, and at their core was the gradual transformation of the social position of township populations with relation to rural populations within a structural duality defined by the "urban-rural divide."[1] There were initially two important objectives of this reform: (1) to liberate the people's communes through state-sponsored redistribution of land and the implementation of the household responsibility system; (2) to work through state/policy coordination to raise the prices of rural products, encourage consumption in the rural areas, and develop rural industry so as to transform the system of urban industrialization that had initially produced the urban-rural divide during the Maoist period. As a consequence, from 1978 to 1984, income gaps between rural and urban residents gradually decreased. These two reform successes followed the gradual easing of small market relations, but, in essence, they were founded upon traditional Chinese land-distribution practices and principles of equality. We can encapsulate them as a "small peasant socialist" model, posed as a repudiation of the people's commune, a model whose main ingredient was state monopoly. The increased productivity of peasants largely originated from flexibility in production and the decrease in the urban-rural gap; it was not attributable purely to the opening of markets. On the contrary, the rural reform policy created security for the local communal markets, for which the adjustment of agricultural product prices was an important regulatory measure. That is, rural society had not yet been reorganized around the principle of urban-centered market-economic relations. High productivity, limited surplus products and an undeveloped urban commodity economy prevented rural polarization and poverty from growing too extreme; at the same time, price adjustments and the protection of small markets allowed for the transformation of the dual urban-rural structural relations. The rapid closing of the urban-rural divide quickly resulted in the polarization of rural society, but this did not in turn lead to rapid social destabilization, precisely due to the factors just listed above.[2] The market was merely one important element of the rural reforms of the 1980s; at the time, the economist who described the agricultural reforms as "developing agriculture through the important tool of policy" was generally correct in his assessment of reality.

This rural reform process offers a background against which we can begin to comprehend the onset of the post-1984 urban reform phase; it shaped the historical conditions in which urban economic reform proceeded and the difficulties it faced. Urban reform covers a myriad of aspects, and most people understand it as being centered on the introduction of market mechanisms. However, from the perspective of its real social content, its core was the "decentralization of power and interests" (*fangquan rangli*): that is, social advantages and interests were reorganized through the dispersal and transfer of certain social resources previously controlled and coordinated by the state.[3] Research shows that in the twenty-six years between 1953 and 1978, the proportion of public spending in China in relation to the gross national product was, on average, 34.2 percent (this includes the 37.2 percent of 1978); from 1978 onward, this proportion dropped every year, and by 1988 it stood at 19.3 percent. In deflationary conditions, where the scope of foreign investment and capital was greatly increasing, local governments were being given more independence and power over their interests and organization.[4] Side effects of this process were tax evasion, mandatory fundraising for local government expenses (*tanpai chengfeng*), local government control over bank payments, and even the large-scale development of smuggling.[5]

The major emphasis in urban reform was the reform of state-owned enterprises: they first increased the independence of these enterprises (the state gave a measure of power back to the enterprises), then permitted some enterprises to close, freeze, combine, transfer, or redistribute, and finally, altered the mode of management, transforming productive relations themselves. Under the pressure of unemployment and layoffs, the state had no choice but to employ a policy strategy that emphasized consolidation and transfer over closures and stoppages, but the basic direction was not changed. Of course, urban reform was more complex than rural reform, for two reasons. First, the process of accounting for industrial resources is more difficult than for rural land; and the question of how to redistribute industrial resources involves extremely complex issues of technological and structural conditions, while also touching upon issues of employment, the division of labor, and regional and other disparities (and the inequalities produced by these disparities). Second, the premises of rural reform and the reform of state-owned industries are completely different. Under the old industrial system, the state distributed resources based upon plans, but command of resources did not coincide with economic, collective and individual benefit. For example, the resources commanded by large-scale state-owned factories had the advantage of monopolies, yet the difference between their workers' real benefits and those of small and medium-sized factories was not large. Thus, once the state began to relinquish its control over the organization of industry and commerce—adjusting rather than defining or implementing plans—the old inequalities in the control over resources immediately turned into unequal benefits. For this reason, urban industrial reform did not merely involve the question of state ownership, but became a problem of the whole national economic structure. In these complex conditions, and in the absence of any suitable process of democratic supervision or suitable economic structure, it was almost inevitable that the redistribution of resources and production would result in extreme social inequities. There diverse factors can explain why urban reforms did not yield the same type of equality as the rural reforms initially did. Moreover, the position and interests of workers as a group, and even of government officials as a stratum, were seriously undermined in this process. Sociological studies have shown that this was manifested above all in their reduced economic positions, internal polarization within strata, the stagnation of workers' benefits, and employment insecurity among old, weak, ill, disabled, and pregnant people, among other effects.[6]

From 1985 to 1989, a debate broke out in the field of economy in China between so-called reform (transformed into radical property reform) and adjustment (adjusting the structure under state interference). There was also an ongoing debate over whether China's reforms should be led by price reforms (moving away from the old planned-economy pricing system and toward a market pricing system) or whether they should be led by reforms in the system of state ownership (that is, large-scale privatization of state-owned enterprises).[7] One of the reasons for these debates was that, beginning in 1985, the Chinese economy was consistently plagued by inflation and economic chaos; it was thought that widespread social instability would result through reforms in the system of enterprise ownership, absent appropriate price adjustments and the cultivation of suitable market conditions. The policy that resulted from this debate was that price reforms led market conditions while the government simultaneously reformed enterprises (mainly through the contract system). This reform path was largely successful because price reform posed obstacles to the old structural monopolies, while also animating market mechanisms. Compared to Russia's "spontaneous privatization," the significance of these successes should be fully appreciated.

However, this process had its own internal dangers, and it also set off a series of particular social problems. From the perspective of market conditions, this reform had been initiated on the basis of a so-called two-track price system (that is, state-plan prices sat alongside market prices, with the former primarily applied to means of production—which included any capital and natural resources left over from the completed state plans—and the latter primarily applied to consumer items; yet this price dichotomy also created the perfect conditions for corruption and official malfeasance (that is, corrupt and underground activities carried out by state cadres and official organs who could use the dual-price structure to their advantage). From the perspective of enterprise reform, the contract system emerged alongside the separation of politics and enterprise functions, but, in the context of an unchanging political structure, implementing the latter proved very difficult. The rhetorical separation of politics from business did not in actuality translate to the separation of politics from the economy, but rather ownership from management. In the midst of this murky transition in rights, a majority of state-owned resources were transferred, legally and illegally, to benefit a small minority's economic interests.

Many economists called 1988 the "year of the contract," because the contract system was expanded from enterprise contracts to foreign trade contracts, department contracts, finance contracts, and so on, and this process of "contracting" afforded more independence to enterprises, localities, and government departments (*bumen*). Yet it also intensified the contradictions resulting from the "two-track price system": localities and interest groups utilized their new rights and a variety of other methods to convert products within the state plan into market products, resulting in inflation, extreme instability and social inequality.[8] In this process, some of the more frequently seen manifestations of corruption were tax evasion, kickbacks, abuse of public funds and the conversion of power into money (such as using power to set contracts in return for bribes). Following the reforms, collectives experienced an increase in sustained purchasing ability and bonuses were more frequently granted, resulting in a terrible imbalance between overall supply and overall demand, with the central government lacking the necessary will to adjust and control financial resources. From May to June 1988, the state loudly proclaimed itself a worthy opponent, and declared that it would close up the price differentials by abolishing state-plan pricing and completely implementing market pricing. This, however, led to panic purchasing and large-scale social instability. In the period immediately following, the state was forced to return to its previous policy of strengthening state supervision; yet this led to contradictions between the state and the creatures of its own creation: the localities and departmental special interest groups.[9]

Even as this period of reform had a number of successes, it also produced certain new conditions that, in different ways, reflected new social inequalities. These became motivating factors for the eruption of the 1989 social movement. First, the two-track system and the marketization of power brought about both inequalities in distribution and "rent-seeking" behavior that was achieved by exploiting the gap between the two forms of pricing. According to scholars, in 1988 the gap created between the two types of price under this dual system (that is, "rent") exceeded 3.5 trillion yuan, representing roughly 30 percent of that year's gross national product.[10] In reality, publicly owned resources found their way into the pockets of rent-seekers through corrupt (power-for-money) exchanges. The formation of local and departmental interest groups (which were the primary sources of corruption in the 1990s) was closely tied to this process. Meanwhile, the contradictions between local governments and the central government began to deepen as a result. Second, the economic disparities between different social strata were greatly exacerbated in urban areas; the workers' "iron rice bowl" came under urgent threat, and incomes went down; and although the unemployment rate and the number of laid-off workers had not yet reached today's levels, its particular effect on workers in state-owned enterprises was already recognized. Third, adjustments in the taxing structure and the marketization of power, changed the composition of the commercial stratum, where the recently won advantages of individual entrepreneurs were being drastically reduced. Fourth, reforms in housing, healthcare, salaries, and other social benefits were not promoted extensively, while inflation threatened any sense of social security. Not only was the salaried class dissatisfied as a result, but the lives of ordinary cadres were profoundly affected as well, particularly due to income gaps between ordinary government workers and other workers, as well as the increasing income gap between government workers that entered the market and those who didn't.[11]

It is worth noting that the 1989 social movement was essentially an urban social movement, and that it was intimately and internally related to the history of the post-1984 phase of reform commonly referred to as "urban reform," and to the expansion of the market. However, we should not forget that the other background condition for this movement was that, as the urban reforms were being promoted, the rural reforms stagnated (particularly visible in the pricing system, the household-registration system, the pension system, the birth control problem, and the problem of the organization of grassroots society, among other things), all of which increased the urban-rural divide. From 1985 to 1989, peasant incomes had already begun to fall, but rural society had not yet been as fully incorporated into market processes and crises as it would become in the 1990s, and there were not yet as many immigrants in the cities as there are today. This stratum was not involved in the social movement of the late 1980s.

The stability of the state in the 1980s was established upon its strong ability to control society; but this ability to control cannot be reductively understood as a purely state-coercive power. At that time, the state was promoting economic reform, intellectuals were participating in and devising ideologies of reform, and grassroots society (especially peasants) were directly experiencing the advantages of reform; these three factors gave the 1980s reform process the aura of legitimacy. Yet, immediately preceding and following 1989, some new situations emerged: First, within the state, there emerged clashes of interests, such as those between different departments, different strata, and different power centers, as well as contradictions between the localities and the center. Second, divisions within the state produced divisions among intellectuals. Intellectuals directly participating in defining the reform process and devising reform ideology and propaganda were actually completely incorporated into the state system, and were highly susceptible to divisions within the state.[12] Also included in the intrastate divisions were the transformations in state function and in the system of the social division of labor, which, in important ways, were altering employment trends and social attitudes among intellectuals. Third, certain urban strata began directly to sense the diminution of their benefits in the reform process, and thus stopped believing wholeheartedly in the mythologies of reform (even while retaining a basically positive attitude toward reform). Fourth, in the development of the urban reforms and the consequent rearticulation of rural-urban relations, new crises in the rural arena were becoming more apparent. These factors helped constitute a new crisis of legitimacy. That is, not only did the residues of the planned economy inform the crisis of legitimacy, but the very social transition toward the market also shaped it. Here, what people questioned was not the consequences of the planned economy (of course, this does not mean that people approved of the planned economy, just that, in the course of systemic transformation, the immediately pressing problems of life led people to question the process of transformation itself). Rather, they questioned the legitimacy of the redistribution of benefits that was proceeding in the name of reform (who was the state representing in its efforts to redistribute benefits?) as well as the legitimacy of the course of the redistribution process itself (in accordance with what? according to which administrative procedures? under whose/what supervision? legal or illegal?), and so on.

These situations formed the backdrop to and conditions for the social movement and social mobilization of 1989. The basic demands of the students and intellectuals included such constitutional rights as workable democratic politics, press freedom, freedom of speech, freedom of assembly, and the rule of law (as opposed to the "rule of man"), among other demands; there was, in addition, the demand that the state recognize the legality of the movement (as a patriotic student movement). While the various other social strata supported the abstract demands, they also filled the demands with much more concrete social content, such as opposition to corruption and official malfeasance, opposition to the princeling party (special privileged class), demands for stable prices, restrictions on Yangpu Peninsula on Hainan Island (an area that was rented out to foreign capital), and demands for social guarantees and social justice—in short, the demand for the use of democratic methods to supervise the process and progress of the reorganization of social benefits, and to guarantee the impartiality of the reform process.

The issue we must squarely face is that, while the 1989 social mobilization clearly criticized the traditional system, what was before it was no longer the old state but rather the reform-minded state, or that state that was gradually moving toward the market and social transformation, and thus the consequences of those policies. I do not make this distinction—between the old state and the reform-minded state—in order to deny the continuities between the two types of state, but rather to point out the transformations in state functions and their social conditions. For, in reality, the very state that was promoting markets and social transformation was utterly dependent upon the political legacy of the old state and its method of ideological rule. The guise of equality the old state maintained in the areas of ideology and benefit allocation belied its dependence upon coercion and planning for the protection of systemic inequality. Under reform conditions, this systemic inequality quickly translated into income differences between classes and social strata, which gave rise to social polarization. As such, the distinction is a heuristic one.

As a movement for social self-preservation, the 1989 social movement was inherently a spontaneous protest against the proliferating inequalities spawned by market expansion, and a critique of the state's handling of the process of reform; as a movement of social protest, however, it also pursued a critique of authoritarianism and the methods of authoritarian rule.[13] However, just as the distinction between types of state does not mean that there were in reality two states, the social protest movement was also one movement that contained a number of complex elements.

It is particularly worth noting the following complexities. Among those strata participating in the 1989 social movement were those special interest groups that had massively benefited from the decentralization of power and benefits in the 1980s, and who were now dissatisfied with the impending adjustment policies. These special interest groups attempted to push for their own demands through the medium of the social movement, with the intention of pressuring the state to carry out yet more radical privatization reforms. These special interest groups were not only products of the reform era, but also the direct reflections of the reform-era transformations of market relations into power. In this sense, their demands unfolded in the space between the upper echelons of the state and the social movement: they used their abilities to attract funds and gain a speaking platform to convey information and messages between the movement and the state. Hence they were able to use the social movement to force shifts in internal power arrangements within the state for their own benefit, as a stratum and as an interest group (although we should not ignore the role played in the movement itself by such groups as the Kanghua Company and the Sitong Company, which were two of the "four big companies" known to have close ties to the top leaders in the CCP). This phenomenon was also in evidence among those intellectuals who had an intimate relationship to state power, which was also closely related to divisiveness within the state and its factionalization at the time. What is now called neoliberal ideology in Chinese discourse had its roots here. At its core was the radicalization of trends toward the decentralization of power, benefits, and the contract system. In the absence of democratic supervision, the ideology also promoted the spontaneous pushing forward of all aspects of privatization, and thus the use of legislative procedures to legalize these entirely constructed processes of class and interest polarization.

For this reason, an important aspect of neoliberalism (or neoconservatism) is the intertwining of the processes of state factionalization and the formation of social factions and special interests; indeed, certain neoliberal principles had already been drawn into the web of state policies through administrative and economic power relations. The implementation of this market radicalism at precisely the moment of crisis in state legitimacy was initially articulated as neo-authoritarianism and neoconservatism (that is, the use of state power and elites to expand the market radically). It is this market radicalism that has come to be known as neoliberalism. To be sure, there exists here a certain shift in the meaning of power or authority: In the context of globalization, neoliberals believe that it is possible to use the strength of multinational and domestic capital to reconfigure Chinese society and the market; they recognize that the state plays a certain protective, favorable mediating role in the context of the relations between globalization and the expansion of the domestic market. Thus they no longer simply charge the state with motivating market expansion: this is the secret history of the mutual entanglement of neoliberalism and neo-authoritarianism. In this sense, certain conflicts between neoliberalism and the state are different from the relationship between liberalism and the state in the nineteenth and early twentieth centuries; they are the product of new relations of interests.

The most that can be said about the conflicts between Chinese neoliberalism and the extraordinarily conservative state organs of ideology is that they reflect the contradictions within state practice, while in numerous ways and in various forums proponents of each side paint themselves as "oppositional" or "dissident." Yet this does not at all prove that there is some fundamental conflict between market ideology and state practice; on the contrary, there is a complex mutual dependence. It is therefore necessary for me to note here that what I am calling neoliberalism is an ideology, and that all scholarly perspectives will have many points of convergence with it. In light of this, what I am analyzing is not any one person's perspective. Aside from this, what I mean by ideology is a guiding thought through which people can understand different issues.[14]

In the sense outlined above, the crisis in the traditional state-planned economy was transformed into a new crisis of the monopolization of market relations. The 1989 social movement cannot therefore be encapsulated as a conflict between state-led reform and social opposition to reform; on the contrary, in the context of the decline of the old system, the demand was for a deepening of reform. The crux of the problem, however, was the question of what type of reform. Students, intellectuals, and other movement participants all supported reform (including political and economic reform) and demands for democracy; but they differed widely in their expectations and understanding of the reforms, as well as how they stood to benefit from them. From a wider perspective, what the masses expected from reform and what they understood democracy and the rule of law to be were not merely a set of proceduralist political arrangements and legal documents; rather, it was the hope to reorganize politics and the legal system to guarantee social justice and the democratization of economic life. What people were demanding was to proceed with economic reform, albeit upon the basis of democracy and justice; they were not demanding so-called absolute egalitarianism or moral idealism. These demands were in fundamental conflict with those put forward by the special interest groups demanding more radical privatization, even though the full extent of this conflict was not understood at the time. The conditions briefly outlined above also explain why those special interest groups who had gained most from the reform process also participated in the social movement, as well as why many state officials and government cadres marched on Chang'an Avenue and participated in the demonstrations and protests that spanned across China's many social strata. In this sense, it is quite impossible to use a paradigm of pro- and contra-reform to understand the characteristics of the 1989 movement. According to the above analysis, we can say that the values of democracy and freedom were part of the ideology of social mobilization in 1989, along with perspectives on equality in everyday life. Indeed, precisely at this moment, traditional socialist ideology became a form of critical mobilizational strength; but as regards the broad participation of various social strata, everyday equality constituted an easily forgotten and yet very important factor, one that was deeply embedded in everyday life.

For this reason, 1989 was for me significant in many ways: it was a farewell to the old era as well as a protest against the internal social contradictions of the new era; it was (for students and intellectuals) a cry for democracy and freedom; and it was (for workers and other urbanites) a kind of plea for social equality and justice. This multifacetedness significantly amplified the movement's demands for democracy. However, the dominant analysis of the 1989 social movement in the world was one most advantageous to those special interests advocating radical privatization. This is due to Cold War ideology, state violence, and a corresponding crisis in legitimacy. In addition, the students and intellectuals lacked an understanding of the above historical conditions, whereas the most conservative elements of the movement (that is, those who were able to form a faction by arrogating power in the process of privatization) were able to establish collaborative relations between neoliberalism and the world order. This faction, presenting themselves as "radical reformers" and concealing their complex relations with state power and with certain other special interest groups—that is, concealing their own interests by burying them in the process—presented themselves to the world as the progressive strength of global markets and democracy.

On June 4, 1989, the Tian'anmen incident shook the world; in its wake, Eastern Europe and the Soviet Union were undermined. The Cold War ended and "history came to an end." The upheavals of 1989 exposed the signs of social disintegration, and, precisely in this context, the state made its own stability the premise of legitimacy, as the state organs of violence were understood as the only force that could maintain stability. Ultimately, this helped conceal the state's legitimacy crisis, which had gradually grown since the onset of the reforms. Here, one basic historical truth, or perversion, is that the state-led neoliberal economic policies led to the social upheaval, while the post-upheaval stabilization became the proof of the social expansion of the legitimacy of state power. After the violence of 1989, people concentrated their attention on the "June 4th" incident; meanwhile, the disintegration of Eastern Europe and the Soviet Union and, above all, the end of the Cold War pushed to one side the historical conditions this period established and the basic demands of China's social movement. In this way, the historical possibilities contained within the movement in China were lost with its failure.

As I have mentioned, the social mobilization of 1989 was based on protests against the uneven decentralization of power and interests; it was based on the dissatisfaction with the conflicts between the central state's readjustment policies and local and special interest groups; it was based on intrastate divisions; and it was based on the relations between different social strata and the organs of state. In the case of the media, we are compelled to ask how reports on the mobilization of all social strata and the demands for democracy could have found their way into the state-controlled media? I believe that the following three factors are most important. First, divisions among political factions and between the central state and local governments made it impossible for the media to provide a monological report on the progress of the movement. Second, the breadth of social mobilization made it impossible for the state to use its traditional methods to control the proliferation of news. Third, the demands for democracy and equality had subtle overlaps with state ideology (otherwise, it would be difficult to explain why the students persisted in demanding that the state recognize them as a "patriotic movement"), and the movement drew a certain legitimacy from it as a result. These three factors destabilized relations between the social movement and the state. In other words, the brief moment of press freedom during the month of May was made possible by the mutual reinforcement of the forces of the state, special interest groups, and the various social strata; its collapse was precisely the collapse of this precarious balance.

The failure of the movement is directly attributable to its violent suppression by the state. Yet, indirectly, it is also attributable to the movement's inability to establish bridges between demands for democratic politics and demands for equality, as well as its inability to form a stable social force. This made it impossible to link the movement's direct goals with its material conditions. In this context, the brief mutual reinforcement of the three factors listed above was too precarious, and could not generate any sort of systemic protection. Nevertheless, that brief moment does remind us that the progress of democracy resides precisely at the intersection of those three conditions; most importantly, it reminds us of how and through what forces such a precariously reinforced relationship can be institutionalized.

If one contexualizes the 1989 social movement within the expansion of the domestic and global markets, then one can see the links between it and the protests of November–December 1999 (in Seattle) and April–May 2000 (in Washington) against the WTO and International Monetary Fund (IMF), as all of these targeted a whole set of plans for the political management of people's everyday lives (even though this management is said to be in the name of the free market). The aims of these protests are dispersed and complex, and they are marked by various trends. Thus, to view them as a repudiation of a relationship between reform and freedom would be mistaken, because the most important element of these movements' and protests' demands is their utopian hope for an association between egalitarian, democratic reform and freedom.

However, the rise of the "end of history thesis" after 1989 also provided a very clear explanation for the social movement: The Western social system would prove victorious in the end, with China merely an orphaned holdout against this historical conclusion. The two ways in which the 1989 social movement were significant were thus reduced to a single narrative and, in my opinion, its critical edge and importance were thereby lost. From the numerous media explanations of the social movement to the new analyses of the protest overseas, all have hewed to the following basic tendency: in the context of the "end of history" globally, China's 1989 social movement was aberrant. Indeed, they have never recognized that 1989 was not only a massive turning point but also a critique and a protest against the new historical relations, the new hegemony, and the new tyranny.

As for the neoliberal antihistorical commentaries, I must raise several sharp, timely, and perhaps even sarcastically inflected questions here. First, the formation of the modern market did not emerge spontaneously; rather, it is the product of state intervention and violence. After 1989 the state continued to pursue reform and readjustment, and because of the threat of violence, expressions of social dissatisfaction with the crises identified above were only aired for a short period of time; indeed, the two unsuccessful price reforms of the 1980s were completed in the aftermath of 1989. We can summarize the readjustment of 1988–91—particularly the post-1989 economic changes—in the following ways: currency policy became one important tool of control; foreign exchange rates were significantly adjusted as they began to converge, which promoted exports in turn; this rate adjustment also increased competition in foreign trade, which gave rise to the birth and growth of management companies; differences between the "dual-track prices" were reduced; Shanghai's Pudong District was opened for development, and development areas soon appeared everywhere. In this sense, the mutual perfecting of the formation of the market pricing system and the market system itself was the result of policies and measures that had been implemented before 1989; on the other hand, this perfection also resulted from state control and violence. The violence of 1989 ended the social upheaval that had arisen in this process, and the pricing system was completed. It is worth noting that the pricing reforms that were forced into suspension at the end of 1988 were implemented in September 1989—that is, three months after June 4. At the time, it was primarily prices, exchange rates, and interest rates that were adjusted. In other words, the new market system and its all-important pricing system did not emerge through spontaneous or independent procedures; rather, they were the products of political intervention and political arrangement. The transfer of this relationship between structures of political power and market relations into the new economic system was thus inevitable. For example, in this process, income gaps among all strata of society, groups, and regions expanded, and poverty quickly grew.[15] This historical turning point placed the old ideology (the socialist ideology aimed toward achieving equality) into direct contradiction with practice, and the old functions of ideology could not be salvaged. At the same time, the failure of the 1989 social movement followed the failure of state ideology, which is important for understanding Chinese ideology at the time: the "strong on two fronts" (*liangshou yin*) strategy[16] implemented after 1989 alongside the economic reforms became tyrannical (in comparison to the previous ideological methods, anyhow); this made it clear that the basic functions and efficacy of the old state ideology were already moribund. It was only under these conditions that neoliberalism was able to take the place of state ideology to become a new ruling ideology, thus providing basic direction and rationality to state policy, international relations, and the emerging values of the media; it also provided the systemic and ideological premises for certain neoliberal intellectuals to play important, albeit dual, roles in the domestic and international media (that is, as advocates of state policy and as so-called public intellectuals).

Second, as a set of political arrangements, the formation of market society has not only failed to eradicate those very historical conditions targeted by the 1989 social movement but has in fact legalized those arrangements. Because intellectuals since 1989 have incorporated the social movement into the end of history thesis (albeit alongside the lamentation that "history" has not yet ended on the mainland), there have been very few detailed investigations into the historical conditions and the basic demands of the social movement. In 1992, when Deng Xiaoping made his Southern Tour and promoted anew the economic reforms, he received the general approbation of local interest groups, intellectuals, and overseas pundits—following an economic slump and political suppression lasting three years, this reaction was completely understandable. However, it is worth noting that the basic problems highlighted by the 1989 social movement were never resolved in any way. For this reason, the main social crises of the 1990s are closely related to pre-1989 social conditions. A brief glance at the fallout— corruption, privatization, the influence of special interest groups in public policymaking, overheated development (such as real estate in Shanghai, Hainan, and other places) and the resulting financial crises, problems in the social welfare system, ecological crises, and many other social problems—immediately reveals the internal relationship between the two periods, although the scope is now greater and, because of the impact of "globalization," the arenas involved are now much wider. For example, systemic corruption is still closely connected to the two-track system; capital flight, factionalized privatization, and the formation of local and departmental special interest groups are completely caught up with the foreign trade and contract systems; the crisis in the financial system was instigated by real estate investments, alongside other overheated development projects; and the worsening situation for state-owned enterprises was also related to the deterioration (rather than the perfection) of the market environment mentioned above. The problems introduced through the newest twist in the financial reforms, and the measures to correct them, were also very closely wrapped up in the dual-track system of the time, although their concrete manifestations and the arenas they affected were obviously completely different. It is in this sense that market expansion has played a large role in creating social polarization and unevenness—by destabilizing the foundations of society—thus helping to create the conditions for authoritarianism and monopoly. It is also precisely in this sense that the process of privatization—even including certain of its contradictions with the state—has never been able to hide either its will toward authoritarian politics or its deep hostility to democracy.

Third, the 1989 social movement was an urban social movement. It exposed the internal contradictions in urban economic reform as well as the social contradictions created in the course of market expansion. Most people discuss the rural and urban reforms as relatively independent phenomena and phases, although few note the relationship between the two. In 1989 the movement participants did not give a thought to the problems of the rural people, who constitute the majority of the Chinese population. But whether one is considering 1989 or today, understanding the rural reforms is a prerequisite for understanding contemporary China's uneven market expansion. Urban reforms were first initiated in 1984, and the rural/urban divide started to grow in 1985; by 1989–91, peasant incomes had basically stagnated, and the income gap between urban and rural areas had reached pre-1978 levels.[17] In the latter half of the 1980s, the percentage of peasants who migrated out of the rural areas grew. Most people understand this phenomenon as a sharpening of the contradictions between the rural population and land, but the problem is more complex. Here I want to mention a few systemic reasons for this phenomenon. First, urban reforms expanded the scope of infrastructural projects, while open-door policies attracted a large amount of foreign investment. These two situations increased the need for labor. Second, village and rural reforms were not deepened in the process of urban reform; on the contrary, the basic structures of the rural and urban systems remained unchanged. This increased the rural-urban income gap, accelerating the rate of migration of the rural population to the cities as well as encouraging a wider segment of this population to migrate. Third, the loosening of the household registration system created conditions of relative freedom for migration (the commodification of rural labor power), but none of this resulted in a new system or appropriate measures for labor security under the rapidly changing conditions. For this reason, deflationary and poor economic conditions led urban, regional, and local governments to place strict limits on in-migration, thereby reviving discriminatory policies based upon socially fixed identities. These fluctuating levels of restriction on rural labor power guaranteed the labor supply, while also limiting the pressures of population migrations on urban life. This is the fundamental cause of contemporary China's "uneven development."

The following exemplifies how urban-rural relations were institutionalized: in 1993, agricultural incomes rose slightly when the state raised the price of grain once again to help rural industries and stem out-migration; but from 1996 to 1999 (particularly after the financial crisis), the efficiency and productivity of rural industries decreased, and large surpluses appeared in the availability of urban labor, and as a consequence, workers in the rural industries and out-migrants began to return to their home villages. In many regions, migration and overheated development made it impossible to recover the previous composition of rural villages, producing a vicious circle: on the one hand, the contraction in the amount of arable land occurred at the same time as the rural population increased by 78 million in 1978; on the other hand, because of the lack of labor security and the household-registration system, peasant laborers could not but periodically migrate back and forth in accordance with the urban economic declines. Today, at any given time, one tenth of China's huge population is in the midst of cross-provincial migration; if we were to include migration within provinces, this number would increase dramatically.[18] We must therefore understand 1990s rural migration and poverty through this lens. These differing directions between urban and rural reform resulted most manifestly in the problem of unevenness; to borrow the words of experts on the rural question, the central cause of today's rural crisis is "diverging rule for urban and rural areas under the system of one country, two policies."[19] This systemic unevenness is based upon market expansion in and development of urban areas; it has already created and indeed continues to perpetuate structural differences between rural and urban areas, which have had a serious and even inestimable impact.

The rural problem was not at all the direct cause behind the 1989 social crisis. However, the contemporary rural crisis became deepened under "post-1989" conditions—that is, under the expansion of urban markets. China's rural crisis not only demonstrates that free labor contracting and social equity are internally related and mutual dependent (that is, not antagonistic), but also explains the depth of the crisis faced by rural regions, for the uneven expansion of the market has rendered peasants and land semi-free commodities. This has undermined both the organization of rural village society and the ability of rural society to rehabilitate itself. China's rural crisis thus presents a perfect example of uneven development.[20] For this reason, it is necessary to consider the following issues: First, one of the most important issues for understanding the relationship between the market system and free labor contracting is rural labor power and the systems for its protection. Second, the freedom of movement for rural labor has nothing to do with drifting; rather, it is systemically entrenched, and it must therefore be investigated alongside strong efforts to eradicate unevenness in the structural systems (and not merely of the household-registration system). The problem of the freedom to contract labor (we could indicate the freedom to migrate as an example) is not merely a Chinese problem; indeed, it is one of the most important measures for evaluating whether the contemporary global market is truly free. As Amartya Sen has noted in the framework for his thesis of "free development," the two most important aspects of development are, on the one hand, to remove constraints on labor to achieve an open and free labor market; and, on the other hand, to stop understanding this process as antithetical to the existence of social security, public management or government intervention policies. In the era of multinational production and consumption, this formulation requires expansion, elaboration, and amplification, for a number of reasons: first, the freedom to contract labor is not only required at the domestic level but also within global economic relations; second, one of the main driving forces of the capitalist expansion is the combination of free and unfree labor power, which means that the relationship between free and unfree labor and social development must be investigated; and third, market expansion is accompanied by an intrusion of exchange activities and their values into all aspects of life, which break apart all pre-existing social structures (such as communities and their values), and reduces all forms of communal life (including minority communities) to their lowest common denominator. In this sense, discussing development merely from the perspective of the freedom to contract labor, while ignoring the relationship between development and social conditions, could indeed result in the disintegration of society.

In defending the freedom to contract labor and the institutionalization of social equity, we must respect the deep relationship between cultural pluralism and the problem of development; we must also investigate rural problems alongside urban ones. The free movement of labor, public management, and government intervention are all necessary conditions for the market system; but how to limit its destruction on the environment, traditions, customs, rituals, and other aspects of life and values is a major problem for the study of development today. This will also be crucial for the liberation of the value of freedom itself from its imprisonment in a monological understanding of economic relations, and for placing this concept in a broader framework of understanding. From an even more radical perspective, the historical progress represented by the freedom to contract labor (that is, the emergence of an exchange relationship in the use of contracts for individual labor), which enabled the creation of surplus value and thereby doing away with the dependence upon political or coercive personal systems of extraction, does not eliminate the necessity to think about market contract relations (try thinking about the coastal regions, where the contract form of labor has led to the emergence of slave labor). In other words, the freedom to contract labor is one of today's many pressing social problems, and it should not be seen merely as society's end-goal.

A fourth basis for questioning the antihistorical stance of neoliberalism is that contemporary China's reforms have proceeded in concert with transformations in the shape of global society; they have also grown from the radical readjustment of foreign policy. Reform and the opening of the mainland are two sides of the same coin. It is worth noting that the concept of "opening" has led to a mistaken notion, which is that, prior to opening, China was a completely closed, self-sufficient society. It is thus necessary to make a strict distinction between the motivations of the Cold War period and those of the Qing Dynasty (1644–1911), both of which had isolationist policies at certain times. In the first place, the conflicts between China and the West are mutually reinforcing—particularly the opposition of the United States to China's Communist Party and its rule. The Cold War that immediately followed the Second World War, along with its hot-war episodes, was one of the primary contexts for China's foreign policy of the time: the outbreak of the Korean War in 1950; the embargo of the Taiwan Straits enforced by the American Seventh Fleet; American support for the Indonesian coup and its anti-Chinese aftermath in 1960; the Vietnamese and Indo-Chinese wars—all of these helped to divide Asia into two different worlds. Ideological and geopolitical considerations led China to turn to the Soviet Union and Eastern Europe, with which it had differing degrees of alliance; following the Sino-Soviet split, China continued to pursue its post-Bandung foreign policy and energetically developed broad political, economic, and cultural relations with the Third World and non-aligned countries. In 1972 the Chinese mainland government became the United Nations representative for China; this was made possible almost entirely because of the support of the Third World and the small countries, and was an expression of the great successes achieved by Chinese mainland foreign policy in the post-Bandung world. It was also widely welcomed by the Chinese people themselves. The policy of openness began during the Cultural Revolution; the establishment of diplomatic relations with many countries was also achieved at this time. The main motivation for this policy toward the West was the strategic readjustment of China's position vis-à-vis East and West, toward an alliance with the United States in order to oppose the threat of Soviet attack.

After 1978 the Chinese government gradually abandoned its policy of alignment with the Third World and the non-aligned countries; it placed its relationship with the United States, Japan, and other developed capitalist countries at the center of its foreign policy. In this period, China's policy of openness developed by leaps and bounds, particularly in the economic and political arenas; China and the developed Western nations formed ever-deepening trade and exchange relationships. However, the establishment of these relationships did not come without conditions. From February to March 1979, China attacked Vietnam. This war was unlike any that had erupted since 1949, including the Sino-Indian and Sino-Soviet wars or the Chinese assistance to Korea and Vietnam. While the reasons behind the war are complex, one element is especially important: it was precisely at this juncture that Sino-American relations experienced a huge transformation, and their shared opposition to the Soviet Union and its allies began to emerge in the form of a tentative alliance. China and the United States announced the establishment of diplomatic relations just before the Chinese government declared war on Vietnam. The war was thus the true beginning of China's entry and assimilation into the American-led economic order; from another angle, the war also demonstrates the relationship between marketization and violence. From this moment on, the old socialist stance of internationalism gradually faded from the scene, and China's previous one-sided policy of openness was transformed into another one-sided policy of openness—that is, openness toward the West (including Japan and other developed countries). There is nothing that demonstrates this problem better than the 1999 NATO (American) bombing of the Chinese embassy in Yugoslavia: in the extraordinary meeting of the United Nations discussing the bombing, not only did the Western alliance stand together, but the traditionally sympathetic Third World alliance was unwilling to voice support for China.

The 1980s policy of openness—which freed China's policies from their previous constraints and from the distortions of the Cultural Revolution—has had some liberating effects; for this reason, it has been welcomed broadly by the entire nation, and particularly by intellectuals. As regards China's reform, its policies of openness and their successes, I, like many intellectuals, welcome them. However, in engaging in historical analysis, we cannot ignore the deep scars and consequences resulting from this process, as it perfectly exposes the biased nature of the world map created by state ideology. Beginning with the generation that grew up after the Cultural Revolution, the only worthwhile knowledge comes from the West, particularly from the United States (and, as before, this too is a sort of bias). Asia, Africa, and Latin America, not to mention Eastern and Southern Europe—those places that used to be the sources of such vital knowledge and culture—have now basically fallen out of the purview of popular knowledge. In the literary production and reassessments of the Vietnam War in the 1980s, what dominates is not a consideration of the relationship between foreign relations and the war, but rather considerations of the Cultural Revolution, as if repudiating

the Cultural Revolution could lend these reassessments all the rational
support they needed. This is a perfect example of how repudiating the
Cultural Revolution has turned into a defense of ruling ideology and
state policy. And this method has only gained in popularity: almost
all critiques of the contemporary period are seen as regressions to the
Cultural Revolution, and thus basically irrational.

Even though the shift from the 1980s to the 1990s was preceded
by ten years of reform and opening, the space of Chinese intellectual
discussion is still limited by the framework of national modernization; it
lacks even basic internationalist sensibilities. Nationalism, the national/
ethnic problem, globalization, and other questions cannot therefore be
placed within the context of ongoing discussions of democracy. This
intellectual situation clearly demonstrates why, in the aftermath of the
failure of the 1989 social movement, people have been unable to find
any critical stance from which to think about the movement and its
failure. It also demonstrates why people predominantly understand the
problem of globalization through the experiences of the United States,
Western Europe, Japan, and the "four East Asian dragons" (that is, the
developed capitalist regions), never touching upon the other sides of
these experiences: India, the Middle East, Africa, Latin America. In
addition, it also demonstrates why the historical moment of the 1989
social movement has not been understood in relation to the different
social conditions and concrete goals of such related events as Gorbachev's
perestroika, the People's Power movement in the Philippines, and the
Korean student movement. It is precisely in this context that the study
of the conjunctural moment of the 1990s, the rethinking of modernity,
and new historical perspectives could have far-reaching effects and
emancipatory potential. I will have more to say on this point in the last
part of this essay.

Three intellectual phases of the 1990s and their major issues

1989–1993: Rethinking "Radicalism"

If one links the 1989 social movement to the historical conditions from
which it came, it is possible to see clearly why its demands for democratic
freedom were connected to demands for social equality. We can also
appreciate that the broad understanding of democracy advanced in

the movement itself constituted a sharp critique of contemporary life. Looking retrospectively from this perspective at the several intellectual debates that occurred in the 1990s—particularly those dealing with the 1989 social movement—it is impossible for me not to feel that these debates were nowhere near as substantive and profound as the movement itself. For analytical convenience, I will provisionally divide the period from 1989 to the present into three interrelated phases—"provisionally" because these phases are not self-contained periods, nor do they constitute internal teleologies; rather, they are interrelated and overlap.

The first phase covers the period from 1989 to 1993, during which many summaries and conclusions about the 1989 social movement were reached, and a general critique of radicalism formulated. The failure of the 1989 social movement provoked massive emotional shock in China: the intellectual world was forced to face the abyss of historical circumstances and rethink the reasons for the movement's failure. In this process, a gap gradually opened between intellectuals and the student movement: intellectuals came to consider the movement's failure as rooted in the students' radicalism and in their shallow grasp of democracy.

The considerations of "radicalism" were intimately linked to the social role that "intellectuals," individually and collectively, had played through the 1980s. In the 1980s there were various strata of intellectuals: at the upper levels, they played a very important role in the reform process, as they directly participated not only in devising a reform ideology, but also in designing state reform plans at every level. They thus overlapped closely with intrastate political and other interested groups. Through this long-term working relationship, these intellectuals had come to believe that, if only the reform factions within the state could gain power, all problems would be solved. For this reason, they staked their reputations upon the hope that intrastate conflicts would be resolved in favor of "reform," while they worried that the increasing radicalism of the student movement would destroy the precarious power balances underpinning the state reform process, thus ushering in the return of conservative forces onto the political stage. However, in their considerations of 1989, many intellectuals brought to bear the reassessments of modern Chinese history that had begun during the 1980s enlightenment movement, through which they established connections between the history of the modern revolutionary movement and their own moral support for new social movements. For these reasons, the critique of radicalism quickly developed into a broad reconsideration of the whole problem of revolution and reform in modern Chinese history, in which radicalism was linked to socialism, with political and cultural revolution as its major characteristics. As one famous scholar stated: even though China had embarked on its revolutionary path through the Xinhai Revolution in 1911, the 1898 *wuxu* reform movement and the new policy reforms of 1901–11 were more worthy of historical approbation. A younger intellectual, meanwhile, criticized the emphasis on science and democracy from the May Fourth period onward, along with the relative neglect in this period of the more fundamental problems of freedom and order.[21]

If one were to view the above historical considerations as reassessments of the political strategy of the 1989 social movement, or as investigations into the very concept of democracy, then these might continue to be relevant points today. However, these analyses were mostly established upon ahistorical premises, as they never once touched upon the 1989 social movement's historical conditions or the motivating forces behind its radicalization. They completely conflated the analysis of the movement's strategies with reconsiderations of historical events, thereby laying out the main outlines of neoconservatism's (or neoliberalism's) legitimating historical narrative. In the context of serious social polarization, the "rethinking of radicalism" thus became the most important and decisive concern of intellectual debate of the early 1990s. By 1998, some scholars saw this discussion as evidence for a more systematic discussion of post-*wuxu* (1898) modern Chinese history, as well as a theoretical paradigm for discussions of contemporary democracy. The predominant perspective in this case was that, ever since the institutional reforms that had begun with the *wuxu* period, Kang Youwei, Liang Qichao and others had mistakenly chosen radicalism; all the while, it was only the local elites, who had promoted reformist gradualism, that had actually achieved reform success.[22] Thus, in the name of repudiating "direct democracy" and opposing the participation of grassroots society in politics, these studies intended to specify indirect (elite) methods as the basic premise for political democracy.[23] Of most enduring significance is the fact that, in the past several years, neoliberals have reconfigured the radical demands of the 1980s political reforms into a "constitutional revision movement" centered on private property rights—whereas, in actual practice, what they did was to legitimize the irrationalities of distributive relations through legislative means, through which the illegal confiscation of public resources was made legal. Beginning from such a historical perspective, it was all but inevitable that social equality and democratic relations would be rejected completely.

This intellectual trend of "rethinking radicalism" was far from unified. For example, in the beginning of the 1990s, scholarly discussions of history mostly addressed the scholarly environment of the 1980s; and, as there was no coherent philosophy of conservatism as its premise, the critique of scholarly trends did not prevent critics from all political persuasions from drawing on conservative philosophies to support their arguments. So-called neoliberal ideology was thus constructed upon common ground between radical marketization ideologies, neoconservatism, and neo-authoritarianism—that is, the radicalization of the decentralization of power and interests under conditions of social stability. But contrary to its ideological representation, the major characteristic of neoliberalism was the withdrawal of the state from society under conditions of social upheaval, and on the tides of globalization.

In 1989, Samuel Huntington's book *Political Order in Changing Societies* was translated into Chinese, whereupon political theorists of conservatism began to draw upon the rethinking of radicalism, from which neo-authoritarianism derived its force. Under these conditions, and in the narration of history, the basic issues of the 1989 social movement were conflated with modern revolution and reform radicalism, even though Fukuyama's end of history thesis had been accepted ideologically and embraced. What was actually formulated was a critique of the relatively radical and Westernized reform paradigm that had been established during the enlightenment movement of the 1980s. The rhetoric of liberalism, now containing many elements of conservatism (which, for some people, was directly translatable into neo-authoritarianism), therefore came to dominate debates on liberalism during the period. After 1989, the Chinese version of Scottish liberalism, or "classical liberalism," turned out to be merely a Chinese version of conservatism, which began leveling attacks against the strategies, timing and morals of the student movement, while enthusiastically deconstructing the radicalism of the Chinese Revolution, as well as a critique of the radical nature of social movements in general. However, what conservatism did not do was formulate any profound hypotheses about the relationship between the basic motives behind the 1989 social movement and its social conditions. Faced by the dual forces of the rethinking of radicalism and the conservatism of modernization theory, the ideology of neoliberalism began to accommodate corruption and its systemic manifestations while abandoning opportunities to promote, through systemic reform, any sort of democratic process through social movements and the building of democracy. Neoliberals were thus unable to contribute to the establishment of democracy, either in China or in the global arena.

For precisely these reasons, in 1992, after three years of economic readjustment, when Deng Xiaoping made his Southern Tour and reanimated the reforms, intellectuals welcomed these initiatives but came up with no new constructive analyses. Local and central government factions welcomed these initiatives, because the new reforms meant more decentralization of power and interests—processes through which the contradictions that had arisen between local interests and the center during the readjustment period could be resolved; intellectuals welcomed them because they believed that, if only reform could proceed and a market economy could be established, then the democratization of China would gradually proceed apace; overseas pundits welcomed the initiatives because China was now back on the path toward the predestined "end of history." The basic issues raised by the 1989 social movement were shunted aside.

From 1992 to 1993, market conditions were relatively ripe and the economy quickly grew, due to the resolution of the price issue through a combination of the three-year readjustment period and the use of force, as well as the development of rural industries in non-state-owned industries in the southeast. However, many systemic problems remained unsolved, such as that of reforming overburdened state-owned industries, rural development, and the new and related problems of unemployment and consumerism. But conversely, after 1992 and with the establishment of the pricing system, the increase in local autonomy along with other factors of accumulation were not accompanied by a commensurate emergence of democratic supervision; neither were these developments incorporated through the reform of state-owned industries into structural innovations. This whole process thus created a hotbed for the growth of systemic corruption, large-scale privatization, a downturn in the financial environment, and an increase in poverty. The direct result of the Southern Tour was the emergence of large numbers of "special development zones" and the development of futures markets, stock markets, and the real estate market. This gave rise to market conditions and became a pretext for the strategic emergence, through systemic corruption, of contemporary China's new wealthy class. They also gave rise, to some extent, to the historical conditions resulting in the "two combining into one" (*heer eryi*) of (domestic and international) political and economic elites. In short, this was a process through which social and class polarizations were simply re-created through unequal conditions, and which harbors within it the long-term prospect of social crisis.[24] Despite this, related intellectual discussions from 1989 to 1992 were unable to address these issues, and in spite of three years of debates over radicalism, intellectuals never considered whether these reform processes were themselves radical, or whether the social conditions leading to the 1989 student movement were being exacerbated through the post-1989 reforms themselves. What I wish to point out here is that it was precisely such discussions that provided the narrative premises and historical rationalizations for the neoliberalism of the second half of the 1990s.

Neither the 1989 student movement nor intellectuals were able to propose any practical avenues for action, provide any self-conscious theoretical critiques of this complex historical process or propose any political practices that could improve it. This cultural context explains why the internal links between the demands for social equality and democracy in the 1989 social movement were ultimately considered as spontaneous elements in the historical narrative; it also explains why, in intellectual discussions of the time and even after, student political demands were never linked theoretically to the broad-based social mobilizations. Here, the biggest problem is that the very concepts of radicalism and conservatism concealed the real character of and social conditions for the 1989 social movement. In the post-1989 environment that marked the movement's failure, many young intellectuals began to study and consider modern Chinese history, and their studies of Chinese academic and scholarly traditions to an extent provided material for subsequent reconsiderations of modernity and intellectual practice.[25] However, these investigations were unable to provide any overall analysis of the internal contradictions of contemporary Chinese society. In my view, divisions gradually appeared after 1994 between intellectuals who had performed self-reflection through direct participation in this process, and those who had not.[26]

1993–1997: Market ideology, the case of privati̧ation, and its critique

The second phase lasted from 1993 to 1997. It began with Deng Xiaoping's Southern Tour, and ended with what has been called the Asian financial crisis. Many intellectual debates emerged during this period, which did not for the most part result in any consensus. Indeed, the divisions between intellectuals actually sharpened. In order to understand the intellectual situation of this period, I will briefly explain the major events of 1993–97 and review the discussions that surrounded them.

First, in the wake of Deng Xiaoping's Southern Tour, the pace of economic development and opening-up quickened, while urban commercial culture (particularly consumer culture) began its long-term development. A large number of consumer-oriented TV series were aired, with Beijing TV, Central TV, and other local TV stations leading the way; the "Wang Shuo phenomenon"—the "writer-as-rebel" phenomenon—along with other intellectual and artistic products, gave impetus to the development of so-called mass culture. Second, with the surge in economic and commercial activity, some intellectuals and scholars also turned to the market—a turn called "jumping into the sea" (*xia hai*)—and the income gap between intellectuals working within and working outside the system increased rapidly, producing a crisis in the social position of intellectuals. Third, the development of township and rural industries, the crisis in state-owned industries, and the difficulties in state tax collection all occurred simultaneously, even as the East Asian development model received new attention, sparking new interest in exploring various different paths for China's social and economic development.

In the global arena there were also several incidents that left a subtle but marked impact on Chinese social psychology, and particularly on the sentiments of intellectuals. It was in 1993 that the Chinese government, seeking to leave behind the international sanctions imposed on China after the 1989 events, sought to win the 2000 Olympics for the city of Beijing. Because of the serious corruption scandals that had surrounded previous Asian Olympics, most intellectuals were quite critical of this pursuit, and in the end, political interference with China's bid by Western nations—particularly the American government—led to its rejection. This blatant enmity was shocking for Chinese society. It was also in October of that same year that the president of Russia, Boris Yeltsin, ordered a military attack and suppression of the legally elected Duma. This violent and anti-constitutional behavior, undertaken by someone who had staked his reputation on rhetorical opposition to communism, not only exposed the grave crisis of Russian reforms— and particularly of the "spontaneous privatization process" promoted by American and other Western advisers—but also reflected the deep contradictions within Western, and particularly American, policies toward democracy and human rights, among other things, thus belying the extreme selfishness and anti-democratic character that lay at their core. American support for this violence was immediately compared to the American response to the Chinese violence of 1989. The import of Russia's October Incident was profoundly felt, especially by idealists possessing a rosy view of the West, those who believed that history had already come to an end, and those who saw the Cold War as already over. At almost exactly the same time, Samuel Huntington published his long essay "The Clash of Civilizations?" in *Foreign Affairs*, which was immediately translated and published as a special issue in both Hong Kong's *Twenty-First Century* (*Ershiyi shiji*) and Beijing's *Research News* (*Cankao xiaoxi*), drawing widespread attention and intellectual debate.[27] These international events were deeply upsetting intellectually for those scholars who had been attempting to analyze globalization based upon Confucian one-worldism (*datong guannian*), enlightenment ideals of "perpetual peace," and the supposedly universal path of mankind.

In this context, a whole series of parallel and successive discussions took place in the intellectual world, which I discussed in my essay "Contemporary Chinese Thought and the Question of Modernity."[28] Here I wish only to supplement that analysis with two points directly related to neoliberalism.

First is the discussion about markets and civil society.[29] This discussion was clearly a continuation of the rethinking of radicalism during the previous period; it was significant in two ways. In light of the major setbacks in political reform, it was posited that transformations in the structures of the state would naturally follow if economic reforms continued to develop smoothly; this would spontaneously bring about democracy (since its real basis was understood as the formation of civil society) so that as soon as civil society was formed, the social division of power would be complete. I cannot analyze here in any detail the theoretical background that informed this discussion, but it is worth pointing out that it represented a shift from the 1980s analyses of political change. That is, the 1990s discussion shifted from a conviction that the establishment of democracy could be achieved only through a radical transformation of the political framework, to a conviction that reliance upon market processes, the formation of local and departmental special interest factions, and the uprooting of clan and other traditional resources would ultimately lead to political democracy. This discussion of civil society did little to explore or excavate any new popular resources; moreover, as an extension of the rethinking of radicalism, it also offered no detailed analysis of its own expectations for the formation of a middle class through the connection between markets and civil society. Nor did it offer any detailed analysis of the social role to be played by the newly formed interest groups, or of the complex relationship between these new economic forces and the state, or of consequent intrastate divisions (between central and local governments, through the factionalization of state interests and state intervention in society). It therefore overlooked completely the potentially serious crises that might be precipitated through this process itself, and therefore had no way to analyze the gradually accumulating social contradictions that had been set in motion in the 1980s.

Here the real issue is that, in the context of rethinking radicalism, the discussion of civil society completely ignored the new alliance between the state and special interest groups in their common desire to combat social movements. In locating "society" outside the category of the state, the conceptualization and imagining of civil society rested upon the assumption that the spontaneous activities of the market would naturally lead to democracy, which presented an obstacle to any political consideration of regular democracy. From the rethinking of radicalism to the discussion of civil society, intellectuals were unable to reach any summary conclusions about the relationship between the process of social movements and preconditions for democracy. The original goal in conceptualizing civil society had been to investigate the possibilities and necessary conditions for democracy, yet because no clear distinction was made between a normative narrative and actual historical processes, this discussion quickly slipped into a theoretical black hole. That is, it conflated the demands of theory with actual historical process, going so far as to rationalize market unevenness as some natural process of achieving democracy.

Thus, while Deng Xiaoping's 1992 Southern Tour helped to ameliorate the tense relationships that had developed between the central state and localities (along with departmental interest factions) throughout the readjustment period of 1988–91, it also undermined the possibility of social mobilization in its support for a division of interests. As a consequence, the following factors are what I understand to be the reasons for the preemptive stagnation of the democratic process in the 1990s: first, the complete undermining of the newly emerging mutual dependence between social movements and political reform in 1989 rendered it impossible for a consolidation of political force across various social strata, one that could force the state to intervene in the relationships between interested groups; second, state violence eliminated any possibility for social mobilization toward promoting a democratic process or the formation of a democratic supervisory system over local and departmental special interest factions, consequently eliminating any forces that could pressure the state; and third, local governments and the central state government struck a much broader alliance via the market, so that local governments and departmental interest factions were no longer required to mobilize social strength to force the central state to continue its decentralization policies—conversely, they were able to utilize this convergence of interests as a solid position from which to influence state public policymaking.[30] Under the monopolization of market relations, common laborers protested against the relationship between monopoly prices and special interests; they demanded that the state adjust prices and also provide security against market competition. However, the state once again became the defender of monopoly. In this sense, any theory of political democracy should have been premised upon the guarantee of the interests of common citizens and the construction of systemic obstacles to the double-sided alliance between the state and special interest groups—this is a basic condition for the formation of a fair marketplace.

It is therefore worth considering the idea that a case for democracy can be made only on the premise of a mixed system (that is, a tripartite system consisting of the state, elites, and the masses), with the participation of common citizens at its core.[31] What the idea of a tripartite system emphasizes is how mass demands can be transformed into state policy, from which a new system of privilege and the double-sided alliance between the state and local or departmental special interest groups can be forestalled. It is precisely this political ideal that is promoted by theories of civil society, and I believe that this is an area that we should pay attention to and continue to discuss. Here it is particularly important to explore how the interactions between social movements and structural reorganization could yield a democratic supervisory system, from which would come not some simple reliance upon state supervision of the upper classes, but rather the mobilization of democratic mechanisms at all levels of society to obstruct the usurpation of power by the state, as well as local corruption. In this sense, it is urgent and important to identify which forces and methods can open up social spaces to various social strata. In my opinion, there is one basic premise required for the establishment of such a mixed system: the promotion among different levels of society of open discussions about public policy through social movements and policy discussions by common citizens. In this context, one particularly important intermediary step is the creation of spaces for social movements and public discussions at different levels of society. That is, social movements and public discussions are necessary not only in the national context but also in local public spaces. In this way, common citizens might participate in discussions that are intimately connected to their everyday concerns.[32] This would be a concrete manifestation of demands for democracy and freedom; it would also be effective in preventing democracy and freedom from becoming radical but empty slogans. This ideal, created out of the actual conditions of contemporary China, is in direct opposition to the conceptualization of civil society that, in reality, only increases the distance between the state and the citizenry; the latter takes democracy as an extra-political, spontaneous process, thereby undermining any possibility for cumulative interaction between social mobilization and systemic innovation.

Second is the discussion of systemic innovation, theoretical innovation, and the problem of state capacity (*guojia nengli*). From 1993 to 1997, some critically minded intellectuals in China began to consider the problem of social justice; they undertook a multifaceted investigation, with reforms in Russia and Eastern Europe as well as the experiences of Southeast Asia and township enterprises as the backdrop.[33] This discussion was in some ways related to a previous discussion in 1992 that encouraged research into the problem of state capacity, although the direction it took and its theoretical framework were different in important ways. The problem of state capacity touches upon the systemic forces that caused unevenness in 1990s society; or, in other words, it refers to the problem of the relationship between the central state and the local and departmental special interest factions. In the debates of 1991–93, the problem of state capacity was commonly considered to be associated with statist-oriented policy research; research on this widely important and valuable topic was therefore not officially taken up by most intellectuals.[34] The eruption of the 1997 global economic crisis forced people to notice the mobility of financial capital and its capacity to destroy domestic and social economies; this helped prompt some scholars to reconsider the question of the significance of the "state" in social security, to rethink the relationship between democracy and the state, and to discuss the multiplicity of state forms, the contradictions in a dichotomous capital-state structure, and so on.[35] There are thus two contexts for raising the problem of the state: in 1991, the problem of the state or state capacity referred to the central state, and it targeted the issue of the reform policies and the consequences of the decentralization of power and interests; by contrast, after 1997, the core problem of the state became that of the utility and position of the state in the context of globalization. However, these two approaches are still internally connected to one another, and both took development and social security as their central issues. The state question in contemporary China is extremely sensitive and complex: corruption, monopoly, polarization of wealth, the disintegration of the social security system, authoritarianism, and the bulk of the state apparatus—all of these are intimately connected to phenomena that have resulted through state policy (the so-called marketization of power and the infiltration of power into the market). However, it was only the financial crisis of 1997 and the way it highlighted the issue of social security that finally made the issue of the protective capacity of the state visible. Here, the irony is that the decline of state capacity was completely tied to state intervention in grassroots society and the marketplace (including its administrative partitioning of the market), the free market, and transnational activity—or, all those issues that transcend the state while constituting the premise that state activity is necessary. Under these perverse historical conditions, within the movement demanding democracy, critiques of the state cannot be separated from critiques of the movement toward market society. The most profound parts of the multifaceted discussions of 1996 were those relating to systemic and theoretical innovation, through which the actual crises in Chinese reform processes since the 1980s were specified at both theoretical and practical levels, and which urgently presented suggestions for the democratization of reform.[36] At the crux of these discussions was opposition to the system's fetishization of neoliberal concepts, as well as to the view that the destiny of all peoples is bound up with authoritarianism and foreign-imposed systems; they intended to explore methods of democratizing market economies. In this discussion, modern socioeconomics and experiences of democracy were understood as multiple, and from that position numerous theoretical possibilities were proposed regarding choices and innovations derived from concrete historical conditions. Most importantly, they harshly criticized the spontaneous privatization that had already occurred in Russia and was just being promoted in China under the control of the central powers; they exposed the profoundly anti-democratic nature of this market-economy model; and they proved that there are insuperable contradictions between ongoing processes of privatization and democracy. They thus proposed new directions that might foster mass participation, alliances between technologically advanced and technologically underdeveloped countries, and the reform of industry and the political system.

Between 1993 and 1997, China's economy grew at its fastest rate; economists and some cultural theorists, having resorted in their theories to Confucian capitalist and Southeast Asian models of development, were left completely unprepared for the extent and urgency of the financial crisis. Indeed, globalization itself posed a sharp challenge to neoliberal ideology. Meanwhile, the aforementioned discussion linked the issues of political democracy and economic democratization, which summarized China's experiences of the 1980s and even earlier. The emergence in this period of discussions on the humanistic spirit, on postcolonialism, and on the theoretical problem of modernity were completely resonant with the discussions described above about civil society, free markets, and system innovation; it was against this theoretical background that the sharp intellectual polarizations of the post-1997 period took shape.

The third period runs from 1997 to the present, and is mistakenly designated by some as a period of debate between neoliberals and new leftists. In reality, the point of departure for the post-1997 intellectual debates is the sharpening social contradictions in contemporary China that have emerged against the background of the "Asian" financial crisis, which had ripple effects spanning across the globe. During the crisis, the economies of Korea, Hong Kong, and Southeast Asia were profoundly damaged. At almost exactly the same time, China's township enterprises went into tailspin, and the internal contradictions within the Chinese economy—particularly its financial sectors—were exposed. But what factors, in the final analysis, prevented China from succumbing immediately? In this context, we are forced to face squarely the internal contradictions within the capitalist system, to seriously consider the meaning of what has long been designated the market paradigm in its concrete manifestation in China, to observe with dispassion how the attempt to legitimize special interest relations has been repeatedly concealed under the rhetoric of legal reform and demands for democracy. Indeed, it is now necessary to rethink all the intellectual formulations that have, since the 1980s, successively provided the premises for reform. It is precisely in this historical perspective that the end of history thesis receives its true comeuppance, and the democratic proposition is theoretically elaborated in a contemporary way.[37]

The 1997 Kosovo War; the bombing of the Chinese embassy in Belgrade; over the uproar against the WTO, unemployment and layoffs; the systemic corruption that is daily becoming more globalized (from privatization to money-laundering, from individual corruption to institutional corruption); the polarization of wealth; the environmental crisis; and other social contradictions that have emerged and deepened in the process of reform—all of these have destroyed any naive or theoretical illusions about modern society. This process has fully demonstrated that globalization is not in any sense external to Chinese society but rather fully internal to it. The relationship between political power and market arrangements, new social poverty and unequal structures; the links between old webs of power and new market expansions: these provide a new opportunity to reconsider the whole course of modern (including both *jindai* and *xiandai*[38]) history, and a new opportunity to understand and discuss creatively the legacies of socialism. The sedimented and spontaneous factors that were deeply buried within the 1989 social movement are now gradually becoming clear. Hence, on the one hand, numerous internally differentiated public discussions and debates have emerged on such issues as the economic crisis, developmentalism, political democracy, globalization, social equity, feminism, education, war and revolution, neoliberalism and colonialism, among others, especially in the journals *Dushu* and *Tianya*; on the other hand, the translation and publication of what were considered classics of neoliberalism (also sometimes directly presented as classical liberalism), alongside the sharp turn by some liberal writers and essayists toward conservatism, pushed neoliberalism suddenly into a period of systemic exploration and analysis of its own ideological assumptions.

Neoliberalism is a broad categorical ideology that is primarily interested in the economy; it permeates every aspect of contemporary society and has enormous ideological coordinative capacity. Hence any critique of neoliberalism or neoconservatism must engage in a differentiation of its various aspects. In the past twenty years, in the history of social thought on the Chinese mainland, there has never emerged quite such an intricate and complex situation as this one; in my opinion, this phenomenon is a reflection of the very fissures and crises within dominant relations. I must explain several things. First, the scope of these critiques is extremely broad, and they are not limited to a direct critique of neoliberalism; however, the social relations to which they refer are all somehow connected to neoliberalism. Second, these critiques are not unified, nor do they possess a consistent logic; frequently, there contain significant internal disjunctures and contradictions, which include elements of a critique of liberalism and elements of orthodox Marxism, internationalism, nationalism, traditional scholarship and culture, postmodernism, and other trends. Hence we cannot see the critique of neoliberalism as a unified intellectual movement.

Since 1997, the discussion has concentrated on the following points. First, there is the discussion about the liberal tradition and its contemporary problematic. Neoliberalism advocates distribution in the name of the free market against a planned society, which has created large-scale corruption and social polarization; this has prompted intellectuals to delineate, from within liberal theory, the coercive and constructed nature of the marketization of power.[39] In contemporary Chinese discourse, neoliberalism not only excludes all types of critical theory in a tyrannical and monopolistic fashion, but also completely ignores alternative possibilities from within liberal theory, such as the egalitarian tendencies of Rawls and Dworkin, or theories related to communitarianism and republicanism. In this era of the marketization of power, and in partitioning public resources through privatization schemes, such binaries as freedom/equality, freedom/democracy, and individual/society are clearly constructed, and it is of enduring significance that neoliberals construct theoretical methods and arguments that maintain that "democracy obstructs freedom."[40] The only parts of Hayek's theories used by neoliberals are those that prove the legitimacy of the "free market"; they have thus rearticulated all the radical market planning internal to traditional society and conflated it with freedom, thereby completely ignoring the discussion of historicization inherent in Hayek's theories. One theoretical characteristic of neoliberalism is to deny that there is an intimate relationship between market and political processes and, in the name of the disarticulation of the state, to force the abandonment of all investigations into the problem of democracy under the conditions of marketization. It is precisely in this context that, beginning in 1997, some scholars began to arrive at a new understanding of the liberal tradition, and to discover from within liberalism the antidemocratic tendencies in neoliberal theories. Such discussions drew upon such thinkers as Tocqueville, Isaiah Berlin, Arendt, Hayek, Habermas, Rawls, and Charles Taylor to rearticulate the liberal tradition of politics in modern Europe and contemporary liberal theory; at the same time as they were analyzing liberalism's internal difficulties, they recovered and developed the egalitarian trends within liberal theory from many angles and at various levels. There thus emerged the phenomenon of what was called the "liberal left wing." In the pursuit of this discussion, the legitimacy of neoliberalism was subverted from within the liberal tradition itself, while these subversions also injected some new elements into the discussions of liberalism.[41]

Second, the discussion of historical capitalism and historical analysis. Neoliberals understand the market system to be a kind of "spontaneous order"; they understand free trade to be the natural law of a market economy, and they perceive the doctrine of the greatest expansion of interests as the sole ethical guide for the market era. The historical horizon of this theory is thrown into sharp relief when set against the polarization of wealth that increases each day, the ever-deepening economic crisis, and the never-ending processes of corruption and marketization of power. In the context of China's reform process, neoliberal advocates refuse to consider the connections between the formation of market mechanisms and mass democratic participation, or even basic demands for equality; hence, by partitioning state-owned resources, by monopolizing gain and super-profits, and by linking the possession of market resources and benefits with special-interest power and transnational or national capital, they have formed a sort of conspiring alliance. Neoliberalism, self-consciously or not, has in fact strengthened monopoly and antimarket tendencies.

However, it is precisely at the level of morality that we discover the toothlessness of neoliberalism, and this is the main reason that liberal economists reject any type of moral critique in the name of science.[42] In this situation, a transcendent moral critique carried out at the levels of theory, history and practice is urgently required to respond to neoliberalism's basic theoretical designs. Beginning in 1998, the journals *Dushu* and *Tianya*, among others, continued the reassessment of globalization and modernity of the previous period and published successive essays on theories of history and historical capitalism which, from the angles of theory, history and practice, stringently attacked the market mystifications of neoliberalism. The theories of Karl Polyani and Braudel, as well as those of traditional Marxist political economists, were important intellectual resources that offered a critical historical horizon informed by political economy and the critique of economism. These critical intellectuals intended to reopen an investigation into the major characteristics of historical capitalism and its links to the contemporary economic crisis, as well as to analyze neoliberalism's theoretical binaries, including politics/economy, state/market, nature/ society, and state/society. These theories were all demonstrated to be historical constructions and ideologies. Such research helped lay out a smoother path that was of immediate importance to a direct critique of neoliberalism.[43] What stands out most from these discussions are the internal linkages established between capitalist markets and power, violence, intervention, and monopoly, all of which demonstrated that the relationship between politics, economy, and culture have never been disrupted. In addition, a necessary distinction was made between markets and capitalism. These discussions were not merely an effort to imagine a historical vision that would incorporate market relations that were characterized by equality and mass participation along with a democratic political framework, but were also an effort to offer new historical possibilities through a rethinking of the experience of traditional socialism.

Third was the discussion of the WTO and developmentalism, which was directly connected to the analysis of historical capitalism.

It was here that the internal linkages between neoliberalism and the state, special interest factions, and transnational capital were exposed in their most concentrated form. The state and its media presented a united propaganda front on the long-term negotiations surrounding the WTO, echoing exactly its representation in the American media. Some intellectuals investigated the problem of the WTO using the Internet and journals, but practically all critical views of the WTO were shut out of the public media, and thus a public debate about the WTO never occurred. Neoliberals saw in the WTO the greatest development of plans for "free trade"; they thought that this plan would pave China's road to democracy. But this political arrangement, which would have such an impact on billions of people's everyday lives, were never publicly discussed, to the extent that after the Sino-American negotiations there was not even any public disclosure of information.[44] On my reading, this is because most of the scholars who were critical of the WTO deal were fundamentally unopposed to China's entry into the WTO; they were also not unconditionally or even abstractly opposed to globalization. Rather, in their concrete analyses, they concentrated on two major issues: first, the conditions under which China should enter the WTO; and second, whether or not there was a public discussion that would yield a concrete analysis and a critique of what the WTO represented for the world order. Here the real question was democracy: whether or not there was a democratic and open discussion; whether or not there were any democratic controls on shaping global procedures. We need to ask: Are the WTO procedures subject to public and democratic controls? We also need to ask: Are China's entry into the WTO and its method of entry in accordance with any principles of democracy and mass participation? In the absence of such democratic and public participation, the overblown claims made about the relationship between globalization and democracy are merely draping themselves in the cloak of democratic rhetoric in order to legitimize a set of tyrannical procedures.

These discussions have been echoed in the debates carried out by humanist scholars and social scientists about developmentalism, which have all exposed how the utopian myth of development and the mystifications of "transition" have masked the urgency of problems such as political freedom and democracy.[45] The critique of developmentalism is not a critique of development; rather, it is an effort to reconstruct the internal relations between development and freedom, and to reaffirm the importance of democracy and pluralism in the development process. By the same token, neoliberalism understands development as a narrow problem of economic growth and is not concerned with the relationship between this growth and political freedom and social security. It thus ignores, whether consciously or not, the political premises for economic growth. Developmentalism is not only the core concern of domestic policy, but also the premise upon which the WTO, IMF, and other international organizations base their global plans—and its theoretical support is precisely provided by neoliberalism and radical marketization. Developmentalism universalizes successful development models, thereby concealing the fact that these development models were themselves based upon uneven core/periphery relations; it thus disrupts any internal relationship between the freedom of choice and development. Even as this plan for the "free market" creates an ecological crisis and wealth polarization, it also reconsolidates one or another form of colonial relations within nations and internationally, in its rejection of democratic controls over society.[46] The debates about the WTO profoundly reflect the necessity for freedom of speech and public discussion. At the same time, the emergence of the WTO and other important social questions have presented new challenges to intellectuals struggling for the right to free speech: in light of the extremely complex contemporary social situation, the struggle for freedom of speech and of the press must be located within the historical horizon of broader democratic demands, from which would arise a much tighter connection between the demands for constitutional rights outlined above and demands by other social strata and social movements. The crux of the problem here is that, in order to obstruct the monopolization of benefits by special interest factions and the re-feudalization of the public sphere, we must in actual practice expand our social space of activity.[47]

Fourth are the discussions about nationalism. These discussions were continuations of the 1993 discourse about nationalism and the problem of globalization, but they reemerged during the Kosovo War and after the bombing of the Chinese embassy on May 8, 1998 incited university students and urban residents in Beijing and other cities to protest and throw stones at the embassies of the United States and other NATO countries. The discussions surrounding the "May Fourth" enlightenment movement, which had been going on since the 1980s, once again called for "saving overriding enlightenment" (*jiuwang yadao qimeng*); in 1999, seemingly in lockstep with this, people began once again to consider whether modern China's two biggest historical problems had been "nationalism" and "national essentialism" all along. Intellectuals published papers reflecting on the new situation, as well as the critiques and enthusiastic promotions of Chinese nationalism from inside and outside China, often in opposition to the works of other intellectuals. In the first place was the interventionist nature of NATO: Was this a humanist intervention or ultimately an expression of political interest, making it an ultra-imperialist holy war? The high-tech weaponry used by NATO troops, the mobilization of the media, and the different goals of the war all made this intervention appear differently from classical imperialism, yet these were wholly incapable of concealing its imperialist essence and of papering over the theoretical and historical relationship between this military action and traditional imperialism.[48] There was also the problem of national self-determination and human rights. The Yugoslavia crisis cannot be encapsulated or analyzed using the simple category of nationalism; rather, any analysis needs to situate both the country and the world within the context of international political and economic relations. Such an analysis would completely deconstruct the weak links between a "humanitarian assistance" in the form of wanton and indiscriminate bombing, and demands for human rights.[49]

The protest movement incited by the Kosovo War became entangled with all types of nationalism; to prevent these protests from becoming completely assimilated into the structures coordinated and designated by the state, it is necessary to make a theoretical and practical distinction between social protest movements and ethnocentrism. Hence we must ask: Despite the biased accounts offered by both the Chinese and the Western media, is it nevertheless necessary to distinguish, in theory, between protests against hegemonic behavior and critiques of state-mobilized nationalism? The state media reported widely on the bombing incident, all the while concealing the internal crisis in Yugoslavia and the severity of the ethnic clashes that occurred; the government used public opinion to bargain with the Americans and Western nations. However, just as the protest movements were reaching their apex, the Chinese government immediately took leadership of the movement, reorganizing it and limiting its scope. At the same time, the Western media concealed the true nature of the bombing, as well as the broadening scope of the "humanitarian disaster" brought about by the war itself—that is, the Western media were too busy conflating the real anger of common people toward the violence with nationalist hysteria. As for the protest movement, it is thus necessary to explain the theoretical difference between protest against hegemonic behavior and violence, on the one hand, and anti-foreignism on the other; it is necessary to explain the significance of the political participation of the masses and the place of social movements in the Chinese democracy movement. Only having made such a theoretical distinction between anti-violent protest and nationalism will it be possible to mobilize active support for, and critique of, the multiple possibilities inherent in social movements.

In this sense, to conflate mass participation in and demands on society, and to conflate protests against hegemonic behavior with "national essentialism" or "nationalism," or even with "radicalism" (thus placing them outside the reform system), is to understand the state and nationalism to be mutually antagonistic. Yet the logic of both are the same. These two political tendencies (the state logic and the analytic logic) have, from separate directions, sabotaged the democratic capacities and demands for equality brewing within social movements.[50]

Since the rethinking of radicalism that began after 1989 and continued through the post-1997 debates on neoliberalism, the understanding reached by Chinese mainland intellectuals about Chinese realities has clearly deepened. However, after 1989, intellectual considerations began from a reassessment of radical social movements, and, in certain respects, this point of departure has only strengthened the premises of conservatism and neoliberalism. The examination of the relationship between social movements and systemic reform has thus not received the theoretical weight it should have. The problem of the interests of workers, peasants, women, and other social groups has gradually gained some hearing in the course of these intellectual discussions, but the self-preservation movements that have sprung up among these groups and the relationship of these groups to systemic reform have been elaborated at the level of theory. In many senses, the systemic reforms of the post-1978 period were part of the processes by which the division of social labor became specialized, and social classes re-stratified. As one of the privileged classes of the reform period, intellectuals have gradually been repositioned as elements internal to the state, educational institutions, think tanks, commercial activities, high-tech arenas and the media, among others; the historical linkages between intellectuals and the worker and peasant classes have now seemingly been broken. Intellectuals are concerned with the fate of such constitutional rights as the freedom of thought, speech, and assembly, among others, and have not yet been able to connect these pursuits with those of other social strata, namely the struggle for survival and the right to development. Even those intellectuals who are critical of the movement for social security have been unable to find efficient methods for constructing theoretical praxes that connect systemic innovation to social movements.

In my opinion, it is for this reason that efforts to think through systemic and theoretical innovation, and to build a participatory economic and political framework, have stagnated at the level of abstraction, even while contemporary social contradictions have continued to sharpen at expontential rates. My point in bringing this up is not to repudiate the importance of theoretical work, nor to advocate unconditional support for all social movements (as the experience of 1989 has shown, there are all sorts of complex elements and tendencies inherent in movements themselves); on the contrary, I believe it is precisely the inability to theorize the relationship between social movements and systemic reform that has prevented us from seeing the real junctures that connect a dovetailing theory and practice at an internal level. It has prevented us from constructing a historical understanding of social change and social movements, and from finding a real path toward democratic processes that can avoid both social polarization and social disintegration.[51]

Why start from the question of modernity?

Within mainland Chinese discourse of the 1990s, the critique of neoliberalism has been intimately connected to the reassessment of the problem of modernity, which is its necessary handmaiden. In my view (one I hope to develop elsewhere at a greater length), these ongoing critiques must at least include the following points.

First, we must rethink the position of socialism within the horizon of modernity. The critique of our contemporary course cannot be made from somewhere outside this framework, since it is only within this horizon that the intimate connections between socialism and contemporary crises can be seen.

Second, European capitalism and its history of global expansion must not become the standard against which China is measured. We should make these the objects of our critique and rethinking as well. Indeed, it is precisely on this terrain that the intimate connections between the Chinese historical problematic and historical capitalism can become visible, and the legacies of China's past and the experiences of modernity, along with their contemporary significance, can be understood.

Third, the reassessment of modernity should not be understood as the totalistic rejection of modern experience. On the contrary, it should be seen as an effort to transform the historical experiences of China and other societies into sources and resources for theoretical and systemic innovation. It is exactly in this sense that the critique of neoliberalism is first and foremost a historical critique—a process of interrogating modernization narratives from the perspective of actual historical processes.

Fourth, the reassessment of modernity represents a critique of modernization. In the absence of this theoretical horizon, contemporary Chinese intellectuals have no way to deepen their theoretical analyses of developmentalism, nationalism and other related questions. For the same reason, the internal connection between the reassessment of modernity and the horizon of globalism makes it necessary to extend beyond the unitary frameworks of bounded nation-states.

Thus, modernity here forms a point of departure for discussion, and provides the grounds upon which more concrete discussions might be elaborated. This is my hope: it is a hope that we might transcend theoretical formalism to examine actual historical relations; a hope to transcend the gulf between theory and practice; and a hope to overcome prejudices and biases of all kinds. But, like my attitude toward history, I have never held a nostalgic or romanticized attitude toward theory, the reassessment of empirical and theoretical questions, or even communication itself. History, experience and knowledge are resources we must use to overcome ourselves in our present state, as we must continuously do, yet they also pose unavoidable limits on this pursuit.

MODERNITY AND METHODOLOGY

3

An Interview Concerning Modernity: A Conversation with Ke Kaijun

Ke Kaijun: *In this past few years, the concept of modernity has appeared in various different newspapers and publications. It is used by critics of post-modernity and critics of the Enlightenment, yet they often fail to define the concept, using it instead in a general manner. It is as if those who use it lack clarity about its meaning, while those who criticize it are equally confused. Our newspaper is preparing to start a column discussing the question of modernity. Can you discuss this concept with us before we begin?*

Wang Hui: The question of modernity is a very broad one that has been discussed by many theorists and historians from a variety of different angles. Marx's concern about the capitalist mode of production and distribution and Weber's concern about rationality can both be read as responses to this same question, even if they don't necessarily utilize this concept explicitly. To provide a concise definition or to standardize the concept of modernity would be extremely difficult, however. But I do believe that the discourse on modernity involves two interrelated aspects.

The first is an examination of the theory of modernity, while the second is an examination of the development of modern society. These two aspects cannot be considered separately.

If we were to summarize the discourse on modernity, we could perhaps understand some of the important usages of this concept. First of all, the concept of modernity originated in Europe and was initially used to signify a kind of temporality, one that progressed in a linear fashion and represents a non-circular consciousness of historical time. Matei Calinescu's *Five Faces of Modernity* describes in detail the origins of the concept of the "modern," claiming that, though it is linked to the secularization of European history, it can in fact be traced to Christianity's eschatological worldview, whose implied temporal consciousness is characteristically non-circular. During the Renaissance, the concept of the modern was frequently used as a complement to the concept of the ancient, and then, in the eighteenth century, to signify architecture, clothing and language in a fundamentally derogatory way. It wasn't until the nineteenth century, and even more so the twentieth century, that the concept began to shed its derogatory connotations.

Beginning in the nineteenth century, modernity as a conception of time came to be linked to a phrase that continues to be popular today, which is the concept of the "age" or "new age." Hegel's historicism (his concept of the "age") was the most complete expression of this sort of temporality. Habermas pointed out in *The Philosophical Discourse of Modernity* that the concept of modernity became in Hegel's work a concept concerning an "age." This "new age" was the modern age, while the Rennaisance, the Reformation and the discovery of the "new world"—events that occurred roughly around 1500—were used to distinguish the Modern Age from the Middle Ages. In this sense, the concept of the "modern" was given meaning by becoming distinct from the Middle Ages and ancient times, and it manifested the belief that the future had already begun. This was an age that existed for the future and welcomed the novelty the future might bring. This conception of time as evolving, progressive and irreversible not only provided us with a way of reading history and reality, but also incorporated the entire meaning of our existence and struggles into a progression of time, a sequence of ages, and a set of future goals.

We still like to say things like "fallen behind the times," and use phrases like shijiechaoliu haohaodangdang shunzhizhechang nizhizhewang *("as the world progresses along certain lines, those that swim with the tide will thrive while those that go against it perish") when discussing contemporary issues. Will this temporality become a standard for judgment in our daily lives?*

Yes. In "What is the Enlightenment?" Foucault characterized modernity as an attitude—one that connects itself to both the present age and the future. Modern artists sometimes dress and wear their hair in ways that might appear quite unusual to outsiders, but for them these are necessary expressions of their times and for getting at the essence of a future-oriented art or way of life. These everyday cultural forms are therefore significant. Our history and our daily lives contain countless different instances in which we invoke the present age and the future to validate our behavior—not even the nineteenth-century decadents can match our pompous behavior, our grandiose proclamations and our rash way of speaking. But the pursuit of trends by artists is still often taken to be a personal character trait. More importantly, the various different communal movements and social practices all derive their force from the inspiration of both the present age and the future. The people of the Middle Ages derived the reasons for their existence and the meaning of their lives from God, so that with the "death of God" the transformations in human history could only then legitimize themselves through promises of a better, freer and more liberated future.

Our everyday lives, studies and work have all been organized within this future-oriented time, so much so that without this teleological narrative of time, we no longer know their significance. Yet, having been hit with a stream of crises in all these domains, the promise of freedom has become freedom's demise. In observing this, theorists such as Lyotard interpreted modernity as a grand narrative, one that was constructed in actuality by particular "senders" (authorities), even if they did so in the name of freedom and liberation. This is the relation between narrative and power. With the aid of such narratives, those things, methods and people that do not conform are all cast out, as described by *shunzhizechang nizhizewang* ("those that swim with the tide will thrive while those that go against it perish"). This grand narrative is monopolizing and compulsory, becoming the argument for the legitimacy of a modern despotism. From the perspective of discursive practices, each of modernity's values are linked to the process of its implementation, so that freedom and liberty are interpreted concretely as practices as well. In his series of works, including *Discipline and Punish*, *Madness and Civilization* and *History of Sexuality*, Foucault proclaims that our promises of liberty, humanism and freedom conceal power relations, exclusions, surveillance, and disciplinary mechanisms. To borrow Nietzsche's words, morality originates in evil, not good. Thus, from an archeological or genealogical standpoint, do those grand narratives finally originate from "good" or from "evil"? The reply is the latter.

I have seen a few journal articles that seem to have lots of criticisms of Lyotard's works. Why have such criticisms been advanced?

Many theoreticians who criticize Lyotard's concept of postmodernity also construct new "grand narratives" themselves, and this perspective has been accepted by many people. Such "grand narratives" are frameworks for understanding the world, and many feel that there would be no way to organize our world and our lives without them; social life in its entirety would be impossible. But this is not the most important reason—it is, rather, how we view the tradition of the Enlightenment and how we understand the crisis of modernity. In his essay "Modernity: An Incomplete Project," Habermas defined modernity as a "project" which only became a central aspect of life during the eighteenth century and belonged to the Enlightenment. In *The Condition of Postmodernity*, David Harvey summed up what Habermas said about this project, which was that it was an extraordinary intellectual feat for the Enlightenment thinkers, through which an objective science, a universal morality and law, and an independent art with its own internal logic were developed. Within this project, the point of knowledge is not only to enrich our everyday lives but also to liberate humanity. In other words, this project includes the promise of science to free us from domination by nature, including our deficiencies, our needs, and natural disasters. The rationalization of social organization and the rational model of thought promises to extricate us from the irrationality of myth, religion and superstition. Only through this project can a universal, eternal and unchanging essence of human nature emerge. Habermas saw the accomplishment of this "subjective freedom" as the symbol of the project of modernity. This kind of "subjective freedom" appears in social life in a number of ways—for instance, in the social domain, in the guarantee of a space under civil law within which one can pursue one's own rational benefit. In the political domain, it appears in the formation of political will through participation and equal rights in formulating public policy. In the private sphere, it appears in ethical freedom and self-realization. In the public sphere, it can appear in the process of the rationalization of social and political power. The Enlightenment project fundamentally finds expression in the form of the nation-state, but in my opinion, what Habermas calls "subjective freedom" is also expressed in the establishment of nation-state sovereignty. In light of this, the project of modernity is not only a particular temporal consciousness, but also the anticipation of a social condition to come.

Habermas thus says that this is an "incomplete" project. He makes the distinction between this project and the progression of modern history, claiming that the latter cannot be seen as the total implementation of the former. Instead, that progression contains distortions, differences, and constraints upon the project. Habermas's awareness of this problem derives from Weber and Kant. To summarize briefly, instrumental reason has come to dominate and has taken the place of a rational division between knowledge (science), practice (morality) and judgment (aesthetics). Pure reason has taken over all the spheres of life, leaving behind all questions of practical reason or aesthetic judgment. This is certainly an extreme simplification, however, and further analysis of this matter can still be performed. I bring up this point because, while Habermas affirms the value of modernity, he continues to maintain a highly critical attitude toward it as well. Habermas accepted Weber's conception of modernity without reservation, understanding it as a differentiated domain of value. However, as early as Weber, the contradictions internal to the project of modernity had already become the cause of theoretical concern. This kind of project did not have the ability to protect the life-world from erosion and confinement by the market and the bureaucratic system, and for this reason he was profoundly suspicious of this differentiation of value domains. In other words, the "incompleteness" of this project of modernity is in itself extremely suspicious, since this process contains two mutually opposed principles, namely the principles of specialization and secularization. Weber was already aware of the irresolvable contradiction between these two principles. How then can we expect the "completion" of a complete project of modernity? Or, what is the significance of discussing the "completion" of a project containing such intrinsic contradictions?

Habermas, however, is unlike the many Chinese theorists who defend "modernization" today. They jumble modernity and the process of modernization into one heap, giving them the appearance of being apologists. As soon as the question of modernity is brought up, they become suspicious that you are suggesting a return to older times or to the Cultural Revolution, among other eras, showing in their reflections that they don't see modernity as a system with internal conflicts but as a unified goal to be affirmed. In doing so, they defend the most hegemonic ideology of our times.

Can you explain briefly how the concept of modernity was spread to China?

The concept of modernity came into use in China soon after it came into use elsewhere. When this began, people were using the concepts of elders vs. youths to express the meaning of progress. Liang Qichao's "Shaonian Zhongguoshuo" ("Ode to Young China") was an example of this. In 1898, Yan Fu translated and published Thomas Henry Huxley's *Evolution and Ethics*, after which the concepts of evolution, natural selection and the survival of the fittest made their way into Chinese history. Yan Fu's concept of *tianyan* ("evolution") is actually more complex, blending together the *I Ching*, *Shiji* ("Records of the Grand Historian") and other traditional elements, and it is hardly pure from a temporal perspective. I gave a detailed analysis of this in "Yan Fu de Sangeshijie" ("The Three Worlds of Yan Fu"—*Xueren*, Issue 12). However, if you have read Lu Xun and others recounting how they felt when they read *Evolution and Ethics*, you will know how large an impact this work had on the youth of the day. In the last years of the Qing Dynasty, the concept of the "new" began to gain in popularity with the important publications of the "May Fourth" movement, such as *Xinqingnian* (*New Youth*) and *Xinchao* (*Avant-Garde*), which all had names beginning with "new" (*xin*). Afterwards, the concept of the "modern" began to appear. These concepts appeared within the dichotomies of traditional/modern and China/West. At the time, there were journals that were critical of such conceptions of progress and time, such as *Xueheng* (*Critical Review*) and *Jiayin*, yet they did not appear to be much different from those that supported the other sides of the dichotomies. Around the time of the May Fourth incident, Bergson's creative evolution theory made its way to China, claiming first that history, politics and economics were evolutionary, then later developing to include consciousness as well. History came to have goals and to include a moral dimension. Later on, Marxists would critique capitalism's various projects, yet they too saw themselves as "new" and believed that historical progress would develop toward a definite future. Marxism is a modernist project that critiques modernity—it too is established upon a logic of historical teleology. Marx's views on history are influenced by Hegel, and carry the imprint of Eurocentrism. The irreversibility of the temporality of European history was constructed upon the European model. In more recent studies—for instance, in Said's *Orientalism*—this sort of Western self-image was also constructed against an image of the East. In Chinese history, the concepts of the "new," the modern and modernity are tangled together with concepts of Europeanization and Westernization in dense and opaque ways.

So is modernity therefore a negative concept?

No. The concept of modernity is in itself paradoxical, containing intrinsic tensions and contradictions. In Europe, modernity is closely connected to the process of secularization, and as a result it finds its most potent expressions in the worship of reason; in its faith in economic development, the market system and the legal-political system; in its faith in the rationalization of law and order. We can understand these beliefs as a kind of ideology of modernity. However, the rise of modernist literature, which has progressed in an identical way, has intense anti-capitalist and secularizing tendencies, with the aesthetic critique of bourgeois philistinism always having been a feature of German romanticism. Nineteenth-century European realist literature and twentieth-century modernist literature both provided critical views of modernity. Marx and Weber's systems of thought also included profound insights and critiques of the process of modernization, even if at the same time they continued to utilize the historical perspectives and various methods of modernity. Moreover, the struggles in modernity between scientism and humanism and between rationalism and irrationalism, to which people often refer, demonstrate the inherent contradictions of modernity. Modernity is a tradition of opposing oneself, as the renowned Mexican poet Octavio Paz has said.

In the mid nineteenth century, Marx and Engels transformed the aesthetic critiques advanced by German romanticism into a kind of ideological and political-economical critique, from which a clear separation between "revolutionary" and "philistine" emerged. The "revolutionary" conception of history represented a modernity critical of elitism, whereas the "philistine" way of life represented the bourgeois standard of living. Today, many of the most intense and profound critics of capitalism also provide the strongest interpretations of modernity. This is why, in their examinations of modernity, some contemporary theories also take aim at its most intense critics. However, trends have reversed, so that in the contemporary age the apparent cultural characteristic of modernity is to use a kitsch modernity against a grand modernity. This kitsch modernity isn't equivalent to everyday life, but is nonetheless a representation of the lack of alternatives to everyday life. If we simply look at how the ever-increasing array of newspapers and magazines introduce, promote and advertise the "new, contemporary way of life," along with the major film productions and television shows, we can get a good sense of this. Newspapers and magazines have already transformed a purely politically controlled domain into one controlled by money, profits and power. Some people regard this as the disintegration of authority, yet it is simply its reconstitution. The valuable critical space achieved through Enlightenment thought has degenerated, with increasing commercial control over ideas in the name of the people. Some former members of the elite have done a complete about-face, ridiculing their former fellow elites.

Thus, modernity can also be separated into elite and popular, and this dichotomy can be regarded as its symbol. The fundamental logic of modernity cannot be shed either by opposing what is popular from the position of the elite, nor by opposing the elite from the position of the mass public. But to point this out is not a sufficient explanation of the historical meaning of these two attitudes. What is important is the ideal represented in the elite, as well as the actual content and mode of secular life. In a society that holds up the elite ideal everywhere, it can become a tool of suppression. But in a society inundated by the forces of secularization, the combination of kitsch and secular power has stifled any critical potential for challenging the authority of this system. In traditional despotic society, state power took on the guise of an ideal in order to cleanse society of its existing foundations, and in the "civil society" of market societies, real critical space has been eliminated in the name of the secular. But the third sort of situation in which both exist is the most complex, for with the coexistence of civil society and despotism, civil society ends up constituting an elitist "anti-elite" critique of secular despotism, while despotism at the same time crushes all forms of social protest in the name of an idealist secular modernity. The modernity of the elites is primarily the continuous forging of the grand narrative of modernity, in which they play the heroes of history. Popular modernity, however, is related to various "modern" trends, each of which permeate everyday life and material civilization. Calinescu therefore ascribes five different faces to modernity, including

Modernism, the Avant-Garde, Decadence, Kitsch, and Postmodernism. Both kitsch and grand modernism are cultural characteristics of modernity. These two aspects sometimes contradict one another, and at other times mesh—yet they also share some important premises. Most of all, they both worship developmentalism.

In "Contemporary Chinese Thought and the Question of Modernity," I suggested that modern Chinese thought is characterized by an anti-modern modernity. China's search for modernity began during a time of colonialism, so that its historical meaning involved a resistance against it and a critique of capitalism. However, this sort of resistance and critique has not led the next generation of nation-states to shed the logic of modernity, but has simply proved to a certain extent that modernity is a global phenomenon. The crises it precipitates cannot be completely overcome in isolated contexts. But this should certainly not lead to the opposite conclusion that we needn't therefore reflect on the question of modernity. What is most important is how the critical thought and thinkers I have discussed presented their critiques of the "modern" from the perspective of the "modern." During the late Qing Dynasty, Yan Fu, for instance, was an important architect of the project of modernity, yet his thinking melded various different elements of thought. His concept of *tianyan* ("progress/evolution") therefore contains the contradictions between progression and reoccurrence, movement and stasis.

In 1907, Zhang Taiyan published a series of very important essays, including "Jufen Jinghualun" ("Two-Way Evolution"), in which he presented a scathing critique of the evolutionary conception of history and Hegel's teleology. In the same year, his student Lu Xun published "Wenhua Pianzhilun" ("On Cultural Paranoia"), which presented a harsh critique of various projects of modernity, including the French Revolution and its principles of freedom and equality. In another essay, "Po Eshenglun" ("Destroying the Voices of Evil"), Lu Xun asserts that superstitions could be maintained, though hypocrisy had to be eradicated, among other wildly unfashionable things—a wonderful claim when we think about it now! In the same vein, Liang Qichao, in the twentieth century, criticized the modern education system and the nation-state system, as well as reflecting upon the abuses of modern history in its founding upon the theory of evolution and environmental determinism. Sun Yatsen's "government for the people" (*minsheng zhuyi*) was a socialist project as well as a critique of capitalist modernity. Mao Zedong's many theoretical projects were established within the logic of modernity, yet he too was unable to avoid the problems associated with the question of modernity in the West. Chinese modernization began during the age of empire, as did the formulation of the project of modernity, and both originally contained revolutionary potential, though they no longer involve such historical analyses of resistance. However, we should certainly consider whether the calamities of modern history work to achieve modernity or anti-modernity, or whether the anti-modern orientation finally works to achieve modernity? Or all of the above?

We may as well look at European and US history for reference, including the relation between various social movements—labor movements, women's movements and minority movements, which struggled for political and economic rights—and the reform of modern social systems. We should also look at the relation between national independence movements and the domestic reform of Western societies. Without these social movements, the European democratic system would never have been achieved. This is also an illustration of how modernity contains its own mechanisms of self-improvement, which is also to say that the conflicts of modernity are the vital force that has sustained modernity to this day. This internal driving force originates from the critiques and conflicts themselves. The significance of this is that we cannot simply view the American, European or Australian systems as capitalist systems. It is just the opposite, in fact, for they contain many socialist elements as well. In other words, without those lasting critiques and resistances against capitalist modernity, the reform and development of our contemporary system, which so many people strive for today, would not be possible. Without lower-class struggles for economic, political and cultural rights, modern democracy would never have been achieved. Without the various national independence movements, the contemporary world would continue to be thoroughly colonial and imperial.

Modernity is a structure that contains internal conflicts. I think that this is a very important point. From this perspective, the reflections and critiques of modernity emerge from modernity itself, while this at the same time demonstrates the inefficacy of critiquing modernity from the perspective of a particular timeline. Many of China's postmodernists and critics of postmodernism fail to understand this fundamental question, thereby failing to acknowledge modernity's internal contradictions and conflicts, and instead adopting a holistic attitude toward modernity. What is essential is that they don't see modernity's internal tensions and contradictions. China's "postmodernists" often think of themselves as standing outside of history, from where they can carry out a critique of modernity. It is from this that the narratives progressing "from modernity to Chinese" or "from modern to postmodern" arose. They think of themselves as "men of the Enlightenment" without understanding the intrinsic anxieties of modernity, but simply embracing modernity wholeheartedly with a minimum degree of reflection. From an intellectual perspective, Chinese postmodernity and the Chinese Enlightenment are in sharp opposition to one another, yet in reality they both view modernity as a whole, and simply disagree with one another on the question of the timeline. China's postmoderns read history as developing linearly from modernity to the Chinese, while the defenders of "modernity" believe that Chinese sentiments have not yet evolved to the same degree that Western sentiments have. As a result, they think that we shouldn't discuss or study the question of modernity. They don't understand the internal contradictions of modernity, nor do they understand that the project of modernity contains principles that oppose one another and are difficult to resolve, or that the critiques of modernity are to be found within the same developmental temporality as the drive to achieve modernity itself. Yan Fu, Sun Yatsen, Zhang Taiyan and Lu Xun all presented critiques of modernity while at the same time seeking out the progress of modernity. It is for this reason that I once said that the critiques and reflections on modernity are one of the most important characteristics of Chinese modernity. Yet it is also for this reason that their critiques of modernity are often at the same time confirmations of its fundamental premises. In the contemporary context, we cannot avoid reflecting on these fundamental premises. In fact, the anti-modern modernity is no longer simply a unique expression of Chinese thought, but is also an expression of the contradictory structure of modernity itself. This self-contradictory structure is the source of modernity's self-renewal, and also the reason it is unable to overcome its own internal contradictions. The project of modernity is inherently paradoxical, and can only therefore be brought to full completion with great difficulty. In my opinion, the necessity of reflecting on modernity is contained here, and this is where we should begin our reconsiderations of it as well.

What then is the significance of examining the question of modernity today?
Could you discuss this from the perspective of history or intellectual thought?

Seeking out a standard definition of modernity is not my interest. We must view modernity as an historical and social construction, looking at how its progressive functions mask the historical relations and forms of oppression characterizing the modern world. We should ask whether modernity in the realm of history and intellectual thought is singular, multiple, or interactional. Modern European history has produced many unique historical models, such as the nation-state and sovereignty model, market society and its corresponding life values, legal structures and their protective mechanisms, and a strict division of labor and specialization. The politics, economics and trade models of European capitalism have been spread across the globe through colonialism, which has also disseminated nationalism, cosmopolitanism and other corresponding ideologies to all "modern societies." But do the ideas of nation-states, market mechanisms, division of labor and even legal mechanisms stem purely from European history? Do other regions not have their own histories? Where was European capitalism actually produced? The hegemony of capitalism is expressed in historiography as Eurocentric and ideological, yet this Eurocentrism is not a purely European phenomenon. The temporality of the modern, for instance, is fundamentally a Eurocentric historical narrative, yet it has also become the fundamental concept in historiography. If we attempt to escape from such a temporality, we find ourselves unable to enter into history.

Since the Thirties, China's many historians have been influenced by such conceptions of modernity, but their work still demonstrates that China's internal history includes historical elements like markets, civil service systems, and division of labor, among others. On the issue of time, these elements may even have appeared earlier than they did in Europe. This is an historical question and not one of whether we should learn from the West. What this means is that these unique elements cannot simply be categorized as "Western" or proper to Western capitalism. A few years ago, Lydia Liu published an essay in *Dushu* entitled "Heisede Yadianna" ("Black Athena"), which described the American scholar Martin Bernal's research on the relation between Greek and African civilization and his critique of Eurocentrism in Western history. When I visited Greece in 1995, the National Museum of Athens was holding an exhibition of ancient Egyptian cultural artifacts, which was located in a hall in front of cultural artifacts from Athens in the archaic period. What Bernal had written about the relations of inheritance between African and Athenian civilization became very clear. In 1995, I attended a conference in America during which the Japanese scholar Koujin Karatani criticized Derrida's phonocentrism, which the latter traced back to ancient Greek thought, neglecting the other regional origins and manifestations of this phenomenon. For instance, Japanese nationalism in its early form was primarily expressed in the cultural movement that sought to write out Chinese characters in the Japanese language. In the eighteenth century, the phonocentrism of scholars of Japanese language and culture (*guoxue*) involved a political struggle against the domination of Chinese "culture." It was also a critique of the bourgeois nature of *bushido*, since Chinese philosophy was the official ideology of the Tokugawa shogunate. The significance of this was that the birth of Japanese nationalism was possibly entirely unrelated to the "West," but rather came into existence within an East Asian world system centered around China.

Of course, this is not to say that the influence of European capitalism upon the rest of the modern world is merely a fiction. Europe's Industrial Revolution, its development of science and technology, and modern democracy have all had a profound impact upon the modern world, and have transformed virtually all "historical nations." Through colonialism and the division of labor, the various regions encompassing the modern world have been organized into what Immanuel Wallerstein has called the "world-system" in *The Modern World-System I, II*, and *III*. However, the systems affect one another mutually, and do not produce effects in a unidirectional way. In the eighth issue of *Dushu* this year, James Hevia wrote an essay that mentions the research performed in the West during the Eighties regarding imperialism, claiming that they did not simply discuss economic questions, but rather situated those economic questions within the multi-level framework of colonialism. For instance, architecture and urban development, record-keeping and census data, population control and family composition, sex and gender, communication, education, leisure, medicine, military organization and technologies, and questions of knowledge-production by the colonized (universities, museums and international conventions, and so on) all demonstrate that colonialism is not simply a unidirectional affair, but an exchange of influences. It has not only been colonized countries that have undergone transformation, but also the central belt of Europe's suzerain states. What this suggests is that the reading of history as a fixed sequence of stages, and of the global trajectory of historical development, must be reconsidered and revised.

In fact, as early as the Forties (and perhaps even earlier), Japanese scholars were already discussing the "capitalist" elements of the Song Dynasty (960–1279) by looking at widespread relations of transport. They thought that the development of modern world history after the Song Dynasty could provide a background for understanding the modern history of the West. Still, these scholars were in the habit of describing Chinese and Asian history from the perspective of European history and concepts, and so were hampered by other shortcomings. However, they did forge a new historical viewpoint that interpreted the phenomenon of European capitalism through a history of transport and communications. They asked: How did the spices produced in the South China Sea come to be favored by Europeans, in turn stirring up their courage to embark on marine adventures? The nomadic people to the north have a strong liking for Chinese tea. How was this connection forged, and how did it then become a threat to China? They even suggested examining the construction of the Grand Canal not simply from the standpoint of China, but rather by considering how, in promoting China's domestic transport, it also linked the two (northern and southern) land-and-sea routes traversing Asia at each of its easternmost tips. China was no longer the endpoint of east-west transport, but a link in the various global transport circuits. The opening up of the Grand Canal is viewed here as a significant enterprise in the context of world history. Referring to Europe's Industrial Revolution and the political revolutions centered around France in the eighteenth century, an outstanding historian named Ishisata Miyazaki suggested that the Orient, and particularly China, not only supplied a market and resources for the Industrial Revolution, but also nurtured the humanist aspect of the French Revolution. The logical conclusion is therefore that if there is only European history, then Europe's Industrial Revolution could never have occurred, because this is not only a question of machinery but of the entire structure of society. The rise of the petty bourgeoisie was the necessary background to the Industrial Revolution, as was capital accumulated through trade from the East. To operate machines required more than power. It also required cotton for materials and a market in which to sell the product, both of which were in actuality provided by the East. Without links to the East, the Industrial Revolution probably could not have occurred.

The significance of these transport networks is not in binding together rigidly separated worlds, but rather, as Miyazaki wrote: it is as if the two gears were linked together using a belt, so that the rotation of one induces rotation in the other. Thus, I personally support understanding modernity through these interactive relations. Eurocentrism in the world of knowledge is a kind of universalistic monism, while a pluralistic view of civilization also runs the risk of falling into the trap of essentialism as well, one that sees civilizations—and especially modern civilizations—as systems isolated from one another, each with their own unique essences. Since the late Qing, East/West dualism has been commonly accepted among several generations of Chinese intellectuals, including both conservatives and radicals, traditionalists and modernists. Cultural pluralism allows us to see the particular characteristics and historical conditions of each culture or civilization, yet these characteristics and conditions are certainly not ossified, nor are they singular in form. Asia's process of modernization is like this, as is Europe's as well. We can clearly see, from this kind of perspective on history, that the critiques of Eurocentrism involve some very complex intellectual and historical questions. It is hardly a case of being "anti-West," as some people have intentionally simplified the problem.

I just read Andre Gunder Frank's *ReORIENT: Global Economy in the Asian Age*. The Central Compilation and Translation Press is currently translating this book. Frank has presented an even more systematic expression of the creation of European capitalism, stating that the rise of European capitalism after 1400 (within the world economy and population) corresponded to the decline of the East around 1800. European countries used silver acquired from their American colonies to buy their way into the expanding Asian market. For Europe, unique and extremely effective business and systemic mechanisms were flourishing. It was precisely when Asia entered its period of decline that Western countries, using the import and export mechanisms of the world financial system, became the emerging industrial economies. The significance of this is that modern European capitalism, and what resulted from the transformation of relations of production within European societies, actually came into effect through their relation with Asia. From this worldview, both Frank and Miyazaki were able to achieve a common perspective on modern European history—namely, that although post-Renaissance European history is generally considered to be modern world history, pre–Industrial Revolution Europe differs significantly from post–Industrial Revolution Europe.

The examples I referred to are all particular scholarly examples, which include viewpoints, data sources, and methods that should be discussed. But these works constituted an important new perspective within historical studies, one that broke through the mainstream Western-centric narrative and provided us with new insight regarding our own history. I may have already mentioned that such universal historical narratives are presupposed by theorists of various different schools, including the Enlightenment, liberalism, Marxism and Neo-Confucianism. From the multi-interactive perspective, markets, trade and cash-flow, and division of labor, which have been regarded with hindsight as capitalist elements, did not simply come into being through domestic means of production, but rather through long-distance trade and transport, which enabled interaction between different regions. This method of interpretation has shattered the view of modernity as a universal and unified progression. From a genealogical perspective, these discussions were very similar to the theories of Braudel, Wallerstein and others, showing that even later theorists still had not shed their Eurocentric narratives. Braudel's *Civilization and Capitalism: 15th–18th Century* and *The Mediterranean and the Mediterranean World in the Age of Philip II* have been published by Joint Publishing (Sanlien Bookstore) and Commercial Press—but, sadly, very few people have read them.

You talk about how the birth of historical capitalism and a certain structure of globalization are linked, which means that globalization is neither a new process nor a capitalist phenomenon. If such links already existed in history, then how do you see the problem of globalization?

What I've said is that the process of globalization occurs through several historical stages. This process developed faster and at a larger scale with the onset of the Industrial Revolution and capitalism. The arrival of the information age, the formation of the system of international finance, transport, and tourism have undoubtedly brought the people of different regions of the world much closer together. But this doesn't provide evidence for those Chinese proponents of teleology. These people regard globalization as the ultimate objective of history, and believe that over the past 300 years of human history—after the Enlightenment, to be specific—all of mankind has come to walk a common path and is now making great strides forward in a history of globalization. But what about the past 300 years of colonialism? The past 300 years of war and plundering, monopolization and coercion? The past 300 years of slavery? For 300 years, all of humanity has certainly become more closely linked to one another through colonialism, unequal trade and technological development, yet a common path hardly exists between the colonizer and the colonized, between Africa and the US, or between China and the major powers. Such common histories exist only as fictions that have been achieved at the price of over a billion deaths, everyday enslavement and the loss of traditional homelands. For 300 years, politics, economics and culture have progressed in important ways in many different countries, including both Western and Third World countries, but this wasn't achieved because people throughout the world worked together to implement and complete a great plan established 300 years ago. This progress was achieved through relentless social struggles, through social conservation movements, including socialist and social-democratic movements that struggled for political democracy and equal social rights—including independence movements that struggled for national emancipation; including the civil rights and women's liberation movements that struggled for minority and women's rights. Histories that fail to understand these widespread social movements can never understand the history of democracy. If we want to discuss globalization, we cannot simply gloss over those relations of domination that constitute global relations (by invoking the temporal logic of modernity), but must instead show why globalization is really just a form of "localization," and highlight the relations of domination that characterize this process. If we want true globalization—even if it conforms to the project of modernity or a globalization of values—we must struggle to eliminate such monopolistic frameworks.

In "Contemporary Chinese Thought and the Question of Modernity," I said some things about the question of globalization that didn't sound very optimistic, though an exhaustive discussion of them is beyond the scope of this interview. I'm willing to explain a little, however. What

I said was in reaction to views expressed in Chinese publications from 1994–95. For instance, some scholars viewed globalization as the realization of the *datong* ("grand unification") ideal, while others saw it as the clear way toward Kant's ideal of "perpetual peace." Some people were also concerned with whether "Asian values" could be made to adapt to the values of globalization, and even warned that we would be cast aside if we did not make every effort to get ahead. I think these people regarded the goals of the Enlightenment as an actual process, which is why their elaboration of the concept of globalization was somewhat specious. They all view globalization through a kind of teleological perspective of modernity, and therefore interpret it as the final stage and goal of history, using preexisting historical models to create their own histories. What they don't realize is that, regardless of whether or not we were willing, we have already placed ourselves within the relations of global history. The book *Wenhua yu Gonggongxing* (*Culture and Publicity*), which I edited with Chen Yangu, collects a number of important essays dealing with the question of globalization, among which Arjun Appadurai's essay "Disjuncture and Difference in the Global Cultural Economy" describes globalization through five dimensions of flow and disjuncture, including ethnicity, media, technology, finance, and ideology. Among these five dimensions of flow, nation-states, multinational corporations, diasporic communities and sub-national grouping and movements—even villages, neighborhoods, and families—are all actors of change or at least the promotion of change. The Asian financial turmoil has already allowed us to understand the fluidity of finance and its disastrous consequences. During the process of Chinese liberal reform and opening up (*gaige kaifang*), the transformation of relations between state and market became clearly visible. As for technology, immigrants, and transnational corporations, they are either in the process of becoming or have already become a fundamental reality of contemporary Chinese society, and especially city life. I think that the transnational and trans-regional characteristics of production, trade, and consumption are all fundamental structures for what we call "globalization."

Have I overemphasized globals perspectives, to the detriment of locals perspectives? I don't think so, since the relation between globalization and localities is not a relation of outside to inside. Rather, they are part of the same process. The behavior of corporations has been cited before as an example, for although they fall under American, English, and Japanese authority, their nature and behavior may also have been influenced by globalization as well. Such a view is narrow, however. Since the nation-state system is itself a political form of global production and a trade system, states are now making the previously unprecedented move of intervening in market activities. Its function has undergone important transformations. Some people have linked globalization to the decline of the nation-state, but I don't think that is necessarily accurate. Instead, what has occurred is a transformation of its function, not its decline—parts of it are in decline but others are also on the rise. Without understanding the reality of globalization, we cannot understand the transformations of nation-states from being centralized to being localized, nor can we understand the transformations occurring at the level of cities or villages either. Some have said that the problem of Chinese society is the problem of traditional inheritance, not of globalization. But if you view globalization as a long historical process, we can only then say that the problem of inheriting traditions has shifted in meaning when viewed within the structures of globalization. Corruption frequently occurs today in the domain of international finance and trade, yet putting oneself and one's resources up for sale can only be understood within the new economic relations. Apart from the changes in the national political system, how society institutes democratic controls on resources and wealth is very important in the pursuit of democracy. In the contemporary context, can the question of resources and wealth be discussed apart from the economic structures of globalization? The meaning of bureaucracy and political monopoly has changed today.

The Chinese model of society, politics and economy has taken on different forms in different ages, and its relationship to other countries and regions has also varied. However, this is not to suggest that those differences indicate the externality of those periods to global history; those periods still lie within that same history. Our concept of globalization as having an "inside" and "outside" is one that we must dispose of. We must focus instead on the development of the contemporary world and examine the economic crises, social corruption, and political transformations that Chinese society currently faces. What are the social conditions against which these occurred? In the contemporary world, relations of domination between those with power and those without not only exist between nations but also among the social relations within nation-states; in the relations between domestic monopoly forces and transnational forces; and in patterns of domination within the domestic economy. To provide a critique of the negative impacts of the process of globalization is not to weaken the critique of corruption and anti-democratic conditions within domestic political or economic relations, but precisely the opposite. This perspective provides the necessary conditions for analyzing these domestic relations. Because of this, I have come to regard globalization as a long historical process and not a new and acute phenomenon, much less a value objective. What we call the history of globalization also links each region, society and individual by weaving them into a singular process that is hierarchically and unequally structured. The process of globalization is not therefore a peaceful one that can be achieved purely through a technological revolution. If we conceal the various types of adversity created throughout the world as a result of this process and maintain our colonialist history, simply for the sake of protecting Enlightenment values (this is not without reason, yet we must look at how and what is to be protected) or the dream of globalization, then that would truly be the most fundamental betrayal of Enlightenment values.

It is precisely in seeing the internal contradictions of globalization that some scholars deny the concept, believing that the world is in actuality governed by the concept of localization. Some have reminded us that, for one thing, the current levels of trade and capital flows, along with the level of international financial liberalization, have not completely exceeded the levels reached in 1913, and, for another, that the tendency toward trade integration it relies upon has weakened since the Second World War, and especially since the Sixties. There is a problem here with how to view globalization, and what to use as a benchmark for describing it. Compared with those perspectives that conflate the value objectives of globalization with actual reality, however, the perspectives of these scholars are at least deeper and more accurate than the others.

From a historical point of view, however, I still tend to see this from the perspective of the monopolizing structure of globalization. The Third World countries from the age of colonialism are forced to implement principles of "free trade" while the colonizers themselves practice trade protectionism. The political form of the contemporary world is the nation-state system, in which detached state forms are established into a global political system. Yet they remain detached. In light of this, if we continue to describe this historical process through the concept of globalization, then we must pay close attention to the relation between those that dominate and those that are dominated within that process. I also think that it is equally important for us to distinguish market mechanisms from global capitalism. According to Braudel's research on historical capitalism, capitalism is a monopolizing form whose history is long. Market mechanisms also have a long history, yet they cannot be equated to capitalism. In fact, we should not embrace the monopoly of capitalism if we believe in market mechanisms, but rather oppose it. Capitalism is neither free markets nor market regulations, but rather an anti-market force. In this sense, the increasing tendency of political power to behave according to market principles and the increasing tendency of markets to behave like political authorities are typical of capitalism, even if they aren't a modern phenomenon. It is also in this sense that we must redefine socialism since, having always manifested itself in state form, it is also a monopolizing form and an anti-market force. What this indicates is that these two worlds cannot be fully differentiated from one another. For this reason, we need to overcome (but not simply abandon) these two historical forms and carry out truly creative work.

When some of our colleagues here use Hayek's theory to demonstrate the rationality of the market order, they often ignore his critique of *homo economicus* and his elaboration of the individual nature of exchange, instead emphasizing the former aspect without criticism. For instance, they use the concept of the "spontaneous order" to explain actual phenomena in the market and society while entirely disregarding the fact that contemporary China's market system and social relations were created through large-scale acts of state. Some people have adopted Hayek's theory regarding the incompleteness of individual knowledge and beliefs, questioning why we can't reconfigure Hayek's position on abolishing central banks. If economic processes already belong to the "spontaneous order," then it should be possible to abolish the central banks; or if they already involve various different levels of intervention, then we might ask why the central bank is necessary as well. In fact, many people oppose state intervention without understanding at all that the necessity for interventions arises precisely from the internal activities of the market. Others follow Hayek's views on the question of progressive taxation, opposing the implementation of necessary welfare systems under real conditions. Certainly, to imitate the welfare systems of Western countries under the conditions of modern China would be unrealistic, particularly since those welfare systems are themselves undergoing fundamental crises. However, what would result if we opposed such welfare systems in our actual lives? When a large number of workers become unemployed and social security systems are seriously deficient, social inequality and social agitation will certainly result if we resist carrying out tax reform and establishing a suitable social security system. We should be mindful of the destructive effects of Reaganism and Thatcherism on Western societies. If there are people—and there certainly are such people in reality—who use the theory of free markets to demonstrate the validity or rationality of financial speculation, then in my opinion they are at most demonstrating that they are vulgar "capitalists," since what they advocate is not the freedom of markets but rather their monopoly. I should add here that these are not excuses for corruption, incompetence, and the exchange of power for money on the part of the state and the banking industry. One of the lessons of the Southeast Asian financial crisis is that external causes arise themselves from internal causes. We must begin here from actual phenomena and distinguish state democratization and market reform from the destruction of the state.

China's mainstream contemporary intellectual world refuses to criticize the process of globalization, with many colleagues mistakenly conflating globalization with market freedom. This is a significant misunderstanding, if not actually misleading. *Cankao Xiaoxi* recently reprinted an article from the Japanese magazine *Sekai* entitled "The Global Economy: Can It Be Fixed?" which is a clear expression of this. I may as well quote from it. David Korten writes:

> The underlying belief that global capitalism can be made to work for everyone is based on a deep faith in the theory that markets necessarily allocate society's resources equitably and efficiently. Unfortunately, a market economy and the new global capitalism are not the same thing. On the contrary, the new global capitalism systematically violates nearly every assumption on which market theory is based—including the key assumptions about competition and cost internalization ... A combination of economic globalization, deregulation, and financial concentration has moved the new capitalist economy ever further away from the characteristics that

make a market economy socially efficient. They have as well shifted economic and political power away from people and democratically elected governments to an unstable and predatory system of global finance.[1]

In the introductory remarks to *Wenhua yu Gonggongxing* (*Cultures and Publicity*, Joint Publishing), I used Arendt's theory to analyze the disparities in wealth and property between modern societies. She used a similar logic to analyze the dark side of global capitalism, which is to understand money and wealth under the same category. Such forms of neo-capitalism only focus on creating money, while the real forms of wealth to be found in the world (natural wealth and human capital) are rapidly being destroyed. Within Asia's rapidly changing society, the relations between power and money have provided unique characteristics to this form of neo-capitalism.

The topic of liberalism has now become especially popular, but some people describe the conflicts of contemporary Chinese thought in terms of an opposition between "liberalism" and the "new left." This sort of description simplifies a complex theoretical question, however, and the people that contribute such reflections represent sectarian attitudes, ones that lack specificity in both practical and theoretical questions. I think that there are now very few serious discussions regarding liberalism, and much fetishization of it instead. Within the constantly changing social situation, the divisions in contemporary thought now represent a unique contextual construction. The strivings of contemporary society toward democracy (for instance, freedom of speech, freedom of thought, equal participation in economics, and legal safeguards for the political process), the bankruptcy of the traditional planning system, and the demands by particular social classes that various reforms be included into the legal framework—all of these have been incorporated into the discussions on liberalism. In other words, the social forces in contemporary liberal discourse are actually very diverse, making them difficult to express within abstract discussions of liberalism. What is worth mentioning is that political democracy and civil liberties were the primary slogans and goals for the intellectual and cultural movements beginning in the late Seventies, and cannot be simply summed up as problems of liberalism. A widespread common consensus already exists in contemporary society regarding political democracy and the question of civil liberties, one which was forged at the crossroads of various different intellectual currents and trends. Many intellectuals of the late Seventies to the late Eighties had a poor understanding of the theory of liberalism, embracing instead Marxist humanism, "May Fourth" democracy, science, the liberal tradition (the complexity and multiplicity of this tradition are very apparent, and certainly cannot be simplified as any kind of "tradition of liberalism"), Western Marxism, northern European socialism, the historical legacy of Enlightenment movements (this legacy bred modern liberalism, but cannot be simplified as liberalism itself since it also produced other systems of modern thought), existentialism, and even modernism. Thus, the achievements of China's social reform can be seen as the result of continuous struggles between various social and intellectual forces, rather than as the achievement of one particular intellectual tradition, if they are viewed not from factional viewpoints but rather from a more objective angle. The divisions in contemporary thought were forged through the development and divergence of these widespread trends. The real force of such divisions is in the distribution of benefits within the process of reform, and also in providing different ways of viewing this distribution process, including whether the unfair distribution of social wealth ("spontaneous privatization" and the transformation of acute social divisions into classes) should be used to establish the premises of political democracy—What is the relationship between political and economic democracy? Can market expansion naturally lead to democracy? What are the relations between political, economic, and cultural capital? What is the relation between economic globalization and the nation-state? Should we construct critiques of developmentalism in theory and practice?—and so on. These are the principle issues raised by intellectuals with different backgrounds of critique. I think that these questions are impossible to avoid, yet I also don't think they can be resolved by distorting the other perspectives, vilifying one's adversaries in debate and then declaring oneself a practitioner of a certain school of thought. Such practices have nothing to do with the liberal tradition.

Just like socialism (including social democracy), liberalism is a tradition and not an abstract doctrine. We cannot simply say that liberalism or socialism are right or wrong, since each has its own strengths and limitations. Departing from specific historical practices and practical contexts, we cannot judge these "isms," since they have no inherent legitimacy or rationality. Twentieth-century history has shown that the threats to civil liberties that people are generally concerned about have originated largely from the right—as in Germany, Italy, the fascist satellite states, and China's Kuomingtang during the Forties, and later with McCarthyism and the military dictators of Latin America. They also originated on the left—as in the form of Stalinism and the unforgettable tragedies of contemporary Chinese history. Both the right and the left used the other as excuses to violate civil liberties, and even today such ways of thinking continue to prevent us from viewing them as the sum total of a variety of different internal historical relations. As theories, liberalism and socialism are extremely complex theories, which include many different tendencies and factions, making it very difficult for us to carry out discussions regarding these theories. What this means is that, when someone calls themselves a liberal or a socialist, they must first say what kind of a liberal or socialist they are. I think that there are very few serious discussions of liberalism today, and virtually no serious studies of socialism. Under these conditions, it becomes very difficult to determine what is meant by "liberalism" in these theories self-described as liberal or social. Some theorists have published grandiose manifestos dealing with Chinese history, sometimes involving an astonishing ignorance on the part of Chinese intellectuals pursuing the history of democratic constitutionalism—which is not simply the responsibility of individual scholars but also of us scholars working in related fields, who have yet to present compelling revisions of those foundations. But this must not become an excuse for those who talk nonsense and refuse to take responsibility, for there have been many historians since the Thirties who have provided rich (if not ample) explanations of these questions.

The theoretical divisions, which I have not discussed exhaustively here, are significant. On a theoretical level, we can talk about overcoming the division between left and right and of overcoming the differences between different "isms," but in reality each individual is faced with a choice, which in turn contains an implied choice concerning theoretical position. But what I must emphasize is that, without insight into historical and practical relations, including the relation between theory and practice, the theoretical struggles between liberalism, socialism, and other "isms" are unlikely to reach any conclusions or even lead to genuine discussions. The reason is that those are simply struggles between different fetishisms. With this in mind, I will refrain for the time being from expressing my opinion on the question of liberalism itself, as well as from discussing the complex relation between state and market. But I am willing to say upfront that, if someone is thoroughly committed to the principles of liberalism—for instance, the principle of the market—he or she must then critique capitalism and the market relations that it dominates, instead of advocating capitalism. If someone truly supports individual rights and acknowledges that these are social rights, then he must abandon the atomistic conception of individuals and necessarily embrace the tendency toward socialism. Rawls's books are classic works of contemporary liberalism, and though I am not a Rawlsian, I believe that they are worth examining.

This reminds me of a discussion that occurred a few years back regarding the Russian and Chinese models of reform. I want Chinese intellectuals to return to this topic and reconsider—earnestly and not temperamentally—the theoretical debates of the time. I think that the core of those discussions was neither whether we needed reform nor whether we needed markets—much less whether we needed democracy—but, instead, whether we really wanted to follow a path of reform that was formally oligarchical. Have we come to view the establishment of dependent economic relations as the goal of reform? Do we think that political democracy will require the total rewriting of class divisions as the premise for a new social order? The problem of "spontaneous privatization" was originally brought up during these discussions, but was finally overshadowed by various other disputes. We cannot simply avoid these concrete social questions by proclaiming ourselves to be members of a certain ideology or school of thought; nor should we avoid suggesting concrete social ideas or measures. By breaking through the misunderstandings that have resulted from these ideological debates, we can discover that they have common premises and practical differences. Pinpointing the possible differences that could exist between people who believe in the same general theories or principles could also help us to find our own concrete positions, instead of attempting to establish our own views simply through collective arrogance, using insults and smears to conceal the frailty of our own theory. A long time ago, Alexander Herzen said something of profound and lasting significance, which was: "We are not the doctors. We are the disease." I think this is a phrase worth mulling over.

What actual significance do you think there is in discussing the question of modernity?

Discussing the significance of the question of modernity involves many dimensions. These include, for instance, the relation between contemporary nationalism and modernity, the question of globalization, consumerism, the theory of modernization, and West-centrism. If we are talking about the direct significance of this question, however, then I think that the critique of developmentalism is a very important aspect. The reconsideration of developmentalism is especially urgent today. I am not an expert on this matter but I am still willing to offer a cursory discussion of these perspectives.

In Raymond Williams's *Keywords*, the entry for "modern" ends by listing three related words—"improve," "progress," and "tradition"— suggesting a useful approach through which to grasp this term. This is to say that the modern has come into existence and evolved within a progressive timeline, and sees itself in contrast to its past. In this way, the meaning of progress also contains a sense of development. If we look more closely at the etymology of the term "improve," we will see that in the eighteenth century it overlapped with the economic life geared toward reaping profits. The terms it is connected to in turn are "development," "exploitation," and "interest," which are all terms that later became economic concepts. The concept of development and the problem of efficiency are closely connected, both having been forged within a temporality of modernity, and in particular one that evolves and improves in a linear way. These terms provide the foundation for the concept of "modernization." We know that developmentalism became an important part of the theory of modernization in the post-war period, as well as becoming the prevailing ideology of modern society. It divides the world into developed and developing countries, suggesting a timeline in which the former category is the future of the latter, and in so doing concealing the fact that both exist within unequal relations between center and periphery—relations that involve domination and subordination. Theories of modernization in America, including that of Parsons, have been heavily influenced by Spencerism, whose social theory takes on the typical form of Social Darwinism. In fact, theories of modernization continue to bear the marks of Social Darwinism, albeit with many formal theoretical revisions.

Who today, in China or the many countries of the Third World, is not looking to develop? Societies must develop, nations must develop, individuals must develop and economies certainly must develop as well. The notion of development seems to have great legitimacy in the world today. The critiques of developmentalism do not deny development, but instead demand that it legitimize itself, criticizing the monopolization, coerciveness, short-sightedness and inequality of developmentalism. Thus, the questions we must pose are, first, When a society allows development to prevail over all other goals, does this stifle all other aspects of human life? Second, what is the relation between the economic development of a nation or region and that of other nations or regions? Third, what is the relation between the development of a certain portion of society and that of the remainder? Fourth, how are short-term and long-term development connected?

We may as well begin by discussing the first question. Contemporary society is a competitive age that has the nation-state as its political form. In seeking to carve out a space for themselves within the existing struggle, the leaders and intellectuals of the nation are forced to consider development as the most important task. The movement since the late Qing to *fuguo qiangbing* ("enrich the nation and strengthen the army") is an example of this. In other words, the movement for modernization that takes *fuguo qiangbing* as its symbol is a product of colonialism as well as of the nation-state paradigm. It is also a consequence of modernity. In other times, however, what does development actually mean? The task of "development" is not balanced and does not imply development of all parts, nor is it undertaken for the sake of individual lives. At best, development can come to be for its own sake, regardless of whether its subject is society or individuals; and when development comes to be the only goal of social life, it becomes society's sole cohesive force. At worst, rulers use development or the things that obstruct it as excuses to reject the need for political, economic or cultural reform in a society, along with the democratic control of society. Indonesia and many other Third World countries are the most obvious illustrations of this. This is not insignificant when we are reflecting upon the many problems associated with Chinese society.

Second, another characteristic of developmentalism is the treatment of successful developmental models (such as the American, European, or Japanese models) as universal models for development, thinking that they can be suitably applied in all regions. This is a typical narrative of modernity that places the development of nations or regions on a singular timeline and treats it as an isolated phenomenon, rather than viewing it in relation to the developmental issues of other nations and regions. This type of narrative conceals the dependence that Western societies had upon their colonies for their own development, as well as what this kind of development implies for the right to development of other regions and peoples, even depriving them in many cases of their right to subsistence. Although colonialism has now withdrawn from the arena of history (since it is no longer acceptable to appropriate the land of other regions through military occupation), the developmental model of today remains unequal due to political and military hegemony, and especially to unequal trade and economic relations. Many texts addressing this topic are already available in the Chinese-speaking world: the Commercial Press published several studies on the problem of Third World development many years back, including Raul Prebisch's *Capitalismo Periferico* and Samir Amin's *Unequal Development: An Essay on the Social Formations of Peripheral Capitalism*—and Taiwan's Linking Books published Ian Roxborough's *Theories of Underdevelopment*. All of these have provided important interpretations of these problems. Some Taiwanese scholars have also begun to reflect upon the relationship between Taiwan's development and its border regions. Unequal development exists not only between the Third World and developed countries, but also within regional relations—between the more developed and underdeveloped nations of the Third World. I often hear ideologues remark that certain cultures and models have become universal. However, while the population of many developed countries is actually very small, they control a third of the world's total resources. If we too use resources in the same way to stimulate development and pave the way for consumerism, we are also engaging in the large-scale destruction of resources, and the disappropriation of resources that belong to others. What alternative routes are available? Developmentalism continues to retain a certain logic of imperialism or colonialism.

Third, unequal development not only exists between countries but also between different regions. In the post-war world, colonialism is no longer an acceptable policy; yet developmentalism and the modernization movement do not rely any less upon the use of monopolies or disenfranchisement. Internal colonization can also therefore appear within social collectives. Relations between center and periphery are re-created and re-established within societies when regional development becomes based upon market, labor power, and resource monopolies. Many scholars have discussed how transnational capital has impacted on resource monopolies, though fewer studies have focused on similar issues arising at the domestic level. We often see how the development of a region is accompanied by the devastation of resources in other regions. Trans-regional production and trade are important and virtually irreversible trends for contemporary societies; yet the social and political structures of these societies have yet to become effective, fair, and suitable for trans-regional development. Since those who initiate the bulk of trans-regional development don't often take local responsibility, they can initiate development however they wish, finally sacrificing the possibility of economic development for that region. In reality, once unequal development reaches a certain stage, serious social conflicts and contradictions will result. Karl Polanyi's excellent work *The Great Transformation: The Political and Economic Origins of Our Time* examines the origins of the First World War, and specifically discusses this point.

Fourth, this is a destructive way to develop and open up regions. A friend of mine called this "development without survival." The flooding of the Yangtze and Nenjiang rivers has resulted in historically high water levels. The reasons for this phenomenon are certainly more complicated and include natural factors. But, even despite these, it has also undoubtedly resulted from human industrialization and unlimited infringement upon ecologies. The pursuit of efficiency has led to massive deforestation, the destruction of land and mining resources, and the rerouting of rivers and lakes, and has finally bred large-scale disasters. We could also say that this is the consequence of uneven development. Several months ago, I heard some people say at a conference that these problems were problems of "postmodernity" and not specific to China, and that this "postmodernity" was simply a trend. I don't know how exactly they understood "postmodernity," but they certainly didn't see that developmentalism and political reality were closely linked. A few days ago, I saw three economists analyze China's current economic situation on TV, and their discussion made me think that they were happy about the disaster induced by the floods, since demand and investment were stimulated in their wake, as well as increased macroeconomic control. These economists didn't mention the local destruction these floods produced, nor the long-term pollution that will result on the coast of the Yangtze due to the sand-filled sacks used in disaster relief and the motor boats and vehicles that sank to the bottom of the river—much less the disaster victims, or the factors that led to this disaster and make up its background. We can't help but ask why we don't have a worker's economics, a farmer's economics, an average person's economics, or an ecological economics. Why is it customary for such discussions of China's economy to begin from these "total" or "comprehensive" standpoints, taking the "total" to be the only measurable standard? Does this sole standard and value conceal the position or point of view from which this social vision is constructed? One positive reaction is that reporters and scholars have already begun to discuss who was complicit in the disaster that followed the flood.

The social significance of these developmental questions is quite complex, so I cannot dive into them here in any comprehensive way. Perhaps some will ask what we could possibly do, such being the case? I think that, before we rest upon a strategy, we must first acknowledge this problem, and then reflect upon whether other alternatives or possibilities are contained within our past experiences. Sun Yatsen's saying *zhinan xingyi* ("knowing is difficult, doing is simple") perhaps contains some truth. In reality, the question of development is like the question of modernity in encompassing much more than the concrete fields of study. Studying these questions already requires specialized training and investigation into these fields of knowledge, yet it also requires a scope of investigation that transcends these fields and can reflect upon them all. I often say to friends that we cannot help but "dance with shackles on," meaning that the existing modes of inquiry are insufficient for achieving any deep understanding of these questions, particularly because, in some sense, they are fundamentally products of modernity. However, we are also incapable of thoroughly investigating these questions if we depart from these specialized fields.

Your critiques of developmentalism are centered primarily in the domain of economics. What about the political side of things?

No, my critiques of developmentalism are not only situated in the domain of economics. These questions are certainly economic questions, yet they are also profound political questions. The project of modernity—to use Habermas's terminology—is a process by which some domains achieve independence. The gradual separation of economics from politics, by which it becomes an independent developmental domain, is an example of this. Liberal theorists and Marxist theorists are mutually opposed in many aspects, yet in this respect their views are consistent. Was classical economics not established upon the premise that economics had become an autonomous domain? They all saw the economic process as an autonomous domain. However, in my view, the "separation of economics from politics" does not imply that the two rationalized domains have already developed to become truly autonomous domains. It simply suggests that the relationship between the two domains has undergone very significant transformations. However, such transformations have never developed to the point where the two domains become totally separate. It is therefore necessary for us to reconsider the various contemporary schools of social theory from the perspective of theory and praxis, since these social theories are fundamentally established upon the separation of politics and economics, state and market. We can see this simply by looking at the history of the "free market," since the "free market" has always followed in the wake of power and domination.

We frequently discuss the problem of forced marketization today—but what is forced marketization? This is the ability to transform political capital into economic capital, and vice versa, and to have this occur under market conditions. The significance of this is that market conditions have never been total or complete. Development is uneven and must also therefore be understood from the standpoint of politics, since uneven development has never been a purely economic problem. It is also a significant social and political issue. The nation-state system is the political form of the world market, and is a more active participant in economic activities than in any previous era. For this reason, modern economics has continuously invented new and different models, and is increasingly less able to describe actual economic processes—a fact that is connected to the theoretical premises of the discipline. When I say this, I am not simply criticizing economics—I certainly am not qualified to make such a grand statement. The fact is that every modern discipline of study now accords with the schemes of modernity. It is precisely in light of this that our reflections on modernity must involve discussions on the genealogies and analytical frameworks of our present knowledge.

At the beginning, I spoke of some of the characteristics of the project of modernity, which were to separate the domains of science, morality and aesthetics into autonomous domains. In actuality, this process has also established the autonomy of economics, politics and law, as well as the sovereignty of nation-states, among other areas. Autonomous development has progressive significance, but the concept of autonomy masks a mutual interdependence on the material level. What are we to do when faced with such a phenomenon? From the perspective of theory, the non-freedom of markets could have two opposing consequences— one is intervention, and the other is the fundamental elimination of this form of intervention. However, these two projects are both abstract. The concept of interventionism is theoretically premised upon the existence of a completely self-sufficient and free market; yet, from ancient times to today, such self-sufficient and free markets have yet to appear. In the past, they have always been entangled with religion, politics, and culture. Today, they are closely connected with new beliefs, politics and culture. Under actual market conditions, the complete elimination of other elements influencing economic activities and processes is virtually impossible, and therefore a more concrete and more meaningful question would be: What is the impact of using certain elements to resist or eliminate other influences upon the economic process?

Under modern conditions, intervention is virtually inevitable, yet it may also be advantageous for the practice of monopolies and power. As a result, critiques of interventionism have continued for over a century, while at the same time providing the ideological basis upon which certain monopolies achieve their own particular goals. The recent monopoly lawsuit against the Microsoft Corporation in America is a precise expression of this problem, and this is because the problem of intervention in the contemporary world differs from the problem of intervention in the nineteenth century. Adam Smith's critique of interventionism was primarily directed against national intervention in small- and middle-sized enterprises, while the present era is one of transnational capitalism—South Korean scholars have even called this the "IMF era"—in which the strength of domestic and global capital now exceeds that of most nation-states. What has resulted from this are monopolies, interventions and manipulations within market activities. Under these conditions, how to evaluate the role of the state in economic activities has become a question differing entirely from the one faced by Smith and his followers in the nineteenth century. The state/market dualism conceals the fact that the state is an intrinsic and fundamental factor in market society, as well as that concrete economic activities themselves produce anti-market forces, such as the market manipulations performed by monopolies, the interventions of finance oligarchs, and the various controls exercised by the government. The significance of this discussion for the problem of intervention is political: under actual conditions, what we pursue is the democratization of the state, not its dissolution. To say this is not to argue for intervention, but to show theoretically how modern market activities depend upon supra-economic forces. This is also why so many proponents of the free market happen to be supporters and founders of policies of intervention; why many who call themselves "liberals" actually commend the rule of technocrats as a measure of great progress. Is not the proclamation of technocracy just another form of statism?

What exists here is not simply an economic problem, but also a social and political problem—one that encompasses the social problem of the democratic control of wealth and processes of production from a global perspective. From the domestic perspective, the only real way out following the collapse of state planning and the state monopoly is a transformation of the dependent status of wage laborers—to use the words of a certain philosopher—so that they possess the right to participate in society and politics. Only in this way can a safe, just and happy life be lived in this society. The unequal social conditions of capitalist society should be made more equal through fair distribution of collective wealth. This is the democratic theory of contemporary society and should be expanded into the international dimension. It could establish fairer and more democratic economic relations and political safeguards, promote peace and development, protect the Earth's ecological balance, and forge a new world system that preserves the uniqueness of nations while transcending the nation-state system.

If we don't regard the domains of economy, politics and culture as isolated in any way, then from a theoretical perspective we would need to think of the objective of modern society as being more than simply political democratization. It would have to include economic and cultural democratization as well. For instance, if people demand that the government provide greater protections for their individual property rights—motivated by the wealth they gained in the process of privatization—without demanding that all human rights be protected, the position that individual rights should be protected deteriorates as well.

Some say that economics is only capable of thinking through freedom, and not democracy; but to make this statement is actually to suggest the complete autonomy of these categories. It fails to understand that economic inequality is only the flip side of social inequality. This is precisely the reason that, in "Contemporary Chinese Thought and the Question of Modernity," I critiqued the lopsided political views of intellectuals. Reform processes in many countries have already demonstrated that these aspects of democracy cannot be realized independently of one another. The realities of contemporary Russia and the history of democracy in India are evidence of this point. In light of this, we need to rethink the parochial notion of democracy. The essence of democracy lies in its acknowledgment of the fundamental rights of people and in the public participation of citizens in political, economic, and cultural processes.

If constitutionally defined political rights cannot effectively pave the way for democratic participation by citizens; if these political rights cannot check the inequalities that exist with respect to race, gender and class; if these democratic rights cannot restrict monopolies, power and domination; if they cannot limit the increasingly market-like behavior of political power or the growth in the authority of the market, then we must consider a broader and more complete concept of democracy. Under contemporary conditions, democratic thought will transgress the boundaries of nation-states, and must provide theoretical support to the needs of smaller and weaker societies in their dialogues with the global community. In reality, modern democratic practices, including those of constitutional governments themselves, have already developed beyond what the early Enlightenment had imagined, and certainly cannot be completely explained through an individualistic theory of rights. While modern constitutional governments oppose various types of discrimination, they also make adjustments to social, political, economic and cultural processes through legal democratic means. But these processes are neither balanced nor mature. The first generation of Chinese who sought constitutional democracy arose in the 1920s, and they carefully considered the class and racial conflicts of the West, making efforts to establish the broadest possible degree of political participation. They realized that direct democracy was open to technical problems, but they also recognized the need to include some derivative of it in drawing up the constitution and designing a system that benefited and reflected the will of the lower classes and oppressed communities. If we examine European constitutional history and understand Carsun Chang's discussions regarding constitutional government, it should be easy to understand these issues. Publicness is especially important in regards to democratic control over public policy and affairs. I believe that grass-roots democracy and the formation of a local public sphere are essential in achieving this. A nation's public policies and public affairs must include politics as well as economics and culture—the various aspects of social life.

It is precisely for this reason that our reflections on modernity cannot ignore actual life processes, nor the relation between its projects and the process of implementing them. To reconsider modernity is not to deny all modern life processes or practices, nor is it to abandon all the values of modernity. The importance of such reconsiderations is in explaining the complex relations between modern values and modern society, to break down the "-centric" historical narratives, and to reveal modern society's intrinsic dilemmas and crises. It is in providing the theoretical resources to achieve a broader degree of democracy and healthier forms of freedom.

4

Rethinking
The Rise of Modern Chinese Thought

Although it took thirteen years to publish once the manuscript was complete, the four volumes of *The Rise of Modern Chinese Thought* only took a little over ten years to write, which is a relatively short amount of time, given its total length. Since its publication, there has been some lively discussion surrounding it and several questions raised, some of which I will attempt to address here. This work is difficult, dense and long, while the disciplines to which its readers and commentators belong are also very diverse; so, for the sake of clarification, I will highlight some of its themes and explain the context from which I wrote.

When I began my academic career in the 1980s, China's social and political climate seemed so hopeful and free. Young intellectuals were looking toward the West for inspiration, and the spirit of resistance, particularly against tradition, was strong. The result was that we lacked a deep understanding of our own traditions and history. During this time, I had been studying Lu Xun, and had already begun focusing on intellectual history and the May Fourth Cultural Movement; but then, in 1989, the social and political atmosphere changed, and it was in the years immediately following that *The Rise of Modern Chinese Thought* was born.

Of course, twenty years have since passed, and the atmosphere has changed once more—there is today a strong feeling of confidence in China's developmental prospects, with intellectuals turning their attentions upon our traditions once more; but in the years immediately following 1989, the social climate was repressive and uncertain. No one had a clear view of what the future might hold. It was in the wake of this social crisis that I began to think about China and its historical fate, beginning from its social, political and intellectual roots. My colleagues and I began to recognize the need to examine the climate of the Eighties, and particularly how it had shaped our thought and academic experiences, so that the research and writing process for this book also became a way for me to reflect upon the intellectual path we had taken. We saw the need to rethink our own relationship to history and tradition.

Naturally, I began by researching modern thought and literature. Only later did I begin examining the thought of the late-Qing period, gradually realizing that many important questions could not be adequately explained within these frameworks. An in-depth understanding would require tracing our intellectual roots back even further, and so I wrote backwards, proceeding from the modern to the ancient (from modern to Qing to pre-Qing), and from the end to the beginning. As I wrote, my knowledge of our history and traditions deepened along the way. What this means is that I did not begin writing with a complete and fully-formed vision of the work in mind. Instead, the work was not published for so long because it could not be published in reverse. Volume 4 could not precede Volume 3. Many of my colleagues today are very young, and did not experience the Eighties or the sequence of events that followed in the same way as me, and others speak of that era only anecdotally. But this period was my starting point; it was the historical backdrop before which I wrote.

When writers and academics perform research, regardless of their motives or ideas, they should take care to situate their work within their own academic traditions. Certainly, thoughts emanate from individuals, but if you want to perform research, you should honestly situate your own work within your specific academic influences and tradition. Thus, when I was producing these studies of intellectual history, I was forced to think through the relationship between my writing and the research on intellectual history that already exists.

I think the Nineties were characterized by two different traditions of intellectual history. One tradition is found among the history of philosophy curricula and the intellectual trends in the philosophy departments of China's universities. Many of the studies of Chinese intellectual history are carried out within these departments, and fundamentally belong in the same discipline as studies of philosophical history. For instance, many highly influential intellectual historians from mainland China, including Feng Youlan, Zhang Dainian and He Lin, teach in philosophy departments, and their work is written within philosophical frameworks. They focus particularly on the history of concepts and philosophical categories. This tradition of intellectual history is obviously the product of contemporary academic history. Various philosophical categories were introduced to China under the influence of Western academia, henceforth tying all interpretations of Chinese thought to the fundamental categories of contemporary Western philosophy. Of course, the terms *ʐhexue* and *kitetsugaku* ("philosophy" in Chinese and Japanese, respectively) grew out of Song Dynasty Confucianism, but the use of the term *ʐhexue* as the translation of the Western concept of "philosophy" only came into practice after the Meiji Restoration (1868) in Japan, which ended 256 years of rule under the feudalistic Tokugawa shogunate.

The Japanese intellectual Amane Nishi, part of the Meiji 6 Society (Meirokusha), who lived after the Meiji Restoration, is someone I think of as being very like Yan Fu in China, even if many people today like to compare Yan Fu to Yukichi Fukuzawa. The Meiji 6 Society published a journal called *Meiroku* during the Meiji era, which introduced Western classics on a grand scale, and Amane Nishi translated the *Encyclopaedia Britannica*, called *Hyakugaku renwa* in Japanese, in which the term "philosophy" was translated as *ʐhexue*. Prior to this, it had been translated as *kitetsugaku*. This quickly became the norm in Japan, and spread to China in the late nineteenth century. In the twentieth century, *ʐhexue* gradually became a specialized discipline within the modern academic system. If we read the works of thinkers in this tradition from one generation earlier, we can discern two distinct methodological approaches. One belongs to those who, though they received Western academic training, were immersed in the traditions of their own culture from childhood. Although their reflections on the many particularities, figures and ideas are lively and vivid, their narrative frameworks were ultimately Western—meaning, for instance, that their discussions of "Chinese philosophy" involved questions of ontology, epistemology and realism. In their treatment of ideas, they often placed their own perceptions within Western frameworks. For instance, philosophical studies placed incredibly high value on the thought of the Song Dynasty. Apart from the similarities between the so-called "return to the ancients" during the Song Dynasty and a certain nationalistic form of thought that was popular at the time, an important reason for this was their belief that only during the Song Dynasty had China produced something similar to modern Western philosophy. *Taiji* ("the great ultimate") and *wuji* ("the void") were similar to the concept of essence; *gewu zhizhi* ("the investigation of things to extend knowledge") was similar to epistemology. Of course, Chinese Marxist philosophers drew a clear distinction between the materialistic and idealistic, and examined the existence of dialectical elements. The Chinese categories of *tianli* ("the heavenly principle") and *tiandao* ("the heavenly way") gradually came to be seen as departing from the intellectual categories of daily life.

Of course, Confucius discusses the problem of *tian* ("heaven"), but this problem is also very closely related to the problem of *liyue*, or the system of rites and music, as well as the political system and people's everyday practices. The Confucian scholars of the Song Dynasty were also concerned with this problem, but Song Confucianism was more broadly characterized by many transformations, with the intellectual categories of *tianli* and *tiandao* becoming more abstract during this period. Many scholars writing from a Western philosophical background saw these changes as very important, believing that China experienced a philosophical breakthrough at this time. Previously, they believed, the philosophy practiced was not true philosophy, and although some elements of a true philosophy existed—such as Laozi and Chuangzhi's discussions of *dao* (the way)—what they discovered in the "breakthrough" of Song Confucianism were abstract categories directly correlated with ontology and epistemology, which they viewed as very significant.

This research method existed not only within the intellectual history traditions of China's philosophy departments but also in foreign schools of Neo-Confucianism, which included scholars such as Mou Zongsan, who was trained in the discipline of philosophy. It is also apparent in the Chinese philosophical traditions that emerged from the work of Hsiung Shihli and Feng Youlan, which were themselves developed from the philosophies of Hume, Kant, and Dewey. Although their discussions are certainly unique and profound in their own way, these philosophical traditions should be rethought. I am not saying that their philosophies are completely mechanical applications of categories from the history of Western philosophy. That generation of scholars had experienced Chinese tradition very intimately, so that these applications always involved complex elements as well. But their fundamental narrative frameworks and their discussions of fundamental issues were developed from Hume, Kant, and Hegel. He Lin was a scholar of Hegel; Mou had been shaped by Hume and Kant; Feng Youlan wrote from a neo-realist position; and Hu Shizhi's origins were in pragmatism. Their basic frameworks were ontology, scientific method, and epistemology, as well as practice, which together came to structure all the questions raised in Chinese philosophy. The introduction of Marxist philosophy was accompanied by the further addition of materialist and idealist questions, yet such questions were still discussed within the context of philosophical ontology and epistemology. This was a very important tradition. When I perform research, I must also reflect upon this tradition and place myself within the history of the discipline. This does not imply a simple affirmation or denial of those traditions, but rather an engagement with them. Of course, scholarly research must move forward, and our perspectives and discontent with the existing philosophies must inevitably be stated—though such discontent differs from simple denial—and this is something I will explain. Intellectual history is very difficult simply to deny, since it is a tradition.

The second tradition is that of Marxist intellectual and social history of recent modernity. The tradition of Marxist thought has obviously been an important influence upon the study of intellectual history within China's philosophy departments, yet its influence upon works on intellectual history within history departments has been much more comprehensive. The Institute of History and the Institute for Modern History at the Chinese Academy of Social Sciences, along with the history departments of many other major universities, have all housed scholars that study intellectual history, and their methodologies differ from those used in philosophy departments. This difference is not limited merely to the fact that some of them focus on intellectual history and its sociality, while others focus on philosophical questions. Rather, it is a difference in their methodologies. Within history departments, research on intellectual history is connected to a very important tradition, which is the use of modern social sciences—and particularly the social-historical method that pays particular attention to production methods and social forms—as the fundamental premise and framework for historical research (this tradition is relatively absent in the intellectual traditions of Ancient China). For instance, when they are examining a concept, a form of thought, or a historical figure, they will certainly also look at the transformations that occurred in the methods and forces of production at the time. They will look at the current state of dynastic politics, and at the class that a particular thinker represents—whether aristocrat, land-owner, or peasant. In short, they elaborate history on the basis of social categories. The most important representative of this form of research was the work that Mr. Hou Wailu and his colleagues published in five volumes, *Zhongguo Sixiang Tongshi* (*A Comprehensive History of Chinese Thought*). We can clearly see that the entire discussion of thought is conducted on the basis of social forms, means of production, and class relations. After the end of the Cultural Revolution, and in particular after the Eighties, this method was criticized by many people, who believed that it was problematic in its mechanisms or its ability to reflect upon those mechanisms. But I thought that the Marxist school of social history provided Chinese intellectual history with a very important point of view, and was an important contribution. No previous studies of history focused as much upon the interaction and relation between the creation and discovery of new means of production, the material transformations in people's lives, and intellectual thought. Although this type of research is frequently accompanied by problems of deter-minism and transcendentalism, we cannot say that the work carried out by the Marxist school is not worth reflecting upon. I think that, even to date, it is a tradition of intellectual history that is well worth our taking seriously. We might say that these two traditions are problematic, but neither are they are traditions that we can simply reject.

For one thing, this is true of the tradition of Marxist sociology. After the Eighties, the Chinese academic world came into contact with works on social and intellectual history in the West, and in this world American studies of China were taken to be representative cases of intel-lectual history. These American studies on Chinese intellectual history, performed in Chinese studies departments, can also be divided into two traditions. One tradition was closely related to Neo-Confucianism; this included the work of Professor William Theodore de Bary at Columbia University, which was essentially carried out along Neo-Confucian lines and was therefore deeply connected to the traditions of philosophy and political thought. But once the social movements and sociological trends of the Sixties and Seventies had come to an end in the West, traditional studies of intellectual history came under serious attack. This was because the targets of the radical movements of the Sixties were the elite and upper-class cultures of the ruling classes, while new intellectual trends placed a high value on popular culture. As a result, a generation of scholars initially engaged with intellectual history began to move away from it in its traditional form. They thought of the "Cheng Zhu" school of Neo-Confucianism,[1] and of Confucius himself, as belonging to upper-class elites. Why did we still have to focus on them? We should instead have focused on everyday life and the society of the popular masses, for instance. As a result, they began to examine the anti-imperialist and anti-Christian society, the "Boxers," who were active in violent rebellion from 1898–1901, and the Taiping Heavenly Kingdom, a state established through large-scale rebellion seeking social reform and which lasted from 1851–64. They looked at the studies of scholars such as Philip Kuhn, Joseph Esherick, and Ke Wen on the Boxers, the Taiping Heavenly Kingdom, and folk religion, which used many new social science methodologies, among which I think two are the most prominent.

One is what we call the methodology of social history, which was influenced by Marxism but was politically unlike the Chinese school of Marxism. Most of the scholars in this field were influenced by Weber, Talcott Parsons or Eisenstadt—in short, the school of modern sociology. Later on, we would oppose Marxism to liberalism in the field of political thought, believing that Marx and Weber were very different, despite the fact that in European thought both thinkers belonged to the same school of social history when considered within the larger framework of social methodology. They were both social historians and placed a high value on social history, despite their many interpretive differences. What this means is that this tradition was very influential in the realm of intellectual history. For instance, the work of Benjamin Elman was marked by Weberian influences, even as early as *From Philosophy to Philology*, and afterwards we could see in the works of the Changzhou School that they were becoming gradually more influenced by social history. They wished to dismantle the model of John King Fairbank and the teleological framework of modernization theory. The other methodology was influenced by anthropology and cultural studies, and included Ke Wen's research on the Boxers, as well as Joseph Esherick's and James Hevia's work, which was heavily influenced by anthropological and cultural studies as well. Although these two methodological directions were opposed to the traditional Chinese school of Marxism in their political ideas, their social classifications, and their various critiques of historical teleology, their fundamental social and intellectual approaches remained nearly identical. All three focused upon the interactions of thought with everyday life, social forms, and mass culture.

These were two traditions of intellectual history that were different in many ways, but also contained many points of overlap. I could not avoid dealing with these two traditions in my research. On the one hand, I spoke repeatedly during the Nineties of our dissatisfaction with the tradition of history of philosophy. If we only used the fundamental categories of European—and especially German or modern European—philosophy as a methodological framework for examining Chinese intellectual history, we would surely be introducing many distortions. For instance, can the concept of *tianli* be interpreted by using the category of ontology? Or, is *gewu zhizhi* ("investigation of things and extension of knowledge") an epistemological question? These questions have already been posed and replied to in the negative in works on the history of philosophy—they are not completely new, but at that time everyone thought that the method of the history of philosophy was universally applicable. These lines of thought were regarded as universal. In the Nineties we began to suspect that continuing to use the basic framework of European philosophy to describe Chinese thought was insufficient.

I was personally most influenced by the second of these traditions: social history. If in our inquiries we ignore the social, political, ethical, or moral practices connected to any body of thought, including Neo-Confucianism in China, that tradition will be very difficult to understand. What this means is that in our intellectual histories we cannot neglect the fundamental social conditions that are produced by intellectual activities, the relationship between social movements and these bodies of thought. Thus, my explanatory perspective and methodology came to involve gradually more of the methodology of social history. However, that methodology also brings with it various problems. The fundamental background to this method of social history is the development of modern social science in the West, which is something we can never shed. The theory of social science grew in its entirety from the development of European and Western societies from the nineteenth to the twentieth century. In other words, in the tradition of intellectual history, if we view social sciences as a product of specific historical conditions (despite its reliance on building models, structure, and theories), then we must ask what relation is constituted between such historically specific knowledge and the theories that we are now trying to examine. This has also become an important question.

I cite a simple example: the writing of social history always places a high value on economic history. Whether within the Marxist school of intellectual history or other schools, none can stray far in their explanations from the economic sphere, and only once economics has been discussed can the spheres of politics and society be tackled. Certainly, the concept of "economy" was already present in ancient China—its equivalent was *shengji* ("livelihood"), which developed gradually and was very comprehensive. Until modern times—the late nineteenth to early twentieth century—Liang Qichao and others used the term *shengjixue* ("study of livelihoods," sometimes translated as "political economy") and referenced *guojixue* ("national economies") in their early translations of and introductions to Adam Smith's works, which was only later translated into *jingjixue* ("economics"). This is also to say that categories like "economy," produced by European capitalism in the nineteenth century, only then came to predominate over all the particular categories in the other domains of life. But economy-based studies of social phenomena are also produced under unique historical conditions. Modern social science is established on the basis of a particular social taxonomy and social morphology, including such classifications as economy, politics, society, and culture. Our scholarly research corresponds to this, being divided into the fields of political science, sociology, economics, and cultural anthropology, among others. We can clearly see the connection between modern social science classifications and the modern social division of labor. We study economics, political science, sociology, and cultural studies, and we transform our knowledge from these sciences into universally applicable methods to understand our own times, as well as our ancient history. When we do this, it is in a sense to restructure our past traditions and history, as well as to reconstruct history based upon a particular, modern classification of knowledge. In other words, if we deploy the category of economics, produced through modern social science, to study ancient history, then we will certainly restructure, omit, or add something in the process.

But what I am discussing here is not the question of pure or impure economic concepts. Among modern economic theorists, there are many who insist that pure economic phenomena do not exist but are instead always connected to politics, customs, culture, and other factors. Marx's economic concepts are such a case. What I am discussing here is the fact that people under different sets of social relations will have completely different appraisals of a particular system, so that it is not simply a question of whether the economy is connected with other systems or customs. The specific historical conditions of a particular society contain a specific sort of economic life, one which might not be identical to economic life under modern social conditions. A simple example are the studies of the Well-Field System,[2] which is something many modern scholars have produced, including Hu Hanming and Hu Shizhi.[3] To study land systems during that time, one had to study the Well-Field System. But whether or not this Well-Field System actually existed is historically debatable—scholars worked primarily on the basis of descriptions from Mencius and others. We know from the investigations and research of scholars that the Well-Field System was a kind of land system, yet it was not simply a land system: it was also simultaneously a political and military system, in addition to being a way of defining the relationship between inside (Chinese) and outside (barbarian), and an effective part of the dynastic and musical and ritual systems. In its practical application, the Well-Field System cannot therefore be reduced to a purely economic practice.

I can also cite another simple example: in the ancient system of rites and music, for instance in the Five Rites (*wuli*)[4], the position of "soldier" was ceremonial, so that military practices can also be considered to throw some light on rites and music. In other words, it is fine to speak of the economy, military and culture—"culture" (*wenhua*) certainly also has etymological roots in ancient times, namely *wen* ("literature and learning") and *hua* ("change")—but the category of "culture" itself was only defined explicitly in modern history. It cannot simply be projected in its entirety onto ancient history, or rationalized as a special category. If we look at how the modern concept of "culture" was produced, we can see how deeply it is connected to modern state systems, social systems, and the rationalization of knowledge. We now have ministries of culture, cultural policy, cultural anthropology, cultural vanguards, and cultural conflicts; yet these terms only began gradually to make their way during the late nineteenth century. They are also intimately connected to the construction of modern states. For instance, our cultural categories from that time included *guoxue* ("national studies" or "Chinese studies") under the category of scholarship; *guoyue* ("national music") under music; *guohua* ("national style of painting," or "traditional Chinese painting") under painting; and *guoyi* ("national medicine," or "traditional Chinese medicine"), among others. All these things constituted new standards for cultural categories produced through a specific history, and were products of completely different cultural conditions—it was only upon this basis that related categories of knowledge could be produced.

But problems arose with our universalization of these categories of knowledge and our adoption of them as methods for observing and narrating history. We not only live in these social conditions, but are products of this cultural and social system—yet, as scholars, we are products of this system of academic training, and it is for this latter reason that we took these categories and methods to be natural and universal. Having been naturalized, these categories are no longer historicized, politicized or relativized as ways of viewing ancient history. What this means is that, though every experienced scholar, regardless of the methodology he or she is using, finds different flexible applications and limitations of the universalization of this particular method in working on historical research, each comes up with different concrete solutions for sorting through various problems. This is reminiscent of that first generation of scholars I mentioned a moment ago: they have excellent foundations in traditional Chinese learning, though they were also heavily influenced by Western frameworks of historical interpretation. Many scholars who examine social history and intellectual history today also emphasize China's particularity, but the problem is that such an emphasis always rests upon the presumption of universality. Many people point out in their studies that China is completely unique, with an economic system, for instance, distinctive from Western ones. But although this method of discussion sounds reasonable enough, it nonetheless runs into the same problem: in taking our own perspective to be particular, we are already presuming that the pre-existing framework of knowledge is the universal one. We already recognize the universalization and naturalization of the Western framework of knowledge—we say that it is "natural" or that it is a "natural phenomenon." In light of this, our application of our own particularities to argue against that universality actually affirms it.

This brings with it another problem: in social sciences and history, the many particularities that we point to are not really that particular. We simply compare our own historical experiences with descriptions of modern knowledge and theory, rather than truly contrasting the social experiences of different regions. If we compare Western studies of "premodern" religion and tribes, and especially the particularities they emphasize, with the characteristics of Chinese society that we identify in our own studies, we will often find that the degree of similarity is far greater than we had imagined. Can they really then be taken to be our own particularities? Suppose that our society and the West contain more similarities in our social phenomena than the similarities between the different elements internal to our own society? Or suppose that our current society is more similar to the West than it is to our own society at a different point in time—then can such a particularism still stand? The question is not whether we are unique, but rather how we discuss these particularities; this particularistic form of critique—also a critique of Western universalism—is in reality quite weak. It is also in this sense that all universalisms until now were particularistic universalisms—particular sets of knowledge constructed within a specific culture, society, and period of time. Nothing but its overwhelming hegemony gave Western universalism the appearance of being universal, leading many to believe that it was universal. In this context, all particularisms are universal particularisms: they all take some form of universalism as their premise and then affirm their particularity from that position. What they lack is a recognition of the universality of particular phenomena. All universalisms are actually part of particular phenomena, rather than simply existing within the dichotomy of particular universalisms. Universality only emerges from particularity, so that all universalities are in a sense particular and unique. This is certainly more of a philosophical discussion, but it invites us to think about method as well.

Performing historical, anthropological, or ethnographical research always involves making observations about a particular or limited subject. But it is clear that Western anthropological theory makes observations on particular subjects—so how did it become universal? This is an interesting methodological question. In my opinion, historical texts need to identify a perspective from which to observe the particularity of historical subjects. On this point, I think that this is somewhat similar to the observations of anthropology: my object of study is an object of historical research, but I can also adopt this object as the methodological perspective from which to view its world. The observed subject must be liberated from its position as object so that it also becomes such a methodological perspective—a perspective that you are continuously in dialogue with. In other words, there is no placeless or ahistorical position from which we, as individuals, can achieve historical knowledge, and it is impossible to examine our subjects without applying our own theoretical traditions and disciplinary methodologies in some way. We all have our own individual backgrounds, after all. To borrow the language of hermeneutics, we might say that this is our bias, our "pre-understanding" or "pre-structure," and that without this "pre-structure," we cannot construct understanding. To put it in yet another way, a purely objective, unbiased research perspective simply does not exist, and no one is capable of creating one.

In light of this, to criticize these theories is not to say that we do not draw from them. Although it has become common in Chinese intellectual circles to avoid studying certain theories because they are Western, this practice is completely misguided. We must engage with them in examining any body of knowledge, and only when a method for examining them is established can they be improved upon. Only then can we engage with them and make conscious our own theoretical foundations. Researchers are not devoid of any aspect of "self," but this "self" must be reconfigured as one that respects the object of study and understands it as a subjective perspective in itself, one from which our own limitations might be observed. I just cited the Well-Field System in my discussion of economics, for instance, though it is not simply a set of economic relations or an economic system. The concepts and methods supplied to us by modern social science, including labor, production, and slavery, can explain certain aspects of the system, but they cannot clarify its historical meaning in its entirety. Ancient economic and social life—we can't help but use these classifications—were also an effective part of social ethics and moral life, so that questions of ethics, morals, and human practice were all intimately connected as well. We cannot therefore neglect these practices if we wish to understand the system. Given this, we can see in reflecting upon the conditions of our own knowledge that ethics (moral and ethical theory) is studied in modern universities within philosophy departments, and that these in turn sit alongside economics departments; equally, this sort of economics is completely separate from morals and ethics, geared instead toward describing the logic of economic life. In reality, however, the rules and conditions described by economics more forcefully regulate our modes of action in modern society than those of any other sphere of knowledge—as in the mindset of maximizing benefits, and more generally throughout our modes of action. In other words, economics contains deep ethical characteristics, although it is now formally opposed to ethics, which has been relegated today to a position of total inconsequentiality. This method of understanding sits alongside the establishment of a system of disciplines in which ethical, moral, and even political and economic life are completely separate fields of knowledge, and are products of modern society's movement toward rationalization. But in interpreting history and concrete social life, this method is accompanied by a series of blind spots and weaknesses, which appear in all the different domains. For this reason, studying ancient thought can actually provide us with a critical and reflective perspective, helping us to understand not only ancient life, but also the location of the central problems and principal nodes of our own society. Only if such an introspective perspective is adopted to reflect upon our own society will these become apparent. In this context, historical research can constitute a live intellectual space—it becomes a live historical source, and even a living object of study. It can also be extracted as a methodological perspective and used to think through our questions concerning modernity. This is fundamentally a methodological question.

My first book, entitled *Li Yu Wu* (*Reason and Matter*), overlapped in many places with Wang Mingming's research on *wu* ("matter"). One of my questions was this: What exactly is *wu*? Today, the term means something like "material" or "fact," and the concept of the "material" in modern times presupposes such essential units as atoms. But in the pre-Qin era, this term was used to express *wanwu*, or the myriad things on earth (i.e. everything), and was also a standard of etiquette, so that the question of *wu* was also intimately connected with the question of rites and of the natural order; it was not something that could be abstracted. Nature, and *wu*, must be understood within the category of rites and music, because they are intrinsically connected with the standardization of practices of etiquette. By the Song Dynasty, *wu* gradually came to signify an increasing array of things, and became more alienated from the category of rites and music, while also developing characteristics closer to the *wu* of nature. At the same time, the development of the problem of *tianli* is closely related to the transformation of the category of *wu*. The concept of *li* ("reason") stems from the phrase *wenli*—the lines in a piece of jade—which were important symbols in ancient times. By the Song Dynasty, the status of this concept of *li* had gradually grown to become one of the most important categories. The construction of this abstract category of *li* should be understood as having occurred gradually alongside that of the concept of *wu*, from which it split when they emerged from the domain of rites and music—these were its premises. The *wu* of rites and music was a standardized and intrinsic part of our practices, so that it does not need to be re-examined through cognitional procedures. In other words, moral practices must be viewed within the rites-and-music system and within our daily lives; but if the tradition of rites and music has disintegrated, then *wu* is no longer an effective part of the rites-and-music system but rather an isolated reality. The problem of *wu* then becomes separated from the problem of knowing (or even the question of moral knowledge and practice). People must approach the category of *li* and reason by first understanding the studies of *wu* and matter. Zhu Xi said that "investigating things to extend knowledge" (*gewu zhizhi*) meant seeking out *tianli*[5]—the heavenly principle or heavenly *li*—while at the same time seeking out *tianli* could never be separated from the practice of investigation (*gewu*). The reason is that *wu* does not present itself immediately as morality or knowledge, but at the same time this *li* is an intrinsic part of *wu*. The separation of *wu* and *li* was fundamentally a result of the disintegration of rites and music. In this context, if we attempt to understand the categories of rites, *wu* and *qi* ("tool" or "receptacle"), for instance, simply through epistemology or ontology, then we will lose all analysis of the historical process through which this theory was produced. This historical process is not simply one of materialization, since historical processes will always be human processes of knowledge, cognition, and representation as well. It is not simply to say that "this thing happened at this particular time," but rather to analyze the historical relations and representations under which these events arose. For instance, Confucius used the phrase *libeng yuehuai* ("the collapse of feudal religious rites"[6]) to express the social crises that surrounded him; yet this representation was itself also a moral and theoretical judgment. It was also something capable of shaking up the social practices of those times. Thus, only by observing the continuing interchange between events and representation, representation and action, can we grasp the significance of that era's crises and situations, particularly for its people. Most of these questions are methodological: How do we know history? How do we understand the thought of an era? How do we know a society?

What I wish to speak more concretely about is a question that is quite central to my book, *The Rise of Modern Chinese Thought*, which is the question of empire and the nation-state. This obviously involves methodological questions as well. My book in fact contains two main lines of thought. One is the relation between the evolution of the social system and Confucianism, which runs through the entire book. I examine, for instance, the relation between feudalism and traditional Confucianism, between the prefectural system and the transformations of Confucianism, and between the formation of modern nation-states in late modernity and the development of scientific knowledge. (The prefectural system describes a system of local administration carried out by court-appointed government officials assigned to specific locales for limited terms, rather than through a hereditary system of local rule.) These all occurred within the mutually interacting categories of social systems and knowledge; but I focus my attention more on political systems, one of which concerns empire and the nation-state. When I address the question of political systems in my book, I use two groups of concepts, one being "empire and the nation-state" and the other being "feudalism and the prefectural system." My narrative emerges from somewhere between these two groups of concepts, and perhaps alongside another related dichotomy as well, which is that of "rites and music" versus "systems," the latter in the sense of institutionalized modes of governance.

We know that the concepts of empire and nation-state are products of modern Western knowledge, rather than being internal to our own intellectual tradition, and in the introduction to that book I investigate the origins of the term *diguo* ("empire"). Although it was already in use in ancient times, we have come to use it as a political term, which is a practice that was imported to China from Japan. During the Meiji Restoration, Japan proclaimed itself a *diguo*, and directly translated the Western concept of "empire" into the Chinese characters for the concept *diguo*. In other words, its roots date back to ancient times, but it is not an ancient concept. In my narrative, I use the distinction between "empire and nation-state," yet this description is not an internal one. Why is this so? Let me explain.

In my concrete descriptions, I rarely make use of these categories, instead relying on the categories of feudalism and the prefectural system. Confucian scholars (regardless of whether they hailed from the Song Dynasty school or the Qing Dynasty) primarily used these political categories as well, which are also closely related to another set of Confucian concepts: that of rites and music. If we look at this from the perspective of Confucianism, all the way up to its later periods, we can see that the concept of feudalism became gradually more connected with that of rites and music, while the prefectural system became gradually more connected to the concept of "system" as described in the previous paragraph as well. In other words, feudalism was the way in which the ancient sage-kings governed, and acted as a mechanism whereby moral life became organized completely within the system of rites and music. Once the rites and music system collapsed, the political system gradually separated from it to become a system of its own—which is also to say that it became gradually more remote from individual people. It became increasingly more top-down, being a system constructed by the imperial authority, which viewed itself as the center and built downwards from itself.

The seeds of the prefectural system lie in the Warring States era (476 BCE–221 BCE), though it was not consolidated until the Qin Dynasty. Within history departments, and particularly Japan's Kyoto School, most historians believe that the standardization of the prefectural system was only gradually established in Chinese history after the Song Dynasty. The evidence of this standardization lies in the gradual disintegration of the feudal and aristocratic system from the Wei and Jin Dynasties to the Tang Dynasty. A bureaucratic system was established, formed around the central axes of the prime minister and imperial authority, from which localized government bureaucracies emanated. This system differed significantly from the bureaucratic system of the feudal period. Ancient political thought was thus also closely linked to this prefectural system. When Confucian scholars criticized the political systems of their time, they often invoked the concepts of feudalism and of rites and music; their invocation of feudalism was at the same time an invocation of rites and music, just as their invocation of rites and music was at the same time an invocation of the early years of rule by the mythological sage-kings, under the Three Dynasties (2852 BCE–2205 BCE). In my book, I tease out some of these lines of thought. In the Song

Dynasty, many scholars wrote history in terms of the division between the pre-Three Dynasties and post-Three Dynasties eras, and this included not only Neo-Confucian scholars but also proponents of the New Learning,[7] and other historians—for instance Ouyang Xiu, author of *Xin Wudaishi* (*New History of the Five Dynasties*), and Sima Guang, author of *Zhizhi Tongjian* (*Comprehensive Mirror to Aid in Government*). This periodization was not meant to correspond to external markers of time, but instead referred to the evolution of social relations. In their view, it was through such an evolution that the system emerged from the practice of rites and music, gradually differentiating itself and taking coherent shape in the process. Little by little, it came to resemble what legalists had described, and even more so the system of contemporary nations. This is also to say that political practice came to depart increasingly from our ethical and moral lives.

Thus, when Confucian scholars described the disappearance of feudalism and the rise of the prefectural system, they provided an entire narrative about society and politics. I noticed that the Song Dynasty thinkers deployed two intellectual systems, and two different narrative categories, simultaneously. Zhu Xi and Zhang Zai are among these thinkers. One strand is concerned with *tiandao, tianli, gewu zhizhi, zhiliangzhi* ("extension of innate knowledge") and *zhixing heyi* ("unity of action and knowledge"), which are concepts that we historians of philosophy later came to view as important. The other was concerned with the ideas of the pre-Three Dynasties and post-Three Dynasties periods, the rule of the sage-kings, feudalism, the prefectural system, rites and music, and "systems" in its institutional sense. Yet within this system of rites and music there are further divisions, including the placement of feudalism and the prefectural system in a relationship of opposition; distinguishng the Well-Field (*jingtian*) System from the Equal-Field (*juntian*) System[8]; distinguishing later military systems from the ancient military system; distinguishing the system of imperial examinations from the previous schooling system run under the election and feudal systems; and distinguishing the southern system of rites and music from the northern system—which extends the split that occurred during the time of the Northern and Southern Dynasties (420–589) between the north and south on the question of rites and music into the historical consciousness of the Song Dynasty. At the time, the Song Dynasty was bordered by Mongolia and the Jinn Dynasty (1115–1234), along with nations toward the south, so that this split involved the question of distinguishing north from south, as well as distinguishing the barbarians from China. Thus, the evolution of both rites and music and "systems" is also located within the differentiation of barbarians from Chinese, which gives those categories meaning in terms of identity as well. Those scholars thought that their systems—for instance, the Equal-Field System, or the Double-Tax System and New Military System of the late-Tang Dynasty[9]—were descended from the northern system, although they evaluated these systems from the perspective of rites and music and feudalism. When the Song Confucians criticized their own society, they often said that its system was not really based in feudalism, but rather on the differentiation between Chinese and barbarians, by which the latter were cast as external and illegitimate. They contrasted "systems" in the institutional sense to feudalism, while these differentiations were also meant to refer to contemporary social and political attitudes. For instance, their observations that in ancient times there were "schools" while now there were "civil examinations" were at the same time harsh critiques of civil examinations as something negative. Their descriptions of "rites and music" and of "sage-kings," and of the distinction between the pre-Three Dynasties and post-Three Dynasties eras, included parables and critiques of their own period.

But these critiques were not absolute, nor were they meant as simple negations. As history had evolved, they could not simply return to ancient ways. Zhu Xi said that the civil examinations, Equal-Field System and Double-Tax System could not simply be abolished at that time, each having its own uses and functions, and that what was most important was the fact that they had lost the spirit of the rites and music of the ancient sages. These systems were themselves historical narratives through which those scholars had constructed their political, moral and ethical perspectives. Within Confucian categories, all political, moral, economic, and social critiques were always ethical or moral critiques in the end, or critiques based in rites and music, while Confucian moral and ethical critiques had intrinsic political, economic, and military content as well. They were synthesized in the Confucian categories, and only in this way can we understand why the Song Confucianist system, framed with *tianli* and *tiandao* at its center, could be constructed at that time. It was constructed with a particular conception of history always in the background—a Confucian history—and this narrative is intimately connected with the society and politics of those times, along with their particular social and historical conditions.

But if this explains enough, why then is the question of empire and the nation-state still relevant? Can we not speak simply of the feudal and prefectural systems? Feudalism and the prefectural system, as well as rites and music and systems, are Confucian categories; but relying simply on Confucian knowledge will not give us a complete or objective view of history. In reality, those categories are also forms of knowledge produced through particular social conditions and built on particular motives. For instance, the historical division identified between the pre-Three Dynasties and post-Three Dynasties periods was used by Confucian scholars as a way of intervening upon the questions of their own time. If we simply objectify this division and treat it as a universal mode of interpretation, thinking that this will objectively present to us the evolution of social conditions, then we will lose many things as a result. To give a simple example, narratives based on the categories of feudalism and the prefectural system cannot accurately describe the transformations that occurred from the Qin and Han Dynasties through the Song Dynasty—much less the long and complex systemic transformations that occurred from the Song to Yuan Dynasties, from the Yuan to Ming Dynasties, and from the Ming to Qing Dynasties. These categories can only describe some of these changes, while also producing narratives of change that rely upon a particularistic Confucian worldview. In this context, if we only read the systems of later societies in terms of feudalism and the prefectural system, then we have to ask whether feudalism is only the ideal model of Confucianism, or if it was an institutional form pre-dating the Three Dynasties or the Western Zhou Dynasty. Was the prefectural system a system of the Qin Dynasty, or can it also include the systems constructed in later eras? Using these categories to describe later history is also certainly insufficient, as is describing all historical transformations purely using the concepts of rites and music, or of "systems." We must therefore hope to find concepts that are internal to our traditions and histories in order to describe those histories. But this is not to say that such indigenous concepts can completely represent history: we must recognize that these endemic concepts also represent a particularistic narrative or description in any given context. As a result, the particular ways of seeing that are opened up to us when we attach importance to history are very important in helping us to identify the limitations of our own ways of seeing. But that is not to say that this can enable us to resolve the problems entirely.

This involves an even more fundamental issue, which is the fear that we will not be able to extricate ourselves from the viewpoint of world history in writing narratives of Chinese history. If we consider this history only from the domestic perspective, there will be many issues we cannot think through or resolve, as well as many that simply return us to a particularism—one which, as we have seen, will simply affirm European universalism once more. To discuss the question of world history is to introduce the question of empire and the nation-state, as well as that of what is considered modern—particularly the questions of Asian and Chinese modernity. The categories of empire and nation-state emerged in contemporary history, and particularly during the historical transformation of nineteenth-century Europe. Of course, if we were to trace it back to its origins, we would have to go back even further, at least as far as the sixteenth century, to the power struggle between the European monarchs and the pope, and the conflicts that occurred between the monarchical nations of Europe and the Turkish Empire, under which empires and monarchical nations came to be opposed to one another. However, these categories did not become fully theorized until the nineteenth century, when Western political economists began to emerge. Hegel's political economy and historical philosophy were particularly important in this trend. Hegel divided history into four stages: from Oriental to Greek, from Greek to Roman, from Roman to Germanic, and with the Germanic nation-state constituting the final stage of history. We can also see this model of historical evolution in the theory of Adam Smith, but he divides history according to economics: namely into gathering, hunting, agricultural, and then urban and commercial civilizations. Hegel deployed the categories of Smith's Scottish Historical School, including "civil society" and "economy," but because Germany at that time was not yet unified, he placed greater importance on the nation-state itself.

This "nation-state" was conceived as the highest goal of history, and was opposed to the traditional political system—which was characterized by the Asian "empires." In the nineteenth century, European intellectual historians began to construct their own world history, which meant taking the various parts of world history and organizing them into an organic whole—European history developed from Asian history, and in the process of shedding it, became a universal historical process. Within this process, the nation-state as the goal of history became a negation of the political form of empire in general, and of the political forms of the Chinese, Mughal, Persian, and Ottoman empires in particular. Within the domain of political theory, this negation can be traced back to Machiavelli, who wrote at a time when the European monarchies were engaged in power struggles with the Turkish Empire. He saw the Turkish Empire as an "empire" and the European monarchies as monarchical states, thereby fundamentally differentiating the two on a political level. In the nineteenth century, these monarchical states came to be seen as the embryonic forms of the European nation-state, so that the dichotomy formed within the narrative of European world and political history between the so-called "empires" and "nation-states" was in reality a theory to legitimize the European nation-state. In my book, I occasionally use the concepts of empire and nation-state, but what I really wish to do is to break down this dualism, and to negate the dualistic relation as it appears in nineteenth-century political economy. Neither do I see the transistion between empire and nation-state as a necessary condition for the transformation into political modernity; I would not describe the problem in this way.

Such narratives also arise from a particular background in academic history. In studying the question of Chinese modernity, we tend to see at least two kinds of narratives, one being similar to the Marxist school, as with John King Fairbank's challenge-response model. This viewed the large-scale clash between China and the West following the Opium Wars as the birth of Chinese modernity. Fairbank thought that China was an empire, so that it was characterized by cultural nationalism while lacking political nationalism. The hidden meaning of this is that political nationalism is a premise of the modern nation-state, and that, because China was only characterized by cultural nationalism, it was an empire but not a nation-state. The Marxists thought that the Qing Dynasty ruled over a feudal society, and that its self-transformation necessarily had to occur in the same direction as that of the Western nation-states.

The other, very different narrative was developed gradually by the Kyoto School in the 1920s and 1930s. Kōnan Naitō and Ishisata Miyazaki argued that Asian or *tōyō* (East Asian or Oriental) modernity developed out of the transformations that occurred between the Tang and Song Dynasties, believing that the origins of the latter could be found during this period. Why did they make this claim? The first reason is political. The Kyoto School had very close connections with the expansionist policies under contemporary Japanese imperialism, as well as the later idea of a "Greater East Asia." They created the category of *tōyō* and placed China within its history, starting from political considerations, which dispels any view of China as a colossal and inevitable entity within history. This concept of *tōyō*, among others, is not self-evident, and it developed under very specific political consciousness, and under a particular form and set of social relations, and perhaps even as a concerted political strategy. Certainly, this concept underwent many changes after that time; our use of the term today (*dongyang* in Mandarin, referring to East Asia or the Orient) does not always imply a return to Japanese imperialism.

But even if the historical narrative of East Asia (*tōyō*) is afflicted by being politicized, it also offers many insights. One of these is that it was not until the Song Dynasty (and therefore not during the Tang or even the Five Dynasties either) that China saw its first mature state with a prefectural system. The Kyoto School understood that this mature nation, organized under the prefectural system, had characteristics that had essentially grown from the distintegration of the feudal, aristocratic system, dating from before the Tang Dynasty. As a result, this system built around a core of imperial authority, the prime minister, and the civil service was a highly rationalized state system. In other words, although the Kyoto School also utilized this concept of the prefectural system, their narratives concerning the Song Dynasty were fundamentally built around the Western category of the nation-state. Their description of this system was no more than a particularistic description, the heart of which lay in the fact that Song China was a nation-state and no longer a traditional empire, and particularly not an aristocratic system of empire. Miyazaki identified it as the early years of the "quasi-nation-state." Where monarchical states that could be understood as embryonic nation-states only appeared in Europe in the twelfth and thirteenth centuries, they had already begun to appear and reach a relatively mature state in China in the tenth century. As a result, the Kyoto School asserted that an early form of the nation-state could be found in East Asia, prior to its appearance in the European political world. Its beginnings date to the Song Dynasty, and it developed in the Joseon Dynasty in Korea in the fourteenth century, as well as in Tokugawa Japan in the seventeenth century. A history of political evolution in East Asia was thus formed.

The Kyoto School also saw this political history as being closely linked to Confucianism in the Northern Song Dynasty, and especially to that of Zhu Xi, Cheng Yi and Cheng Hao, which they saw as being produced under the emergence of this new national form. They considered this unique form of Confucianism, differing significantly from Confucianism before the Tang Dynasty, to be a new form of nationalism. The Japanese concept of *kokka shugi* was also translated into the Western phrase "nationalism," so that their descriptions of Song Confucianism were developed within the intellectual context of contemporary nationalism. Even more importantly, however, Kōnan Naitō and Ishisata Miyazaki carried out studies of economic history, among which the most important concerned the currency system, long-distance trade, and urban economies. On the subject of the currency system, and the use of silver and copper currency in various nations during the Five Dynasties, for instance, silver was the currency in use at the time (which is also to say that foreign trade was beginning to occur); by the Song Dynasty, the development of the copper currency system caused the original barter economy to develop into a money economy—which is to say a commodity or early market economy. With the development of the commodity-based economy, new phenomena began to appear in urban life. Long-distance trade, including overseas trade, had already begun to appear. The evidence for this is based on the discovery of shipwrecks in Nansha over the past few years, where spice boxes for export and African ivories were found inside Song Dynasty merchant ships. The fundamental theories behind modern economic history also show that long-distance trade promotes a division of labor, which we know is an important condition for the development of capitalism.

The Kyoto School thought that early forms of the nation-state, nationalism, and long-distance trade had already appeared by the time of the Northern Song Dynasty, along with the bureaucratic system brought into existence with the standardization of civil examinations. They constructed their narrative by placing these things within the traditional categories of civil examination, the prefectural system, and Song Confucianism; but at the same time these narratives were obviously constructed according to the standards of European modernity. The Kyoto School's concepts were established within the framework of contemporary Western social history, and in their narratives we can undeniably see the influences of Hegel, contemporary European historians, and Weberian social theory. But they also used Asian historical narratives to resist that framework and reinterpret the history of China and Asia. In their efforts, they created a new concept of *jingshi* (the "early modern"), and they believed that this new historical form appeared in East Asia during the Song Dynasty.

One positive contribution of the Kyoto School was in shattering the narrative asserting that the Opium Wars in the late-Qing era suddenly brought about modern changes. Certainly, no one denies that Western invasion and expansion had a decisive influence upon the development of modern Chinese history; but this is not equivalent to saying that Chinese history did not undergo its own particular evolutionary process. The seeds of modernity already existed. The Kyoto School stressed that, since the tenth century, the question of modern changes already existed in an early form as China designed its political, economic, artistic, cultural, and intellectual systems. If we attempt to describe these changes within the framework of world history, we would be rewriting history along the lines of Hegel and the political economists of the nineteenth century. The framework of Hegel's narrative of world history was entirely that of a teleology of European nations. But the narratives of the Kyoto School were also very problematic—particularly the opposition they constructed between empire and nation-state according to the framework of European world history. This was essentially to view the nation-state as the only modern framework, and then to disparage any other political form. The nation-states we speak of today are highly structured, and characterized by sovereign entities. The nation-state is a political form that is sovereign whether in its internal or external relations. It is formally defined by relations of equality within the nation-state system; and according to this standard, empires lack these formally equal sovereign relations, instead being characterized by relations of tribute and a hierarchical structure of social relations. According to Fairbank and many Chinese scholars, China could not engage in diplomatic relations because it was an empire, always being self-centered and hierarchical, while modern societies and modern state systems are equal with one another. As a result, they tend to oppose "tribute" to "diplomacy," "tributary systems" to "treaty systems," and "empire" to "nation-state." In fact, these are all manifestations of the dualism between empire and nation-state, appearing at different levels. By this standard, the wide array of traditional social systems are all simply seen as empires, and as pre-modern, anti-modern, backward, or traditional systems.

This is problematic on a number of levels. Firstly, according to this narrative, the Song Dynasty was a nation-state. But was the Yuan Dynasty then an empire or a nation-state? If the Song Dynasty was modern, then what about the Yuan Dynasty? Was it post-modern or pre-modern? Suppose we characterize the Ming Dynasty as a nation-state; then, was the Qing Dynasty anti-modern or anti-nation-state? Or, to put it differently, did it just become more backward? How should we understand it? On the level of political systems, how should we describe the transformation from Song to Yuan, as well as from Ming to Qing? In my view, the Kyoto School did not have the theoretical tools to sort through these questions. Ishisata Miyazaki recognized these problems, and switched perspectives as a result, choosing not to interpret from the perspective of politics but from one of social and legal history. He did this, for instance, in explaining why the Yuan Dynasty was the only Chinese dynasty that did not establish a new legal system, instead using the laws of the Jinn Dynasty in the early years, which were only later abolished. The territory occupied by the Yuan Dynasty was extremely large, and was characterized by extensive internal variation; it thus became impossible to rule all of these different regions and their varying sentiments under Jinn law. What was used instead under the Yuan Dynasty is similar to our contemporary common law system, rather than the standard system of written law, and Miyazaki attributes this to social transformations that necessitated a new system after the Song Dynasty. The Yuan Dynasty and the Song Dynasty were different from one another in many ways, he claimed, and it is difficult to describe the Yuan as having a state model like that of the Song. How then are we to describe it as a uniform and coherent entity? He described the transformations in social life during the Song Dynasty as having continued into the Yuan; and since the increasing deficiencies of Jinn law were due to these changes, there was no way to invoke the models of past dynasties. The Qing and Ming Dynasties differed greatly in their border relations; so if we accept the dualism between empire and nation-state, how are we to describe early-modern China within the scheme of historical transformations that occurred from the Song, Yuan, and Ming to the Qing Dynasties? If the Song Dynasty is considered to be early-modern, then it would seem that the Yuan and Qing Dynasties are closer to being empires. Did things simply reverse themselves? The Kyoto School was plagued with problems of historical teleology and evolutionary theory that prevented them from clarifying these issues.

The second problem is that the theory of the Kyoto School tends not to use descriptions of concrete historical relations. For instance, many historical innovations, including the system of tributes and the *tusi* system,[10] are differed between regions and cannot therefore be understood as homogeneous systems. Students of anthropology and ethnology will certainly be more familiar with this than me. An example of this is the way in which Kangxi Emperor (1654–1722) sent people out to conduct investigations before designing systems, since the laws and systems in each place were different. In Tibet, Qianlong Emperor (1711–99) established the Kashag system that placed the Dalai Lama at the head of the government; but even after conquering the Zhunger Basin he continued to use Islamic law. The *tusi* system in the southwest was also unique. To bring up the tribute system once more, there are in fact several different kinds— the purpose of the Lifan Yuan (the Ministry of Foreign Affairs during the Qing Dynasty) was to manage relations with the Mongols; but then relations with other countries, including Russia, are also included under the "tribute" category. Are these examples of tribute or of diplomacy? Is it tributary trade or foreign trade? Are they hierarchical or equal? The claim is that empires do not have diplomatic relations, while nation-states are characterized by boundaries, diplomatic relations, and administrative jurisdiction; yet China and Russia already clearly deployed methods of drawing boundaries introduced by Western missionaries in the 1689 Treaty of Nerchinsk, which established administrative jurisdiction within these regions. The Treaty's mention of a fugitive slave law (*taoren fa*) signifies that people from each side of the boundary are prohibited from fleeing to the other, and that the governments on each side are prohibited from granting asylum to fugitive slaves. Is this not what we call administrative jurisdiction in frontier territories? The Treaty stipulated a specific volume of trade. Is this not what we call trade access? When modern social theory deals with the difference between nation-state and empire, it always uses boundaries and frontiers to distinguish the two, saying that nation-states have explicit borders, while empires understand both sides of borders or the various shared frontiers as their own. Many regions in the Qing Dynasty had frontiers; yet many regions

also had explicit boundaries, precisely because they had to resolve ownership and trade questions with the minority populations in their border
regions. This was a very complex system and set of practices. If we place
all these practices within the scope of European history—ever since
Weber, concepts of state have all been based on objective standards of
delimitation—we will discover that these objective standards already
existed in the seventeenth century. Is China then a nation-state or an
empire? We probably cannot answer this.

The third problem is that, according to the logic outlined above, the
Kyoto School has no way to describe the relations between nation-states
during this time. For example, in contemporary times, and since the
establishment of the Treaty of Nanking, China has signed many treaties with the West under highly unequal conditions. But these unequal
treaties presuppose a formal equality of sovereignty, since without that
sovereignty one has no authority to sign treaties. In other words, China
was taken to be a modern sovereign state, and its establishment of sovereignty was made apparent by its formal signing of an unequal treaty. Yet
formal equality in sovereignty does not at all describe the equal or unequal
relations of power. A different question we might ask is: Is America an
empire or a nation-state? Does America have boundaries or does it not? It
certainly has boundaries, since one has to go through customs when one
arrives; yet its frontiers may also be in Turkey, Iraq, Afghanistan, and
all along China's periphery. It has frontiers everywhere—in Okinawa,
in the Taiwan Strait—and we might even say that there is nowhere in the
world that is not a US frontier. If American influence is present in every
corner of the world, is it an empire or a nation-state? The standardized
political description we give of two different eras—what we call the pre-
modern and post-modern—are based on the distinction between empire
and nation-state. But can this distinction really describe our reality? Not
only is it unable to describe our history, but neither can it really describe
our present concrete relations.

Have things changed? Certainly. These transformations began in
the eighteenth century with the construction of a universalistic body of
knowledge through particular regimes of power, which was connected
to the Enlightenment and the establishment of modern nation-state
practices in Europe. This universal knowledge was a theory of political
legitimation and egalitarianism in the realm of politics. All contemporary politics must be connected to a politics of equality—"all countries,

large or small, are equal," as the saying goes; yet, in reality, countries are not equal. We know that no regional or international relations are equal in fact, even if they are in form. The development of formalist knowledge played a significant role in this era, and was a gradual change that occurred from the seventeenth to the nineteenth centuries. In any society, political legitimacy must also be established upon foundations of equality, since we are citizens—it cannot take on the form of a feudal or aristocratic system. But we know this is not true in actuality, that this society is in fact unequal and becoming more unequal, and that is in itself responsible for creating yet more inequalities. But it must retain a formal equality in all of its narratives of legitimation.

We all know this society is unequal; yet economists say that it offers equality of opportunity, rather than outcome. Ultimately, however, opportunity is unequal as well. Since we have not yet achieved equality, we can only discuss the origins of and necessary thresholds for achieving equality, which can only be considered theories of legitimation and modern science. None of these equal origins we normally speak of are anything more than narratives of legitimation. In modern society, any political practices that are not linked to equal practices are not legitimate. This is why modern historical narratives always reduce systems, such as those involving tribute, to pre-modern, feudal and backward forms, as well as why the plethora of different systems and ideal practices are all described uniformly as "traditional." The biggest problem with modern society is not one of formal equality, but of whether equality has been achieved in actuality. The question of how formal and actual equality are related exists on both international and domestic scales, but we are hard-pressed to provide an answer to this question in either case.

There is then the question of multiplicity, which is gradually disintegrating among the cultural and social forms and lifestyles of modern society. This is perhaps most readily apparent to those in the field of anthropology, many of whom have realized that the early Mughal and Chinese empires were significantly better at protecting and retaining cultural multiplicity within their societies than modern social systems. This is an observable reality. That is not to say that those systems are all good, but instead that the multiplicity of cultures and lifestyles are being destroyed at an ever-increasing rate, both around the world and within China. The formalized systems of modern nation-states and their high degree of organization are also connected to this fact, while the tendency toward formalized systems has seeped into all other social mechanisms as well. As a result, our studies of these past "empires" provide important perspectives from which to consider modern societies.

For instance, we examine multiplicity as it relates to the tribute system. The Japanese scholar Takeshi Hamashita was primarily interested in viewing the problem from the perspective of trade (especially marine trade). The tribute system was incredibly rich and complex, not being completely opposed to the nation-state system, and Hamashita has suggested that Asia was not characterized by European-style nation-state relations but rather by a dispersed center-periphery system. But did the relations between Qing Dynasty China and Russia, Spain, and Portugal take the form of diplomatic relations between nation-states or tributary relations between empires? On the one hand, we cannot easily claim that they did not behave at all like nation-states, which appeared early in China in nascent form. The presence of nation-state characteristics throughout Chinese history has often been cited as an important indicator of China's historical continuity; for, despite its innumerable breaks, it is certainly also characterized by this stable central political form. At the domestic level, without considering the prefectural system to be the internal core of these states, whether it is the Han or the Tang Dynasty we are referring to, we will find it difficult to understand. Many people today take the opposite position, criticizing the nation-state form and the West, and saying that China would be more accurately described by the term *tianxia*—"all under heaven"—or as an empire, which is equivalent to affirming the empire/ nation-state dichotomy of the West. This is because they neglect the very ancient roots and development of China's nation-state system. The Qin Dynasty was the most important practitioner of the prefectural system, yet it was a highly unified empire that was understood as a nation, rather than conforming to the model of empire opposed to the nation-state. The Qin Dynasty grew from the highly developed state form of the Warring States period, rather than the dispersed empire to which we usually refer. Its internal bureaucratic system was already very well developed.

In *Lianghan Sixiang Shi* (*The History of Thought in the Two Han Dynasties*), Xu Fuguan greatly emphasized the system centered around the prime minister. His research was conducted during the Cultural Revolution, but what he was considering was the problem of "traditional China." The core problem in his research was why China had been unable to shed its autocracy—an autocracy that had been central to imperial authority. In European history, the autocratic or imperial dictatorships disintegrated as systems of bureaucracy developed. But in China, ever since the Han Dynasty (and even more so since the Song Dynasty), a civil service system centered around the prime minister was already highly developed, much like the system in contemporary England. In fact, there are now many studies showing that England's civil service system was inspired to a degree by China's civil service tradition. But why then is China, with such a highly developed civil service system, unable to shed its imperial dictatorship?

At the time, Xu Fuguan was examining the Sino-Korean question, and claimed that Sino-Korean relations were modeled on the relationship of the nuclear family with the wife and mother's side, as well as on the eunuch system in the civil service (who were considered more trustworthy than the scholar officials), while doing away with the executive system of power centered around the prime minister. He was thereby also hinting at the opposition between the Cultural Revolution Group, which consisted of Mao's most radical supporters and had been established in 1966 to direct the Cultural Revolution, and the State Council. If we simply return to the traditional categories of *tianxia* and empire, and take them to be completely distinct from the modern nation-state, then I think that we will fall back into another trap of Eurocentrism—a real trap, since it denies the possibility of our own, internally driven history.

In my book, I examine the Gongyang School[11] as a way of understanding the problem of empire and nation-states, which is also an attempt to explain the theory of political legitimation of that ancient era. An example to clarify the issue more effectively: when I speak of the Gongyang School and New Text Confucianism (*jinwen jingxue*), I give primary emphasis to two perspectives. The first is that most scholars of Qing Dynasty New Text Confucianism believe that it did not appear until that dynasty's later years, under the Emperor Qianlong—that is, only with the scholars Zhuang Cunyu and Liu Fenglu. They believed that New Text Confucian Scholarship had ceased to exist after the time of the Eastern Han, apart from a few individual cases. It was Old Text Confucianism, Song and Ming Confucianism, and also the study of history, that became the dominant framework of Confucianism. When I was reading through the material, and particularly that related to the *Spring and Autumn Annals*, I discovered that the Gongyang School was extremely influential in the political practices of the several dynasties that followed. For instance, the

Jinn Dynasty, which opposed the Southern Song Dynasty, also finally occupied the Central Plains of the Mongolian Yuan Dynasty and, in order to legitimize this occupation, began to appropriate much Confucian knowledge for its own purposes, among which the theory of Grand Unity (*datong*, a vision of grand harmony among all people) and the Theory of Legitimate Succession were most prominent. At that time, many scholar-officials of Han, Mongolian and Jurchen ancestry working for the Jinn and Mongol dynasties petitioned the emperor to continue using Gongyang and New Text Scholarship—which was not really classical scholarship, but rather the application of theory in the service of dynastic politics. The most important aspect of this was the means of delimiting inside (Chinese) from outside (barbarian). *The Chronicle of Zuo* is one work that makes such strict delimitations, although *The Spring and Autumn Annals* and the *Gongyang Commentary* also provide ways of doing this. By the time Dong Zhongshu wrote *Cunqiu Fanlou* (a commentary on the *Spring and Autumn Annals*), Han China had become completely different from the China of the pre-Qin area, due to the large-scale expansion of the Han Dynasty empire. In this book, he significantly revised the boundaries between "China" and the "barbarian" tribes, so that in his account—for instance in the chapter entitled "Zhulin"—the distinction between China and the barbarians began to take on an oppositional characteristic. *Yi* (barbarians) and *xia* (civilized Chinese) were not absolute categories, and their meaning gradually became more dependent upon whether one submitted to the Confucian rites and customs, as being civilized gradually came to be associated with the Confucian tradition. Even though this distinction had already been understood within the category of rites and customs—there was no doubt that Chinese society differed in its rites and customs from its neighboring societies—the adoption of Confucian rites and customs as the standard for distinguishing between the two categories made them oppositional, not simply different. But as ritual music became neutralized—so that those who submitted to rites were considered to be *xia* (while those who transgressed those rites were considered to be *yi*)—theory was thus modified in accordance with historical developments. Within this theory, the distinction between *yi* and *xia* allows for the two categories to transform one another, which is itself a result of those historical changes. There were many petitions of this kind made to the emperor. No new laws were established during the Yuan Dynasty; but how could stable rule be established without new laws? To achieve grand unity and establish their own legitimacy, the new dynasty had to have a system of justice and legitimacy; as a result many scholars began to attempt to use the *Spring and Autumn Annals* as an interpretation of the Yuan Dynasty system of justice, in the hope that it could become a sort of constitution for the dynasty. This had already been done before by the Han Dynasty scholar Dong Zhongshu, who had used them as a legal text. During the Yuan Dynasty, scholar-officials began to suggest this practice, and their subsequent analyses of the inside-outside relationship and of Grand Unity within their interpretations of the *Annals* obviously grew out of Gongyang Studies. As a result, the notion that Gongyang studies disappeared for over 1,000 years, only to reappear during the mid-Qing Dynasty, is simply a conclusion reached from the perspective of disciplinary history—that is, only by identifying an orthodox Gongyang School among these New Text Confucian scholars, and by neglecting all political practices, can we reach this conclusion. The claim that Gongyang studies did not exist after the Eastern Han Dynasty, which is often made by historians of New Text scholarship, is a claim I see as highly problematic.

The second perspective can be represented by Benjamin Elman, who carried out a very creative and excellent study of the Changzhou School[12], and who proposed that the revival of Qing Dynasty New Text scholarship was the result of a political struggle (a court struggle) between Zhuang Cunyu and Heshen. Of course, his explanation was more complex. This is a very important work of Chinese intellectual history from the past twenty years, and one that also influenced me—especially in relation to how we might understand the relationship between Confucian scholarship and politics. His research techniques are well worth applying. But I think that our understanding of the rise of Qing Dynasty New Text scholarship has been limited by the framework of that court struggle, which has in turn greatly limited our political understanding of Qing Dynasty New Text studies. I recently read an article in *Zhonghua Dushu Bao*, which spoke of scholars of Qing history re-examining Zhuang's studies while objecting to Elman's explanation. I too posed this question several years ago, although primarily from the perspective of intellectual history. By carefully re-examining texts by Zhuang Cunyu and others, we can see that the questions raised among them are all very important, and in fact are indirect ways of interpreting the questions of Grand Unity and the Three Traditions (Buddhism, Daoism and Confucianism). The question of how to define the inside-outside relationship is also raised repeatedly within these narratives. The Qing Dynasty was a period in which a minority group held political power in the Central Plains, so that the questions of how to explain one's own legitimacy and how to be able to describe oneself as "Chinese" were very important ones. The phrase "China" (*Zhongguo*) appears repeatedly in Qing Dynasty Gongyang Studies and New Text scholarship. Zhuang Cunyu, and other scholars of the Confucian canon who came after him, interpreted China through the opposition of the categories of *yi* and *xia*—*yidi* (the barbarian tribes to the east and north) could be China, and China could be taken as *yidi*— in a way that invoked a history of mutual influence and transformation between China and the barbarians. This question is intimately connected with that of the legitimacy of the minority Qing Dynasty. When we examine history today, we always do so through the sequence of Song, Yuan, Ming and then Qing, with the Qing period understood within the framework of dynastic cycles; but the legitimation of the Qing Dynasty was not really established until the time of Emperor Qianlong, when it was acknowledged by the vast majority of Chinese scholar-officials and neighboring empires, as well as by most of society, as a Chinese dynasty. The questions of Qing history, of the study of the Confucian canon, and of Confucianism in general, cannot be separated from the question of political legitimacy.

In my book, I examine how these theories were transformed in the context of contemporary social relations. For instance, in examining the West, Wei Yuan and Gong Zizhen (along with many missionaries, such as William Alexander Parsons Martin) used many aspects of these theories to explain Western international law and international relations. Already in the works of Kang Youwei and Liao Ping, the Confucian concept of Grand Unity was explicitly modified to be understood within the categories of international and global relations. Some critics claim that this was a complete misappropriation, but we must at the same time recognize that this appropriation was not without historical precedent, since it is linked up with a set of Confucian theories of legitimacy and with historical practice. When a new set of social relations is established, those theories gradually have to change as well, in order to think through the new questions of the era. This is why I repeatedly discuss questions of methodology when I examine the evolution of Confucianism and contemporary thought. This is roughly what I have been thinking about in reflecting on *The Rise of Modern Chinese Thought*.

5

Scientific Worldview, Culture Debates, and the Reclassification of Knowledge in Twentieth-Century China

The Scientific Worldview and Modern Society

The extensive application of the concept of science is one of the main characteristics of Chinese thought in the twentieth century. Since the late Qing dynasty, science has served as a symbol of and call for liberation, as well as an objective criterion for all social and cultural reform. As a stand-in for a universalist world outlook, science has provided not only arguments for the necessity of the reforms hoped for by advocates of a new culture, but also objectives and paradigms for the reform. The power of science lay in the fact that it established an intimate connection between a universalist worldview and a kind of cosmopolitan/nationalist social system, and, through a rationalized classification of knowledge and social division of labor, incorporated in its broad genealogy human life in all its forms and tendencies.

The concept of science as an understanding of objective truth endowed the New Culture movement's advocacy for social and historical reform with a sense of inevitability, enabling transcendence of the dichotomy between fact and value.[1] The "scientific interests" of mainstream intellectuals of the New Culture movement, such as Chen Duxiu, Hu Shi, Wu Zhihui, Ding Wenjiang, and others—the radical intellectuals of the time—were sparked by their concerns with society, politics, economy, and culture. For example, under the influence of pragmatism, Hu Shi equated science with methodology, but he did not realize that when this method was applied to politics, ethics, and the humanities, it already served as an epistemological model. It was much the same with more marginal groups of the New Culture movement. Intellectual orientations that questioned the absolutely dominant position of science were also incorporated into a rationalized knowledge system. Whether challenges to the Western scientific civilization were informed by "cultural differences," efforts to preserve the independence of the fields of ethics, aesthetics, or affection were all transformed by their incorporation into an institutionalized, rationalized, and scientific framework of knowledge classification and institutions. The intellectual, educational, and social efforts made by Liang Qichao, Liang Shuming, Zhang Junmai, and the Xueheng School (a group of early-twentieth century intellectuals surrounding the journal *Xueheng*, or *Critical Review*) transformed categories such as culture, morality, aesthetics, and feelings into specialized fields at modern educational and research institutions. Science, and the changing view of nature that it has triggered, not only dominates our knowledge of nature, but also prescribes our awareness of society and ourselves.

From this perspective, the process by which a scientific "worldview based on axiomatic principles" (*gongli shijie guan*) reformed and replaced the traditional "worldview based on heavenly principles" (*tianli shijie guan*) constitutes the basic aspect of the transformation of modern thought. This new worldview paves the way for the division and specialization of knowledge and institutions in modern society. Viewed from the perspective of the relationship between science, its social function, and its role in national construction, the issue of science itself is a social issue, and the process by which axiomatic principles replaced heavenly ones embodies a sea change in social sovereignty.

The sovereignty of modern states is a product of the world political system and of economic relations. Along with the establishment of the sovereign position of modern states in trade, military affairs, and diplomacy, economic, political, and moral relations within society have also been transformed. The modern nation-state system has to achieve the following goals. First, it must transform the previous imperial system into a sovereign system based on nation-states and unify the people and the state under the concept of singular sovereignty, which on the one hand dissolves the original multi-centric imperialist system, and on the other establishes on the basis of such a singular sovereignty international relations between nation-states and other political entities. Second, it must incorporate sovereignty and the people with a singular will into the frame of nationality, since the power of the empire or of royalty represents a collective in a multicultural relationship, even though nation-states transform this multicultural collective relationship into a unified subject. This is the origin of the concept of "the people of the nation." The formation of the concept of the people's sovereignty and the formation of the sovereignty of the nation-state system proceed hand in hand. The conception of the people by modern states is not simply an ideological project; it is also a reconstructive project of the society supported by state sovereignty. Third, the modern nation-state system must abstract or separate individuals from their ethnic, local, and religious relations by law in order to reconstruct them as national citizens with equal rights. The latter will participate in activities of national sovereignty either individually or collectively. This political process accompanies industrial development, urban expansion, an increase in the power of money, the formation of guild organizations, the establishment of a market system, and so forth, which have greatly increased the demand for free labor. The fact that the legal systems in modern states use private property as their basis for establishing equal individual rights is the very product of this dual process. In this sense, the principle of blindness to status in the modern legal system embodies the inherent demand of a changing social institution: the sovereignty of nation-states is not compatible with the legal pluralism of the imperialist era, nor can local social networks centered on local gentry and communities adjust to the national and industrial social organizations, since both assume an individual subjectivity defined by the idea of natural rights. Under these circumstances, positivism and an atomistic scientific view provide a new principle for social construction from the perspective of nature, which renders individuals into atoms of society with equal rights, separating individuals from kinship ties, geographical nexus, and other social networks. The idea of self or subjectivity, therefore, deconstructs the intrinsic connection between the worldview of heavenly principles and communities of religion, kinship, and geography, on the one hand, and changes the principle of constituting political sovereignty, on the other. The moral/political superiority that scientific ideas have achieved through attacks on religion and the establishment of republics is based on the changing relations of social sovereignty discussed above. The discussion of the relationship between science and the republic in the scientific discursive community is carried out under the same circumstances.

We can therefore see clearly the inherent connection between the scientific worldview and the legitimacy of the social institution from the relationship between the atomistic scientific idea and the social system: blindness to status in the identification of citizens is a legal abstraction based on atomism, which confirms the legitimacy and rationality of the new moral/political power through naturalism and social immanence. The construction of modern sovereignty is premised on the liberation of individuals from social networks such as locality and kinship. The core of freedom and liberation lies in the subject without status and with equal rights, who provides the basic category in the construction of the state and the social system. In relations of modern sovereignty, individuals and states are two active polarities: whether under capitalist privatization of property or socialist collectivization or nationalization, these two oppositional social systems nevertheless are at one in legally regarding their citizens as individuals without ascriptive identity. The system of citizenship constitutes a great challenge to contractual relations and moral genealogy based on communities and status affiliation. The scientific worldview provides legitimacy for this new sovereignty. From the late Qing to the early Republic, atomism was at the core of the newly fashionable scientific positivism, and dissolved the Confucian worldview that had hitherto provided legitimation for the dynasty's political, religious, and geographic relations. During the May Fourth era, the scientific worldview justified attacks on the family system and its ethical presuppositions, providing a rationale for the legitimacy of atomistic individualism, marriage, and other social affairs. All these show that the scientific worldview is not only the banner of a cultural movement but the legitimate groundwork for modern states. Its theory of rights and its legal basis are premised upon an atomistic idea of abstract individuals. The historical connection between abstract individuals and atomism shows that atomism is not based on positivist principles but on abstract assumptions. The conflict between the atomistic view of nature and the Neo-Confucianist worldview was born in the transformation of the moral and institutional systems: the conditions surrounding the discourses on morality were in the transformation from consanguineous and geographical community relations into the abstract legal relations of the modern state.

Changes in sovereignty and the legal basis of the modern state cannot be separated from the production of new knowledge and ideology. Hence reconstituting the educational institutions and system of knowledge is an important aspect of the construction of modern sovereignty. In 1906, with the abolition of the civil service examination system, which had been maintained for 1,300 years, a new educational system, and the scientific knowledge to go with it, was legally established. After the founding of the Republic of China in 1912, academic reform was carried out in 1912, 1915, and 1923, modeled, respectively, on the academic systems in Japan, Europe, and the United States. Since then, every national reform has been accompanied by changes in educational institutions and the system of knowledge. Despite varying conditions, European universalism unavoidably became the dominant element of the educational and knowledge systems through the process of institutionalization. The establishment of a new educational system in the late Qing and the early Republic was intimately connected with study-abroad policies, as well as international trips of officials and some men of letters. In 1915 the educational system received direct guidance from Europeans. Like the expansion of the nation-state in the establishment of the modern state, the educational system in modern China included two orientations: through the professional division of labor and a new knowledge classification system, it brought together in one process the national and global educational systems, and at the same time it provided institutional protection for a new division of labor in society and its mode of social operation. Within this system, the production of knowledge gradually became professionalized. Even those intellectuals who regarded themselves as enlighteners were professional scholars based in colleges or research institutions. The reform of the educational system and the establishment of a scientific community provided the preconditions for a new power of knowledge. It reevaluated "common sense" under the protection of intellectual authority, eliminated unprincipled knowledge, and set new criteria for knowledge classification. In the new knowledge system, the traditional worldview and its epistemology (morality, traditional education, and so on) continued to exist only as elements of the new knowledge education, and lost their status as a worldview. From "the controversy on Eastern and Western cultures" to "the debate on science and metaphysics," the affirmation of the autonomy, special status, and internal values of culture was incorporated into a rationalized classification of knowledge. The defense of the autonomy of ethics, aesthetics, feelings, and culture finally secured their positions in the rationalized knowledge system, or empire of science.

National education and professional education based on a new social division of labor constitute the basic framework of the educational system.

The crisis of the scientific worldview and the formation of scientific institutions

Tied in with the reform of the educational system, and supported by the state, specialized scientific research institutions gradually came into being. From the late Qing to the early Republic, this system was modeled on the United Kingdom's Royal Society and its principles. For a short time in the late 1920s, France provided a model for the newly established Academia Sinica and several other academic institutions. After the mid twentieth century, new institutions would be modeled after the Academy of Science in the Soviet Union. Since the late twentieth century, there has been a turn once again to Western (mainly US) models. Every institutional reform presupposed the paradigm of universalism. The organizational principle of the scientific community has been analogous to that of the nation-state, and its mode of operation has provided models for the state and its citizens. This is the premise of the homologous relationship between the modern knowledge system, power relations, and the form of modern sovereignty. A scientific research system accelerates the combination of science, industry, and the state, which, on the one hand, provides conditions for increasing industrial productivity, and, on the other, paves the way for states to achieve a privileged position in international competition. For the same reason, the state regards universities and the scientific research system as workshops of knowledge (productivity) and offers certain privileges to these institutions, such as allowing them to follow international standards, to secure some free space for knowledge production under the premise of specialization. In turn, the scientific community seeks a free space for scientific exploration, based on the relationship between truth and national interests. Under stable institutional circumstances, direct interference of states in education and scientific research is limited to those fields that are directly related to sensitive political and social problems, so that a certain degree of autonomy can be guaranteed at universities and in the scientific research system—especially for research in the natural sciences and in technology. But the relationship between the state and the educational and scientific research system is not always stable. In some historical periods, the state and its dominant ideology have fully controlled the direction of education and scientific research, exposing the weak position of the cultural autonomy that is protected by the legal system of the nation-state. The relationship between university intellectuals and the state is different from that of men of letters, who achieved their position through the civil examination and the imperial court, since the former engage in social activities through their specialization but generally do not engage directly in bureaucratic activities. Through the activities of the scientific community and universities, "scientific culture" becomes a peculiar part of social life. The "two cultures" and the line dividing them constitute one of the characteristic aspects of modern society.

The dualistic confrontation between tradition and science constitutes an obvious characteristic of social reform movements launched by modern states, and the process of nation-building may also be viewed as a process of reforming tradition. In this sense, the establishment of the scientific worldview and its institutional hegemony occurs simultaneously with the establishment of the hegemony of the state rationality. At the beginning of the twentieth century, with the appearance of organizations of scientific research such as the Chinese Society of Science (*Zhongguo kexue she*, 1914) and other more specialized schools, characteristics of scientific methodology and specialization became visible. But this methodology and its specialized form of research (as distinct from the conduct of daily social life) did not imply the appearance of nonsocial or nonstate forms. On the contrary, there was a close relation between the system of scientific research and state rationality. It is noteworthy that a scientific worldview established its supreme hegemonic status in Chinese society at a time when European countries were involved in two world wars. The two disastrous wars between sovereign states, developments in science and technology that spawned new forms of violence, and public sentiment on science, morality, and civilization—none of these disrupted the hegemony of the scientific worldview. On the contrary, this competitive world scene has reinforced sovereign states' demands for science and technology, further guaranteeing the development of science and technology, professionalization, state control of science and technology, and the dominant position of the scientific worldview. As a matter of fact, although the two world wars and their catastrophic results provoked some people to reflect on science and technology as well as on their modern application, the application of science and technology in industry and the military has not been reduced, but has become even more widespread in the post-war years. So it is not surprising that we observe the paradoxical historical phenomenon that, when the First World War in Europe encouraged some European intellectuals to reflect critically on science and scientism, China was in the midst of its first enlightenment movement of the twentieth century, which aimed at establishing the hegemonic status of a scientific worldview. When the high-tech carnage displayed during the Second World War astounded the whole world, Chinese intellectuals were preoccupied with national liberation and showed little interest in reflecting on scientific hegemony and its technological application. The nation-state and its competitive paradigm provide a political reason for the expansion of the hegemony of science and technology. The principle of profit-optimization in the capitalist market helps explain the economic dynamics of technological innovation. The latter also helps explain why, even though globalization contributes to the changing status of the nation-state, the hegemonic status of science and technology does not fade away. The social paradigm, with the market principle as its axis, still relies on the non-ascriptive identifiable individual rights system and the principle of profit maximization. The dynamics of the state and the market are closely related to the scientific worldview and its technological extension.

The history of thought in the nineteenth and twentieth centuries was shadowed by dualities of fact/value, cognition/practice, pure rationality/practical rationality. Numerous scholars contributed to drawing a clear boundary between these alternatives, with the motive of confining the hegemony of the world of "things" by this distinction. Science, however, did not retreat from its universalist claims and its status as a universal knowledge system. On the contrary, the boundary of science was expanded greatly by the retreat of positivist science into the domain of natural science. The positivist, atomistic scientific worldview has had to face challenges from two directions: on the one hand, the domain of science is no longer characterized by classical physics; on the other hand, the domain of scientific knowledge is rationally divided into the knowledge of nature, the knowledge of society, the knowledge of morality, and the knowledge of aesthetics. However, the separation between natural science, social science, and the humanities not only replicates the principles of classification in the system of science, but also regulates the professional principles of these fields through a formalized division. In this sense, the challenge to the atomistic and positivist concept of science actually extends rather than limits the hegemony of scientific principles. For example, after the first Chinese revolution and the establishment of the Republic of China, the scientific community, in their own particular way, extensively discussed evolutionist issues in science and morality, science and social politics, and philosophy of life, as well as scientific ideas, mapping out a classified knowledge genealogy in a strict methodological sense. This genealogy of knowledge encapsulated all categories that were related to the old worldview, such as morality, politics, religion, and so forth—but with meanings totally different from the categories of the old worldview. Now they were appearing as special fields in a scientific system, arranged according to their levels of positivity and practicability, from high to low. During the May Fourth period, this positivist knowledge system was critically challenged, so that critiques of the universalist concept of science from Liang Shuming, Zhang Junmai, and the Xueheng School only resulted in the incorporation of the categories of morality, aesthetics, and feelings into the scientific systems and institutions of knowledge, as rationalized fields in their own right. There were changes inside the knowledge system, but the rationalized principle of classification and its process of institutionalization did not change at all. In this sense, the confinement of the field of natural science and the critique of the monolithic scientific worldview became the very warm-up for the unlimited expansion of the domains of science and scientific rationality.

We may best observe how the self-deconstruction of the scientific worldview contributes to the further expansion of scientific rationality and its hegemony from the perspective of internal crises. The first crisis of the scientific worldview is the paradoxical relation between its characteristic as a worldview and its claim to scientific methods. The main instrument that the scientific worldview uses to destroy old values is the positivist method of modern science. According to this methodological principle, all knowledge that cannot be verified by experiment is pseudo-knowledge and metaphysical superstition. However, the scientific worldview cannot break away from its own metaphysical characteristics and totalism. On the one hand, the scientific worldview needs a narrative of totality to defend the dynamics of reform and the legitimacy of the new system; on the other hand, the positivist methods that the scientific worldview uses to destroy the old system and old ideas also challenge its own idea of totality. The former needs support from cosmology, ontology, and religion, but the latter denies the existence of any ultimate truth and unified principles. In the world of Yan Fu, sociology constitutes the core of a knowledge system that encapsulates the universe, nature, and human society, because sociology can provide the knowledge system with a teleology: the value of the collective (*qun*) and the public (*gong*). But the authority of science in sociology is based upon its application of the positivist method, and this method cannot guarantee the moral orientation of the collective or the public. There exists an inherent gap between the characteristics of science as embodied by sociology and its characteristics as a worldview. If there is no inherent connection between knowledge and moral objectives, then the general knowledge system, the positivist method, the professionalization of learning, and its industrial application are all distinctively different from the teleological knowledge system affirmed by Yan Fu and Liang Qichao. We cannot connect Yan Fu's cosmology, derived from the *Book of Changes* (or the *I Ching*), and its operative mode with the process of production and application of science and technology; neither can we connect Liang Qichao's practical method, which can generate moral meanings, with scientific invention and its cognition, creation, and applications. The hegemony of the scientific method is achieved through the denial of the direct relation between science and value (which is the precondition for establishing science as a worldview).

The second crisis that the scientific worldview encounters lies in the paradoxical relation it has with the institutional practices of the state. When the effectiveness of the positivist method undermines the ultimate truth and the unified principle on which the scientific worldview relies, the knowledge system in the modern state hastens the dissolution of this ultimate truth and the unified principle. What the modern state relies on is specialized, professional, practical, and institutionalized (scientific) knowledge practice. Whether this knowledge is knowledge about nature or society, effectiveness and practicality are always the primary criteria that are internalized in the operation of this system. In the context of this system, a serious conflict comes into being between the moral teleology of the early scientific worldview and the scientific system that accepts efficiency and its contribution to the state as the only principle. Scientific journals published before the 1911 revolution—such as *Yaquan zazhi* (*Yaquan Magazine*, 1900), *Kexue shijie* (*World of Science*, 1903), and *Kexue yiban* (*A Glimpse of Science*, 1907)—displayed a functionalist scientific worldview, and the significance of science was put into the discursive paradigms of science/politics, science/civilization, science/epoch. Hence science was naturally endowed with morality and functionalism. However, while a knowledge system based on the division of labor and its institutionalized practice helps the advance of disciplinary knowledge, its principle of classification has nothing to do with specific moral concerns. Thus a gap is produced between function and value.[2] Despite the fact that the state attempts to endow this new knowledge and its occupational modes with moral meaning, the morality thus produced consists merely of functional relations regulated by the state. The separation of morality from the institution is not only the main feature of the modern social system, including the educational system, but also the main objective of this system. It is exactly under these circumstances that Liang Qichao questions the morality of those who are able to enter colleges or study abroad with high grades, or those who have achieved positions of authority in specialized fields. Should school be a place for selling knowledge, or a path to intellectual maturity after the models of the "great learning" (*daxue*) in the three dynasties (Xia, Shang, and Zhou)? Liang Qichao's questions echoed those of Cheng Yi and other Neo-Confucians of the Song dynasty (960–1275 CE), who examined the relationship between the civil examination system and morality.

The case was similar with the establishment of the scientific community. The scientific community (i.e., the Chinese Society of Science) maintains strong interests in society, politics, morality, and ethics, and expands the application of its monistic scientific knowledge from the study of nature to the social field. Its tenet of conducting scientific research by experiments facilitates the technologization of science and its connection with industries. The scientific community, with its belief in the scientific system of natural monism, consolidates dualisms of nature/human being, material/spirit, and physical world/spiritual world, and therefore secures itself a special position in modern society. Under modern conditions, scientific research has been transformed into an organized research system, so state rationality can quickly extend the results and methods of scientific fields into other social fields. For example, 1915, the year the journal

The Youth was founded, also witnessed the birth of the journal *Science Monthly* by the Chinese Society of Science. Taking this journal as their organ, scientists began to study scientific concepts even before *The Youth*, and to use a horizontal form of writing, Western-style punctuation (in 1916), and vernacular Chinese. These experiments were recognized by the state and society, then developed into a state-approved institutional practice (for education and the mass media). Norms of modern Chinese humanistic discourse and daily language (such as punctuation and horizontal writing) were accepted gradually through the practice of scientific language. So in the early stages of the experiments, it is hard to distinguish the language of science from the language of the humanities.[3] This institutional practice implies a certain understanding of the relationship between the development of science and the evolution of civilization: the development of science serves as a paradigm for the progress of civilization, and scientific rationalization becomes the objective of social development. When all kinds of scientific terms entered into people's daily lives through the media and textbooks, efforts to explain science and the world with traditional resources quickly lost their impact.

A discussion of the social and cultural significance of the knowledge practices of the scientific community needs to take note of the continuous expansion of its boundary. In the description of modern cultural activities, the concept of a "discursive community of science" is more effective than that of the scientific community. While the scientific community is important, it is only part of the discursive community of science. The latter refers to the intellectual community that uses scientific or parascientific language and scientific authority to carry out sociocultural activities, which also includes scientific and technological activities. The intellectual groups New Youth and New Tide may be regarded as part and parcel of the discursive community of science, even though they did not engage directly in research and application in the natural sciences. These intellectuals not only endowed their cultural activities with scientific meaning, but also imitated the language of science in their discourse, so that their way of discussing questions and establishing cultural groups emulated the scientific community and its principles. The discursive community of science used colleges, newspapers, and textbooks extensively to express their preferred ideas as well as their value judgments, and attempted thereby to influence social and state practices. The community of scientists regarded themselves as subjects that were distinct from general social subjects, as a group of people who engaged in classified and specialized intellectual institutions. They had cognitive objects, used objective methods, had specialized training, and conducted professional research. The organization and activities of this special social group could serve as a model for society at large, since, according to scientific monism, fields of morality, belief, feelings, instincts, and so on were all components of the scientific knowledge system, and scientific activity itself included the necessity of morality. In other words, the activity of the scientific community included a double principle of generalization and specialization. Intellectuals and humanistic scholars who claimed to limit the scope of application of science adopted the basic standpoint of using the principle of division to attack the principle of generalization. They argued that the fields of social life, such as morality, belief, and aesthetics, should be separated from the universal field of scientific knowledge in order to develop their own autonomy. If we take the subjective turn as the birth of modern Chinese humanities, then the so-called humanities were not born from an understanding of human beings or from an understanding that human beings are complicated social beings, but from the definition and distinction of fields that cannot be explained or regulated by categories of economic rules, political rights, and scientific practices. In this sense, the humanities are not the discovery of human beings, but rather the discovery of fields (individual or collective) of morality, aesthetics, and unconsciousness.[4] Modern humanities represent the disintegration of the human being instead of a reconstruction of the integrity of the human being, because, along with the separation of humanities from science, the concept of the human being is also separated from natural and socioeconomic objectivity. The human being is the subject of morality, a subject that is distinguished from nature. It is the research object of ethics, psychology, literature, and history. This specialized understanding of the human is related to the classification and institutionalization of knowledge: in the genealogy of this knowledge and institution, the actual relations of human beings have to be considered as furnishing the principle of classification.[5]

Culture debates and the classification of knowledge

The autonomy of the humanities thus reaffirms the universality of the principle of division on which the scientific community is built. Discussions of the classification of knowledge—especially education and the reorganization of the scientific institution—have been closely related to the division of labor in modern society. The rational division of the knowledge system, first of all, is a rationalized project for modern society and, secondly, provides a practical program of modernization. In the debate on "science and metaphysics" in 1923, Zhang Junmai's attack on the scientific system and his reconstruction of knowledge on the basis of "division" was by no means a purely intellectual activity. His effort to reestablish a knowledge system stressing "life outlook" implicitly echoed the educational reform that took place after the May Fourth movement—especially the academic reform of the early 1920s. His reconstruction of the "study of the mind" has been widely acknowledged as the very beginning of the modern New Confucianism, but his "study of the mind" broke with Song Confucianism in that it attempted to provide theoretical evidence for the autonomy of morality, aesthetics, and feelings, as well as to reorganize the knowledge system. For Zhang, the function of the "study of the mind" was no different from that of German idealism. In this sense, the prescription for the crisis of modernity from intellectuals of metaphysics became an organic part of the cultural project and the practical outline of modernity.

The universalization of science and its system provided a general criterion for different cultural advocacies and created cultural premises for unequal and hierarchical relations, internationally as well as domestically. The contributors were not only those who spread scientific thought and practice, but included those who criticized and challenged them. In the context of modern China, nationalism in the mode of civilizational discourse constitutes the first serious challenge and critique of the scientific knowledge system. If we take the debate on science and metaphysics in 1923 and the issue of a "life outlook" as a turning point, which prepared a theoretical basis for the reconstruction of the modern knowledge system, and especially the separation of science, morals, and emotions into different domains, then such differentiation arose not from the framework of epistemology, but was conceived and matured through debates on cultural differences between East and West that had originated in the late Qing dynasty. Both sides in the May Fourth cultural controversies took dualisms, such as China/the West, quietistic/dynamic civilization, Chinese/Western learning, and spiritual/material civilization, as the fundamental premises of the debate, and they associated science, knowledge, reason, and utility with Western, dynamic, and material civilization, while identifying morality, spirituality, instincts, and aesthetics with Eastern, Chinese, stable, and spiritual civilization within this framework. Hence, the original dualism of civilization was transformed into a new dualism of epistemology, including oppositions such as science vs. morals, knowledge vs. emotion, reason vs. instinct. In other words, the classification of knowledge greatly relies on the classification of civilizational discourse, but in a more objective and neutral way. In the history of modern China, cultural conflict is fundamental to differentiation in the domain of knowledge. Accordingly, the conflicting ideas on knowledge in "the debate on science and metaphysics" cannot hide the fact that it is basically about cultural conflict. The reflection on science and modernity, in the context of China, is also one of the cultural conflicts China has faced since the late Qing, and is especially a reflection of the relationship between Western and Chinese cultures.

Scholars like Du Yaquan, Liang Shuming, the Xueheng group, and Zhang Junmai created a new system of moral discourse in the 1920s in opposition to mainstream modernist ideology. But the program of modernity and its core philosophical categories also provided their basic premises. Therefore, their antiscientific, morality-centered ideology and cultural theories still included the inherent, essential content of the principles and themes of modernity. The thought current they represented provoked the subjective turn in Chinese thought, but this only resulted in an expansion of a universalist intellectual hegemony. The so-called subjective turn in Western philosophy was represented in critiques and denials of the Hegelian metaphysical system and in the "subject-object" epistemology of the Enlightenment, leading to an exploration of human subjectivity in individuals, personal emotions, moods, and experiences. In modern Chinese thought, such a "subjective turn" is first of all a cultural turn: taking Western modernity as the point of departure for rediscovering the values and significance of Chinese culture. Thus, China vs. the West as a cultural and intellectual dualism becomes the axis of the discussion.

The formation of this axis is provoked by the search for the uniqueness, difference, or authenticity of the national culture, and is much closer to the romantic nationalism developed by Herder. Liang Shuming's concept of "spiritual desire" and Zhang Junmai's concept of a "life outlook" are both premised on a national subjectivity. Both are particular in terms of civilizational discourse, and may be seen as theoretical prerequisites for nationalism. However, a historical paradox is that the differentiation of knowledge derives from the theory of cultural difference; but the form of cultural debate conceals the very cultural implication of such a conflict. Through the stormy debate and the reorganization of the scientific knowledge system, the unequal cultural relationship between China and the West is finally encapsulated in the classification relationships of knowledge domains, and is confirmed in the forms of their institutionalization. This shows that the epistemology and the theory of civilization, both focused on difference and separation, do not weaken but reinforce the premise of the universalism.

The specialized epistemology plays a minor role in the conflict of modern philosophies, but it is a general principle in the formation of the modern social system. The cultural ethos represented by the philosophers mentioned above shows the main trend of the modern moral movement, and without this moral consideration, it is impossible to realize completely the outline of modernity and the principle of specialization in modern world affairs. This is the very position of modern moralism. The scientific principles of anti-traditionalism, the moral- and culture-centered antiscientific theory, and the revolutionary theory of Marxism provide the key theoretical links to the modern social order. In this sense, the outline of modernity is accomplished not by a single philosophical group; neither is its principle of specialization created by certain theorists. By contrast, every part of the outline of modernity and its principle of specialization comes into being gradually within conflicting currents of thought. In order to understand the meaning of these currents, we first need to understand the background of their relationships.

The issue of modernity and the significance of late-Qing thinking

In the sense discussed above, the rise of modern thought may be described as a process not only in which the scientific worldview achieves its hegemonic position, but also in which that worldview itself undergoes a metamorphosis. The principles of knowledge classification and institutional specialization gradually eliminate its characteristics as a worldview. The revolt of the scientific worldview overthrows the outlook of heavenly principles, but in turn faces the fate of disintegration. On the one hand, positivist scientific concepts cannot truly distinguish the domain of science from that of metaphysics, so its resort to the positivist method not only disassembles traditional worldviews but also the metaphysical base upon which the scientific worldview is established. On the other hand, scientific principles are strictly based upon models set by the scientific community and the experimental methods in positivism. Due to the absence of an intrinsic connection between the traditional moral community and the process of scientific practice, there is a deep ambiguity in the relationship of scientific principles to the ethical world. The scientific worldview claims that science has internalized moral imperatives, but neither its methodology nor its institutional practice can be transformed into concrete political, ethical, and aesthetic practice. The "disenchantment" with the scientific worldview indicates that the development of science has become a self-legitimizing process. The withdrawal of scientific practice from the fields of ethics, aesthetics, and so on indicates that the scientific institution and its operation no longer need legitimation from the outside.

Let us observe this process from the construction, internal conflicts, transformation, and disintegration of the axiomatic world outlook of the late Qing period. The main feature of late-Qing thought is the collapse of the outlook based on heavenly principles and efforts to construct a new worldview; we can name this era "the era of worldviews." Late Qing thought approached the question of origin from two directions. One was the return to questions of origin, such as the origin of the universe, the origin of human beings, social principles, and so forth. The other was the return to the great founders and their ideal systems, such as Confucius, Laozi, Mencius, Buddha, rituals and music of the Three Dynasties, and the like. In the form of knowledge, these universalist worldviews can be transformed into orthodoxy through teaching. They seek to reach, from different directions, ultimate truth, unified principles, and a conception of the world as an integral entity (of nature and human society). New Text Confucianism, Old Text Confucianism, the teachings of philosophers Xunzi (313 BCE–238 BCE and Mozi (470 BCE–391 BCE), Consciousness-Only Buddhism, Daoism, legalism—

all experienced a revival in the late Qing period, and suffered the historical changes of the period and of their respective positions in the social ideology. All these movements sought to construct a comprehensive interpretation of the world—that is, a universalist worldview. To some extent, the revival of worldviews can be regarded as the result of Western influence, but they retained a basis in traditional sources and a kinship to popular customs. In this unprecedented situation of change, late-Qing intellectuals attempted to reconstruct a universalist worldview and to find comprehensive explanations for the operative principles of the universe, the rules of change in the world, the base of politics and morality, and criteria for feelings and aesthetics, and sought a general method to discover the truth. Scientific ideas constituted a worldview at the time because they replaced the heavenly principles worldview through its restructuring. The revival of worldviews implied a complete reorganization of traditional ideas of time and space, and the location of the self and its direction of movement in this new time-space dimension.

One of the marks of the revival of worldviews is the proliferation of new concepts. Late-Qing thought adopted the guise of reviving ancient thought, which makes the new concepts often seem like a recycling of ancient concepts, although both the meanings and the usages of these concepts have been changed fundamentally. To borrow a concept from Schopenhauer, the social world refers to the world as "will and representation," so the revival and spread of new concepts and old words marks a reconstruction of the world of representations. The world as will and representation is psychological, as well as theatrical and political. The process of constructing the worldview itself is the process in which the social world and its different forces struggle for words—the change in words is the change in the world of representations, and changing words is therefore one way to change things. If we can argue that it is words, to a great extent, that create things, then reforming politics is essentially a process of reforming words; therefore, political reform and social reform have to begin with the struggle against words. Writers and journalists who have used and spread new words most extensively and most effectively have exerted the biggest influence on modern Chinese thought. New concepts, and their relations to each other, are established in the reconstruction of the representations of modern China, and the establishment of new representations relies on new principles of classification, such as public/collective, nation/race, individual/ society, class/state, nature/society, freedom/dictatorship, government/ people, reform/revolution, and all hierarchical structures in social relations.

The authority of science is gradually established by the historical circumstances of the constant bombardment of modern Western science and technology, and, as a result, new disciplines are set up in the educational system. Accompanying this process is a process in which new words are used to reconstruct the worldview. From the perspective of evolution and positivism, any effective worldview and its claims on universal laws must be preconditioned with science and its concepts. The constructive process of the scientific worldview can be generalized as a process of universalizing or axiomizing science, and its mission is to incorporate science into the discourse of the worldview, thus producing a scientific worldview. There is a difference between universalizing science and scientizing universalism. The latter refers to the fact that, with the establishment of the hegemony of science, any universalistic discourse has to be proved as scientific discourse; the legitimacy of the former, however, still requires a universalistic defense. During the late Qing era, since the authority of science was not yet established, categories such as civilization, progress, development, state, and morality were all applied to the confirmation of the significance of science and its values. For the same reason, what was universalized in the process was not simply science, but all principles of nature, politics, and morality commonly recognized by the people. The trinity of nature, politics, and morality was the general characteristic that emerged from the struggle between, as well as mutual infiltration of, the scientific worldview and the heavenly principles worldview. In this sense, the scientific worldview may have resulted from the importation to the East of Western ideas, but was born in the womb of the Chinese worldview of the heavenly principles. We can find elements of these two worldviews in some crucial themes in late-Qing thought, such as the collective, the public, the individual, axioms, states, and society.

Three important projects helped to reform the modern world and China: Yan Fu's universalistic worldview, which was established upon Neo-Confucianism, the *Book of Changes*, and positivism; Liang Qichao's worldview, which is supported by the Study of the Mind (*Xinxue*), New Text Confucianism, and German idealism; and Zhang Taiyan's anti-universalistic worldview, which combined Consciousness-Only Buddhism and Zhang Zi's Daoism. The paradoxes and mutual deconstruction between them provide a different perspective from which to rethink issues of modernity. In the aforementioned three systems based upon the universalist view, Yan Fu and Liang Qichao represent two mainstream directions in the integration of Neo-Confucianism and a monistic view of nature. Yan Fu's view emphasizes the internal homogeneity of the world. He believes in the possibility of understanding the internal principles of the universe, the world, and human beings through science (*gewu zhizhi*) and positivist methods. The Study of the Mind, New Text Confucianism, and dualist philosophy (German idealism, in particular) make up Liang Qichao's synthesis, which emphasizes the deep gap between the natural world and the moral world. The only way for communication between these two worlds is through the "unity of thought and action" (*zhixing heyi*). Both of these scientific worldviews set up a methodological unity between cognitive science and practical morality. Science and the "unity of thought and action" are not just ways of knowing the world, but are also moral practices to eliminate the private and uphold the public. What deserves special attention is that, as Neo-Confucianism integrated the *li/qi* dualism in cosmology and subject/object dualism in epistemology, in late-Qing thought, the scientific outlook that took Neo-Confucianism as its point of departure was characterized by monism. By contrast, in the debate between the study of the mind and the study of the principles (*lixue*), what is emphasized is the monism of mind and thing; in the genealogy of late-Qing thought, however, most theorists who took Wang Yangming as their point of departure adopted the dualisms of material/spirit and science/morality. In this sense, it is the theoretical difference discussed above that finally leads to the separation of the two worldviews during the May Fourth era.

Yan Fu was the first to introduce evolution and the scientific system of knowledge based on sociology. In his monist cosmological framework, evolution and methods of positivist knowledge include moral meaning and *telos*. Just like the European monist cosmology, this

new cosmology assumes a universe that can extend in time and space endlessly, all the eternal materials inside it mov[ing] according to the law of eternity and necessity, infinitely and aimlessly. This endless universe inherits all the essential qualities of the God, but only with this aimlessness, as everything else has been carried away by the disappearing God.[6]

In contrast to European cosmology, for Yan Fu the new cosmology remains the fundamental framework of the cosmology of the *Book of Changes*. Within this framework, as a natural process, the universe unifies the basic principles of heaven, earth, and human beings, and synthesizes the dual logics of linear evolution and circular change. While, according to Neo-Confucian cosmology, moral truth is the natural embodiment of the operation of the universe, Yan Fu on the one hand endows the progress of the universe with features of totality and teleology, and on the other hand believes that we should establish science, technology, industry, the state, and all kinds of institutions through man's active efforts, which can connect themselves to a higher objective, thus completing the moral objective of the natural progress of the universe. Yan Fu's cosmology of change is thus supported by a knowledge system centered on sociology. His cosmology argues that the operation of the universe can transcendentally set up the ideal of the public, and that the divisions of modern society will finally be incorporated into a rational relationship between *Tianyan* ("heavenly evolution") and *Gongli* ("universal principles"). His optimistic belief is based on the logic of knowledge centered on sociology. In this system, the concept of *Tianyan* cannot be reduced to concepts of evolution or progress, because it also includes a circular history and cosmology inspired by the ideas in the *Book of Changes*.

Why should the modern scientific knowledge system be centered on sociology? The appearance of sociology and its knowledge system in China cannot be viewed simply as an activity in translation and the spread of knowledge. Its coincidence with the rise of society is not accidental. The category of society is a new creation. It is first constructed by those with access to Western knowledge and by those who closely observe modern Western society. One way of constructing society is to construct a knowledge system that is suitable to social programming. Thus, knowledge of society becomes an organic—and the most crucial—part of a universalistic knowledge. In this sense, the separation of society from family, kinship, ethics, and imperial power is more a sudden event, or the result of knowledge programming and state intervention, than a

natural process. The society referred to here is a new order formed by teleological programming rather than by an historical product or an element
in the domain of daily life. In the paradigmatic narration of sociology,
society is a process of programming that can organize historical elements
(such as family, village, and exchange relations) into a new social order.
So, the dualism of society and social organizations, such as family, imperial power, and religious law constitutes an important connotation for the
intellectual discourse of enlightenment and modern states. In her discussion of the rise of European society, Hannah Arendt connects it with the
appearance of economics. Her statement is at odds with the issue of the
knowledge system of sociology that I have discussed above. According
to Arendt, "modern equality is based on the conformism that is internalized in society. The reason for this possibility lies in the substitution of
behavior for action as the most important form of human relationship."
This is the same conformism (which assumes that people are conform-
ists and will not take any action against one another) that paves the
way for modern economics. With the rise of society came the birth of
economics—armed with its main technological instrument: statistics—
and it became a standard social science. Only when people become social
beings, and conform to some given modes of behavior, therefore making
nonconformity antisocial or abnormal, does economics attain the nature
of a science. (Until the modern period, economics was only a minor part
of ethics and politics. Modern economics is based on the assumption that
human beings adopt the same manner of behavior in the field of economic
activities as in other fields.)[7] Political science as a branch of science, as
proposed by Adam Smith, is also directly related to the rise of society,
because the process creates the beings called "economic man" by liberal
economists and "social man" by Marxists. However, in late-Qing China,
economics and other fields of science all belonged to the scientific knowledge system based on sociology. This difference offers a perspective
from which to observe the interaction between the economy and society
in the Chinese context: rather than argue that economic changes facilitate
social transformation, it is better to say that the establishment of modern
economics and its modes of behavior are the result of reconstructing the
social order.

Yan Fu's emphasis on the moral objective internalized in classified
knowledge is closely related to his understanding of the division of labor
and professionalization in modern society. During the process of social

division and knowledge classification developed day by day, if there is no moral necessity for scholarship, then a moral regulation of scholarship has to be reinforced from the outside, which creates an obstacle for the independence of knowledge. Yan Fu, on the one hand, constructs a new, hierarchical knowledge system by his translation activities, and, on the other, attempts to endow this knowledge system with moral meanings in order to connect the natural processes of the universe and scientific research with values such as honesty, publicness, and universal principles. In this sense, the knowledge (as well as social) project accomplished by the system centered on sociology requires not only the development of science, but also a given model for human behavior. It regards those who do not obey these principles and their behavior as antisocial, abnormal, and immoral. The distinction between the normal and abnormal is directly related to the definition of teleological (normal) and nonteleological (abnormal) in the universe and among humans. On this point of using cosmology to uphold the modes of normal and abnormal, Yan Fu's knowledge system is very similar to the Study of the Principles (*lixue*) in Neo-Confucianism. The scientific knowledge system centered on sociology embodies an internal consistency, and what it expresses is not a natural relation but a political ideal of society and its cosmological environment. According to this ideal, society will be overwhelmed by routinized daily life, and will reach harmony through the scientific outlook that it internalizes. Homogenized programming of the universe had already become one of the main characteristics of modern society, but at the time it also contained a denial of the traditional political regime—a regime in which a certain person or a certain kin group governs society. According to the scientific project, modern society should be the natural operation of a specialized system that is organized by many individuals. Obviously, this process of knowledge reconstruction contains a deconstruction of imperial power and religious society, as well as of their legitimacy, and provides the conditions for the birth of mass society. No matter how complicated and even paradoxical Yan Fu's ideas are, the dominant aspect of his social thought is still a comprehensive project of modernity made up by a knowledge system centered on evolution and sociology. It is in this sense that Yan Fu can be regarded as the representative figure in the creation of a project of modernity in Chinese history.

The relationship between knowledge and society is also the main concern of Liang Qichao. He facilitated the establishment of modern society through newspapers, communities, and other methods, and provided legitimate defenses for the construction of this society with a program of knowledge. Based on his idea of moral autonomy, Liang Qichao worried that the over-expansion of science would eventually castrate the moral and aesthetic subjectivity of human beings, and he refused to incorporate society and human behavior into a unified, science-controlled model. For this reason, his idea of society and state was deeply rooted in a moral ideal of collectivity—a community with moral coherence that is akin to traditional communities. If we can argue that Yan Fu's epistemology has characteristics of atomism and positivist physics, then Liang Qichao's epistemology is deeply imbued with moral concerns, and its social categories place greater significance on community and the negotiation between individuals. For example, his concept of society is very similar to the concept of the "school" in Confucian ideals. Flexible social division, the political importance of distinguishing right and wrong, close community relations, and moralism are the fundamental features of this social paradigm. Liang Qichao connected German idealism (especially Kantian dualism) with Wang Yangming's study of the mind and supplemented it with the academic system of the Three Dynasties and educational designs from the Han and Tang dynasties, in order to relieve the moral crisis produced by scientific programming. His description of the evolution of the universe is developed with attention to relations between science and the individual will, the objective universe and cognitive subjectivity, and truth as a set of natural or moral principles, thus drawing a clear line between nature and society, and between pure and practical rationality. As an exponent of modern educational reform, Liang's knowledge classification is based on the structure of politics, education, and technology, which on the one hand promotes the development of natural science, and on the other searches for the establishment of moral autonomy. The social categories of the collectivity and the public, as he conceives them, are reminiscent of communities of ritual (*li*) and music (*yue*) in Confucianism, in the sense that they can connect social behavior organically with the system of moral evaluation. Within this system, the scientific cognitive process can even be transformed into a moral practice that eliminates the private, so that knowledge, methods, and institutions which conflict with moral practice can be eliminated from the category of scientific practice.

If we compare Liang Qichao's ideas with Yan Fu's, the differences lie not in the presumption of universality or the heavenly principles, but in the way they connect human beings and their transcendental essence. Yan Fu thinks that the cognitive relation between human beings and things can be established by way of experiments, and arrives at ultimate truth by a set of cognitive programs. Liang Qichao, however, attempts to establish the concept of truth (conscience or heavenly principles) by practice (the unity of thought and action); that is, he binds together human social and moral practice with issues of scientific universality. This also deeply influences his idea of evolution: evolution for him is not a scientific description of the origin of things in the universe and their evolution, but a proof of the teleology of the universe, so the competition among things and the final selection made by the heavens has an internal objective. If a certain behavior is harmful to the interest of the majority and to moral objectives, then it is against the natural law of evolution and progress; so the criteria of evolution are criteria for the realization of the collective and the public. During the period of the educational system reform in 1923 and 1924, Liang Qichao repeatedly emphasized the significance for modern education of such theories as Wang Yangming's "unity of thought and action" and Yan Yuan (Xizhai)'s "practice and achievement." His goal was to overcome the separation between cognition and model, theory and practice. Compared with Yan Fu's cosmology of change, Liang Qichao's idea has a characteristic of interiority; that is, its universal principles do not come from the operation of the universe, but are embodied by the internal moral practice of human beings. Therefore, in order to judge whether the operation of the universe and the world is following the natural law of evolution or not, we have to establish a set of internal moral criteria. So the key issue is not whether evolution has an objective, but whether it is necessary to establish a social ethics to define the moral meaning of this process. In the world of Liang Qichao, "the collective" is a key concept, in the sense that it refers to a society with a high level of autonomy and freedom, and a bottom-up structure, with the moral principles appropriate to this kind of civil society. Here the collective, or society, is not the counterpart of the state or a category in the civil society/state duality, but a mode of social construction.

The universalization of science originates partly from the legitimate demand of science itself and partly from the moral limits placed on the social consequences of science and technology. However, for Zhang Taiyan, universality is nothing but an oppressive and dominant power, and modern society oppresses individuals in the name of universality to a degree that was unknown in ancient society, where the ethical system centered on the concept of the heavenly principles. Zhang Taiyan also uses the concept of the atom in modern physics, and applies it to the social field. Like atoms, individuals are the primary elements of the world. All affairs and laws of a collective nature are illusions of the oppressive power that suppresses individuals. The concept of the atom itself is an illusion. Drawing on Consciousness-Only Buddhism and Zhuangzi's Qiwu theory (on the equality of things), Zhang constructs an oppositional worldview that is squarely against universalism, which I understand as a negative universalism or a self-denying universalism that negates all projects of modernity, including state-building, as well as social and individual construction. This negative universalism is intended to be a critical worldview; it has no possibility or desire to provide a project of modernity. The attractive power of this view, which took Consciousness-Only Buddhism as its theoretical framework, lies in its opposing Buddhism to Confucianism and Ritualism (*lijiao*), as the latter came to be viewed as the source of imperial power during the late Qing period. Zhang Taiyan incorporates the moral foundation and political agenda of modern revolution into his abstract thinking, which gives it a realistic critical edge. He attacks Confucianism, Ritualism, and imperial power by way of negation, also extending this attack to projects of modernity promoted by his antagonists. If the universalistic worldviews of Yan Fu and Liang Qichao legitimize the narratives of the modern state and the modern state system, then the denial of universality in negative universalism inevitably contains the negation of the nation-state and its system. If most intellectuals in the late Qing period stress only the morbidity of a specific government (in this case, the late-Qing government), and from there proceed to defend the establishment of a proper state, then Zhang Taiyan attempts to connect the denial of the specific government to the denial of the state paradigm itself. This is a nationalist's attack on a nationalist project. This paradox itself reveals the features of Zhang Taiyan's self-denying individualism and nationalism.

Zhang Taiyan's critique of scientific universalism is founded on two basic principles. First, he uses the principle of subjective epistemology to distinguish two concepts of nature. Nature in scientific research is not nature-in-itself, but a nature that is limited to the horizon and category of science (that is, the nature that has been constructed by science), so it lacks the essence of real nature, being without autonomy, and can be manifested only through the law of causation. Starting from this point of view, he arrives at a series of conclusions: the materialist ideas of things and nature are entirely imaginary; science as an interpretive system cannot interpret the world itself; universalism and evolution are not laws of the universe or transcendental principles, but ideological constructs of human beings; the process of the construction of universals is not so much a manifestation of the public as a distorted symbol of the private. So, universalism is just another word for control and domination. Secondly, Zhang rescues the operation of nature from teleology and denies the moral meaning of evolution. He therefore negates the connection between individuals and evolutionistic, historical teleology, the dependency of individual moral orientation on the operating principles of society in general, and the idea that the individual is an instrument of collective evolution. The individual is neither a citizen of the state and the law, a member of family and society, a subject of history and morality, nor a subject of the relationship between the subject (human being) and the object (nature). In short, the individual's significance and status cannot be defined through a relation with other more general entities. The full application of the atomistic idea subverts the concept of society that is based on the positivist scientific view.

The historical significance of Zhang Taiyan's idea of the single subject or individual has to be understood against the background of the constitutive process of modern society. Both Yan Fu and Liang Qichao admit the significance of the individual for social construction. They either begin with liberal politics and economics or with the traditional concept of the private to search for a legitimate basis for the individual. The fundamental paradigm in European politics since the seventeenth century—the social model based on individual elements that is developed from the abstract legal form of contracts and exchange—constitutes the core of their respective social views. In this basic formula, modern (commercial) society is the integration of the contractual relation between isolated legitimate subjects, and the precondition for establishing this contractual relation is the idea of atomism. In Foucault's words, the individual is an entity produced by the special disciplining power of technology: "At that time there existed a technology that could construct individuals into elements related to power and knowledge. The individual no doubt is an imaginary atom embodied in the ideology of the society."[8] In other words, when Yan Fu and Liang Qichao used this knowledge system to build society, they simultaneously constructed the atomic individuals that constitute this very society. Because the scientific knowledge system regards the atom (individual) as the natural basic unit, the individual itself is created and produced in the process of creating society. Zhang Taiyan's concept of the individual is totally contrary to mainstream Chinese thought since the late Qing period. He refuses to admit a logical relationship between individuals and other collective categories such as society and the state. He thus takes individuals as his point of departure for exposing the illusions of society and the state, and ends up with the individual itself as the domain for subjective construction. His concept of the individual is thus not only a temporary concept, but also a self-denying concept. This cognitive insight provides Zhang Taiyan with a special perspective in which all things and phenomena are produced in relational and interactive connections and conditions, and are thus occasional, relative, and transient. Individuals have priority over universals, evolution, and materiality, as well as over government, state, society, and family; but this priority means only that the individual is much closer to, but not equal with, self-nature. After finishing its mission of deconstruction, individuality, like other things without self-nature, returns to nothingness. In Zhang Taiyan's negative universalism, the nihilization of the individual does not equal the emptiness of the whole universe and the world. Taking the self-denial of the individual as his point of departure, he develops the concept of "self without self" and the natural view of "the equality of all things." The so-called self without self refers to the subject or the reality of the world that is independent, unchangeable, self-existent, and self-determined. The phrase "all things are equal" means that the distinguishing aspect of the cosmos is a natural equality. Zhang's demand for "self-knowledge as general principle" (*zishi weizong*) and "respect for self-confidence" (*jingyu zixin*) seems to emphasize the value of individuals; but within his negative universalism, the so-called self-knowledge and the respect for self-confidence refer not to the self-conscious internal experience of the individual but to a self that transcends the individual. This individualized self that transcends the individual negates all the constructions of the actual world. The concept of "the equality of all things" comes from the same idea. Its special task is to expand the category of individuals to encompass things. Zhang Taiyan uses Zhuangzi's concept of Qiwu to interpret the meaning of equality; but his equality is not the modern idea of being equal as in Yan Fu's and Liang Qichao's idea of universality. It is not equality as an endowment of nature to individuals, but as a natural condition—not a condition of human beings, but of nature; not a condition of the world, but of the cosmos. In short, universalism demands the establishment of equal relations, whereas the idea of Qiwu is a negation of all relations. Since relations are always embodied by languages and naming, so a Qiwu situation that aims at destroying all relations implies the deconstruction of all language and naming. When the universe breaks away from the limitation of naming (languages), it is also freed from the differences and relations of self/other, you/me, this/that, internal/external, big/small, love/hate, good/evil, and becomes a self-sufficient, limitless, omnipresent nature. The autonomy of the universe lies in its negativity.

The idea of nature in Qiwu discourse negates the natural ideology of modern science and technology, in which nature is simply another material that cannot be defined in quality, with infinite changes in quantity. In Zhang Taiyan's view, so long as the quality of world relations remains unchanged, there will be extensive hierarchy and inequality among individuals, social groups, states, and nature, and names and hierarchical relations will serve as instruments of domination. The development of science and social construction is related to the struggle for equal rights among the newly risen classes and oppressed states, and carries implications of liberation. But this liberation does not aim at reforming basic social relations in general, and transformation into an egalitarian society itself becomes a new form of hierarchical oppression. Therefore, Zhang Taiyan sought to achieve equality in the relation between phenomenon and noumenon, and thereby to distinguish social theories that were formed out of individual/society, society/state, and state/world binaries. His argument is as follows: (A) all things in the universe are subjects, so there is a homological structure between things, between human beings and things, and between human beings; (B) since both human beings and things are subjects, so the recovery of the sovereignty of things is the precondition for eliminating relations of domination; (C) since the establishment of human sovereignty is preconditioned by unequal relations between human beings and things, it follows that the contractual relations between individuals in atomism do not imply ontic equality. Zhang Taiyan's "ontological universalism," or "the world-view of the equality of things," is a way of imagining not one or another aspect of the world, but its totality. Therefore, when he proposed the new concept of nature, in fact he was proposing a set of principles that were totally different from the projects of modernity advocated by Yan Fu, Kang Youwei, Liang Qichao, Sun Wen, and others. These principles cannot be realized in communities such as states, chambers of commerce, scholarly associations, political parties, village communes, and the like. Rather than articulating principles for reforming existing institutions, his idea represents a negative utopia.

The practical significance of this negative utopia is not fully negative. Take the issues of knowledge and education, for example. Based on his idea of equal nature, Zhang Taiyan emphasized the capability of education to break away from state control, and argued that modern education is still confined by the imperial court or the state, which necessarily leads to the decay of scholarship. Taking as his point of departure the tradition of stressing private learning and opposing official schooling, he continued the rebelliousness of the private academies of the Ming-Qing transition: the "many waves compete with one another and heretical theories rise," correct or not, with scholars free to choose, without any criteria set by the state. What embodies his idea of education is a natural spirit of "being outstanding in the world." Another example of opposition to the modern scientific wave is his promotion of "literary restoration" and the study of "small learning" (*xiaoxue*). Zhang Taiyan eliminated names. He disagreed with the instrumentalization of language by Kang Youwei and Wu Zhihui, who either degraded languages to the level of simple instruments (Kang), or debased Chinese as barbarian (Wu). He did not deny the function of languages in general, but stressed the natural relation between languages and human beings:

> Letters are signs of language, and languages are banners of ideas. Although they are natural words, they did not exist in the universe since the very beginning. They are created by human beings, so they obey human behavior in general. As there are differences in human behaviors, so languages are different from one another.[9]

His worldview that "all things are equal" denies the distinction between civilized/barbarian and divine/mundane, and refuses to accept the hegemony of any language.

Zhang Taiyan's "world of equal things" and Yan Fu's "world of names" are two totally different ways of imagining the world. The "world of names" is a world constitution that can be arrived at by rationalizing knowledge. The relationships of names are mainly based upon the functional relationships of things. The "world of equal things" abandons the logical relationships of names. The relationships of things are based upon the denial of functional relationships established by language. By its definition of functional relationships, "world of names" exerts its control over all kinds of relationships in the world and places them into a hierarchical structure. By contrast, a refusal to define functional relationships entails a denial of all hierarchical structures—hence the denial of the practice of hierarchical structures. In Zhang Taiyan's view, breaking away from obligation and hierarchy is not the same as establishing modern social theory on the basis of society/state dualism (such as in the state's non-intervention in civil society and the market). What he reveals, rather, is the oppressive nature of state structures and social organizations themselves. As discussed above, Zhang Taiyan was a radical nationalist and a founder of the Republic, and there is a large gap between his theory and his practice. His self-negation, or temporary individualism, and self-negating nationalism enable him to avoid the oppression of the individual by the movement that he was deeply and actively involved in, and to emphasize individual sovereignty while practicing self-denial.

There is an internal connection between the two different points of view and the two differently oriented nation-state theories in the late Qing period. One focused on the idea of the public (*gong*) and the collective (*qun*), and then developed theories of the individual, society, and the state on the double foundation of the functional needs of the community (for example, an international context in which only the fittest survive) and moral necessity. The other focused on the idea of the individual, and from the temporary relationships between the individual and the nation developed a temporary self-negating theory of the individual, society, and the state. Both theories borrowed from atomistic individualism to criticize Neo-Confucianism, but they did not stop with atomism. They both recognized the necessity of the state and society, but did not take them, or their relationship, as the ultimate goal. The concepts of the public, the collective, and the individual contained their understanding of the "state of nature," from which they constructed their projects of modernity, but with an accompanying critical reflection on the very same project. This internalized logic of self-negation in the late-Qing worldview is not a product of the modern system of science and its institutional practice; it originated from the discriminating universalisms within the traditional world outlook. At the moment of its denial by social science, this world outlook provided a source of wisdom to reflect critically on modernity and its crisis—especially on the relationship between the modern knowledge system (humanities and social science as reflective sciences) and modernity.

REVOLUTIONARY
INTELLECTUALS

6

Son of the Jinsha River:
In Memory of Xiao Liangzhong

On April 3, two days before Tomb-Sweeping Day, I went to Kunming and Lijiang, and a friend arranged a small truck for me, taking me to Chezhu Village in just over two hours. This village is located along the bank of the Jinsha River, Xiao Liangzhong's hometown and his first subject of study. It lies on the Zhongdian side of the Jinsha River, and under the dim night sky Liangzhong's cousin, Lee Runtang, drove his pickup truck onto the ferry. The ferryman calmly turned the boat around, and then we crossed the Jinsha River under the moonlight, in the shade of the mountains. Sitting beside me, Xiao Peng told me that the memorial plaque the villagers had erected for Liangzhong was on the mountain slope along the river. I raised my eyes, the night air coiling around us, and only then did I sense the shadow of the mountain pressing down upon us. Back on land, we followed a winding road until finally we saw glimmers of light reflecting back. It was Chezhu Village. In the morning I went to visit Liangzhong, hiking along the small path up the hill behind his house, and although his grave was unmarked, and although the memorial plaque was not too far away—the plaque that read "Son of the Jinsha River," but did not include his name—you could unmistakably feel his presence everywhere along the river. Liang zhong still keeps watch there over his Jinsha River; he certainly has not left. And the weight that had been pressing upon me for many months gradually began to subside. I could remember again.

I met Liangzhong because of *Dushu*, and if I remember correctly it was sometime at the end of 2001 or the beginning of 2002. Among the manuscripts submitted to *Dushu* was an essay entitled "Yinyu de Manshuiwan" ("The Metaphor of Manshuiwan"), which was an account of the lively but simple way of life in Manshuiwan Village, a Yi minority village in southern Mianning County, Szechuan Province. It was obvious that the writer was an anthropologist. His calm and collected narrative was intertwined with an anthropologist's inquisitiveness; his intimacy with the people, the land, and the customs of Manshuiwan permeated the space between the lines—particularly in the earnestness with which he had thought through the relationship between Han Chinese society and the transformation of Yi culture. In the last portion of the essay, he clearly stated that the Yi identity of this region was not rooted in some distinctive culture, since the characteristics of their way of life did not differ significantly from those of other ethnic groups (Han Chinese or otherwise). Instead, this constructed identity was a kind of metaphorical cultural characteristic, and it was precisely this kind of characteristic that could inflate or deflate within a concrete environment, eventually differentiating the group from others, and finally becoming their distinguishing feature. I liked and identified with this method of research, which contextualized minority identities within the relations of coexistence with the multiple ethnic groups. This essay was immediately included in the "Field Notes" column of this year's third issue—the fastest *Dushu* had ever sent a manuscript to press.

Only a few days later, once that issue of the journal had gone to press, I ran into a *Dushu* colleague, Li Xuejun, as I was leaving the editorial department, at the entrance to the café in the second-floor bookstore. She was in mid-conversation with a young man who she introduced to me as Xiao Liangzhong, the author of "Yinyu de Manshuiwan." I immediately thanked him and told him that his essay had been published. Liangzhong was of average build, with a square face; he seemed sincere and spoke in a very good-natured way. He was a little surprised, but happy, to hear that his essay had already been published. Having ordered our coffee, we sat chatting casually, for the most part discussing the issues relating to the minority groups of southwest China and their historical fates. He mentioned the ethnic minorities of Yunnan province, as well as the history of the Tibetan people. I had also been reading through some historical materials related to the topic, and in the course of our discussion I discovered that we held many ideas in common. We did not meet many times after that, though each time we did it was in the coffee shop on the second floor of the Joint Publishing building—usually when he had written a new article for *Dushu*, or when he was participating in *Dushu* events.

Once, when he submitted a new piece to me—"Chezhu: Yigeyaoyuan Cunluode Xinminzuzhi" ("Chezhu: A New Ethnography of a Frontier Village")—he also attached the manuscript for a novel called *Tugu*. The essay was published in the third issue of last year's *Dushu*, but the novel remained stored on my computer. I gave it a quick glance and thought it to be elegantly stylized; but because I had too many things to handle and already too much to read, I put it aside. Liangzhong was a very sincere and upfront person, but also very sensitive, and because he had not heard back from me regarding my opinion on his novel, the next time we met he asked me, with an air of loss, whether I had read his novel. I stalled, and, though he didn't press the point, he printed out another copy and brought it to me in person. I always knew that Liangzhong would never forget that incident. He would never forget nor let it go—even though he always seemed so good-natured and amiable.

In the autumn of 2002, I was abroad doing research as a visiting scholar when I received a letter from Liangzhong out of the blue. It was not a submission this time, but rather a letter from a friend. In my memories, this was the moment when my relationship with Liangzhong developed beyond our writer-editor relation. He had on occasion heard people maliciously attacking me—people who didn't know me, and whose statements were totally groundless. Liangzhong was at first bewildered, but later became angry. After reminding me to be careful, he asked whether I would fight back with a response. Liangzhong was still too young, and didn't yet have a good sense of the disputes that occurred among academics, nor of how many of those who called themselves "intellectuals" behave. I thanked Liangzhong for his concern, but did not say much more on the matter. I ran into him once after I returned to Beijing, and he brought up this matter again; but, as before, I didn't respond. In this world, the darkness held within human hearts will always surpass what we could possibly imagine, so why weigh down such a pure-hearted person with more pessimism about the world? For me, having a friend like Liangzhong, who sincerely cared about me, was good enough. Liangzhong never mentioned such things again, but I knew that he had occasionally gotten into heated arguments on the matter with people he knew well.

From the moment I met him, I knew that Liangzhong would never be able to abandon his research, and would never be at peace with himself working in publishing. He met with a few setbacks and considered going into the Department of Sociology, but at the last moment he was denied entry. Liangzhong came to see me about this matter, filled with unease and confusion, and although I made countless calls to find out what had happened, in the end I could be of no help. Last spring, he told me that he had two options: to enter the Center for Research on China's Borderland History and Geography or the China Tibetology Research Center. The procedure for the former was more complicated, the latter more straightforward, and, due to his previous rejection, I suggested he enroll in the latter. But he was hesitant. After last summer, Liangzhong became involved in the movement against the construction of the Tiger Leaping Gorge Dam, while he was in the process of a work transfer. He was concerned that these events would interfere with his work, and mentioned the matter each time we met or spoke on the phone. I knew how much effort he had put into the transfer, and of all the hopes he had placed in it. I too was worried about how his involvement in the movement would affect his transfer. But Liangzhong had insisted to me that he would not push aside and ignore the fate of the Jinsha River simply for this reason, and once he had his wife's support, he became very excited.

Liangzhong first became involved in the anti-Tiger Leaping Gorge Dam movement last spring. He was asked to join by Ma Jianzhong, a Tibetan scholar, and both participated in and helped to organize the "Zangzuwenhua yu Shengtaiduoyangxing" ("Tibetan Cultural and Ecological Diversity") symposium held in Zhongdian. He remembered the discussion we had had when we first met, which is why he wrote and called asking if I would attend the conference. I was certainly interested in Tibetan cultural and ecological diversity, but had no research experience in the field and did not dare to comply hastily. However, Liangzhong told me that the topic of the conference involved questions concerning developmentalism, and that he still wished for me to participate. His effort grew out of his concern for his hometown, and I finally could not turn him down. In May, Liangzhong told me that he would come to deliver a conference invitation letter in person, and though I told him that he need not make the trip—he could just send it by mail— he would not listen. We made plans to meet for lunch in the afternoon, but it was not until 2 p.m. that day that he arrived at my house in haste, sweating profusely. By then, I was already ravenous. As he wiped away his sweat, he explained to me that he had been at an editorial conference with Commercial Press and had been unable to leave. I certainly knew the state of Beijing transportation—and in addition to that Liangzhong had arrived by bus! We had a drink at a small restaurant nearby, and chatted about Zhongdian as planned; yet, at that moment, the lure of this place and Yunnan for me had not been colored by the issue of the Tiger Leaping Gorge.

On June 9, I packed my bags and headed for Zhongdian. In the departure hall of Kunming Airport I caught a glimpse of Liangzhong's silhouette, and with him was the young monk, Master Ti Heng. Master Ti Heng was dressed in the usual monk's robe while Liangzhong was dressed casually in short sleeves, and they had just come from visiting a temple in Kunming. They had with them gifts from the temple abbot. As we were talking in the departure hall, I bought a map of Yunnan, and immediately asked Liangzhong about the situation there and what plans were on the schedule. After we flew into Zhongdian, we put on our jackets, though Liangzhong continued to wear only short sleeves, and his excitement at returning to his hometown was evident upon his face. Before I had left, a friend had called to tell me to be careful to avoid altitude sickness. After we got off the plane, I felt normal and mentioned my luck at not having contracted it, to which Liangzhong replied, with a laugh: How could you get altitude sickness? After we had settled into the hotel, Liangzhong took me to a small inn, where we ordered some food and drank some highland barley wine, sitting on wooden stools.

Liangzhong attended middle school in Zhongdian, and though there was a large population of Tibetan people here, there were also many different residents from the Bai, Yi, Pumi, Nakhi, Lizu, Hui, and Han ethnic groups. He was himself a member of the Bai ethnic group, while Ma Jianzhong, the conference organizer and member of the Nature Conservancy in America, was Tibetan. They had been classmates. After graduating from middle school, Liangzhong had been admitted to the Central University for Nationalities, while Jianzhong went on to attend the Forestry University, and then studied abroad in Thailand. While they each headed along their own respective paths, at that moment they came together once more for the sake of their hometown. In the course of our conversation, Liangzhong invited me to stay with him at his home once the conference had ended. Feeling happy and drunk, I agreed. I originally thought that Liangzhong had come up with this idea on the spur of the moment, but later understood that he had been making plans for it early on. He had simply not mentioned it to me before I arrived in Zhongdian.

I have attended many conferences before, but this one was unique. On the first day the conference was held at the hotel, and apart from some specialists from Beijing, most of the presenters were local academics, many of whom were Tibetan. Mr. Zhambei Gyaltsho was a colleague of mine from the Chinese Academy of Social Sciences who was in the Institute of Ethnic Literature. I was part of the Institute of Literature, and, purely due to this separation, we had never met. But now, in Yunnan, we did. Mr. Zeren Dengzhu, another participant, is a well-known Tibetan scholar who had single-handedly written the one-million-word opus *Zangzhu Tongshi* (*A Comprehensive History of the Tibetan People*), and enjoys a high level of prestige and authority among the Tibetan people. The Buddhist monk from Qinghai had a kind face and did not speak much, but later on, as we traveled to Deqin, I came to admire his erudition very deeply. The few scholars from the Yunnan Academy of Social Sciences had been observing the customs, religion and nature of the local area for a long time. Their papers also reflected the careful research they had performed on plant classification and the ecological conditions of Zhongdian, Deqin, and Lijiang. Several scholars mentioned the worship of sacred natural sites in Tibetan Buddhism, claiming that these rituals were very important for ecological protection. On the morning of the second day, we traveled by car to participate in the inauguration ceremonies for the local center of Tibetan studies, after which we headed to Qiciding Village to participate in group discussions. Liangzhong switched from group to group, finally winding up in mine, where he sat down beside me. During the discussion, Liangzhong made a sudden outburst: the NGOs had now arrived here in abundance, but investment and activity were all concentrated in the Tibetan region—did other ethnic groups not have traditions of protecting nature? He had grown up here and lived here since childhood, he said, with the members of different ethnic groups mingling together, not only as fellow students and colleagues but also as family, since inter-ethnic marriage was very common. But all foreign investment flowed toward the Tibetan region, just as all publicity had been concentrated upon Tibetan culture. Grudges and divisions had now arisen between ethnic groups that had coexisted peacefully for centuries. Was this not a problem?

Liangzhong had discussed this question with me previously, but because I did not understand the situation I was afraid to express my opinion openly. During my conversation with Ma Jianzhong, however, I explicitly asked how he felt regarding this issue. Jianzhong is Tibetan, and works at the Nature Conservancy, and he acknowledged the existence of this problem. He thought it would be difficult to change, however. He complimented Liangzhong on his writing—he had grown into a man of many considerable talents, with a knack for writing that had far exceeded his expectations! Jiangzhong and Liangzhong were like brothers, and although they had studied at different middle schools in Zhongdian, they both achieved top scores on the entrance exams, and were admitted to universities in Beijing. Though they quarreled occasionally, their mutual bond was strong. In August, Jianzhong wrote me a letter from the US pressuring me to submit the essay I had promised him, also mentioning that the struggles of Liangzhong and others against the construction of the Tiger Leaping Gorge Dam were having dramatic effects. The issue that Liangzhong referred to was very acute, and I thought that he saw things in a truly anthropological way, rather than purely from the perspective of environmental conservation. It was not that he didn't support the work of NGOs, but rather that he was concerned about whether NGOs could carry out their various activities while maintaining a truly culturally and ecologically diverse vision. It was obvious that Liangzhong saw ecological and cultural diversity as being very closely linked, and that any attempts to differentiate groups within a community based upon ethnicity and religion would rapidly erode its cultural multiplicity and any other of its organic relations, producing new inequalities. In this context, ecological and cultural diversity are both intrinsically related to the question of equality. Liangzhong's interest in his hometown did not arise from his interest in a particular ethnic or cultural group, but rather in the social networks woven together through history and their multiplicity. While I was in Yunnan, and after I returned, we had several discussions about Yunnan's cultural multiplicity and its significance. Afterwards, as we drafted a proposal opposing the Jinsha River Hydroelectric Development along the first turn of the Yangtze River, this became one of the points he emphasized most strongly.

In the few days I spent in Zhongdian, Liangzhong was extremely busy; yet, apart from taking his teacher Zhuang Kongshao, a younger female colleague, the monk, and I to sample the local cuisine, he also brought some of his local friends up to my room to chat. Liangzhong is an honest person, and when he has an idea he says what he is thinking—often without considering his surroundings. That day in Qiciding Village, a statement let to a discussion, and even after a confrontation, Liangzhong would not give up. He had strong opinions concerning the model Tibetan cultural village that had been constructed in Qiciding Village, and on these issues I approved of his views completely. Although I was limited by my status as a visitor and did not say much more, I still echoed Liangzhong's views in my final speech, expressing my concern at the excessive level of tourist development and market expansion. During my chats with Liangzhong and his friends, it emerged that our main concerns were the historical traditions, cultural standards and social policies that would be the basis for conservation efforts regarding Yunnan's rich and multifaceted ecological and cultural diversity, along with the various ethnic groups that had been able to coexist harmoniously with one another while also conserving their own ethnic characteristics. Would the changes occurring in the modern world—marketization, globalization, modernization—be able to facilitate such transformations? Liangzhong identified strongly with his hometown and ethnic group, but at the same time identified just as strongly with "China." Such feelings of identification also expressed a kind of critical attitude toward the various prejudices preserved within class relations and normalized assumptions. Within his person, various different identifications constituted a unique character and way of thinking. Sometimes you felt that he existed within a contradiction of emotions and attitudes, but in the end those contradictions were always completely unified within the figure of his person. One day, the issue of the crisis of minority language and minority language education came up while we were in my room, and a Tibetan friend he had brought along spoke of how they spoke the Tibetan and Naxi languages as well as *putonghua* (Mandarin)—all of these were their languages. Why then was the latter not called *putonghua* but *hanyu* (Chinese)? Sometimes I thought about how students and scholars of theory should listen to how these individuals looked upon the issue of *putonghua*. The problems precipitated by the rise of NGOs, which Liangzhong pursued with concern, are worth focusing on, especially by those people participating in the movement. Perhaps these issues will have a profound impact upon the future of development.

When the conference was almost over, the attendees were divided into two groups, one taking an expedition to Meili Snow Mountain while the other visited Jade Dragon Gorge, which was much closer. I could not resist the temptation of Meili Snow Mountain, so I decided to head north to Deqin. Liangzhong mentioned to me (tactfully) that his younger brother Liangdong had already prepared a car to take us along the Jinsha River to Chezhu—his hometown. His father was also expecting our visit. I was very hesitant. Perhaps I am influenced in a similar way by the atmosphere of certain cultures, but I have always been deeply curious about Tibetan culture and wanted to investigate the Tibetan region more thoroughly. Liangzhong did not try to force me to go, but neither could he conceal his disappointment. He said that the scenery en route to Deqin was not very nice, that its ecological state was worse than that of the Jinsha River valley, and that the azaleas were in bloom back at home. Seeing me hold stubbornly to my opinions, he added that "we minorities keep our promises," implying blame for my casual remarks and for reneging on promises. I promised Liangzhong that I would certainly go to the Jinsha River valley to visit his home-town in the future. He did not insist again, and said only that, once I returned from Deqin, he would rush back from his hometown to send me off.

The next morning, we split into two cars and headed toward Deqin. Before leaving, Liangzhong came to send me off and specially brought me a package of brown sugar to nibble on as we headed through the Baimang Snow Mountain pass—something that would help to reduce the high-altitude stress. As we set out, he called again to urge Jianzhong to look after me and let Ma Hua switch over from the other car to sit beside me so I would have someone to debrief me on conditions along the way. As we passed Benzilan, Ma Hua told me of previous plans to shift Deqin toward this area, but that if the Tiger Leaping Gorge Dam was constructed, Benzilan would be flooded. These plans could prob-ably not be implemented as a result. This was the first time I got a sense of the scope of possible impacts that would result from the construction of the Tiger Leaping Gorge Dam. Ma Hua had arrived in Deqin a year and a half before, and had volunteered at an elementary school teaching English. We had met once before, also on the second-floor café in the Joint Publishing building, but there were many people there at the time and I had already forgotten the circumstances of our meeting. This time, he made a deep impression upon me, largely because of his devotion to his work and his appearance, which now differed significantly from that of the urban youth of the day. His inner world had, like his appearance, gone through enormous changes. In the editor's notes for the ninth issue of *Dushu* last year, I made a record of our short contact. That night, we had gathered in a small square in central Deqin, where many locals were playing instruments and dancing. Ma Hua appeared to be very happy, his feet moving quickly with the beat, which I greatly admired. There, under the night sky, Ma Hua told me that he would no longer accompany us to Meili Snow Mountain, but was going to rush back to Mingyong Village that very night. That day, as we passed through the Baimang Snow Mountain pass, he described to me the magnificent sight of the Tibetan people making their pilgrimage, the *kora*, around the mountain. The charm of his words will remain with me forever. From the time we first met in the second-floor café at Joint Publishing, until we met once more in the Tibetan region of Yunnan, he had come a very long way and had experienced many things.

While I was in Deqin, Liangzhong spoke with Jianzhong on the phone nearly every day, asking how things were. He was very worried about the safety of our transportation. The next day we arrived in Deqin, headed up to Meili Snow Mountain (Kawagebo) and began climbing in the morning. We hiked forth, but by the time we had completed half our climb the dry rations we had prepared had all been consumed. I began to understand then how physically demanding high-altitude hiking could be. About six hours in, we reached the end of the narrow path, which took us to the edge of a cliff, and as we looked around us Kawagebo was surrounded by thick clouds and fog. We waited a long time for her to emerge, but all we saw were her shoulders and the giant glacier stretched up to just below her peak. Kawagebo is more than 6,800 meters tall, yet although it is still not the tallest snow mountain, it has yet to be conquered. Years earlier, a Chinese and Japanese mountaineering expedition had attempted to reach the summit, but had been hit by an avalanche, resulting in the worst disaster in mountaineering history. No members of the expedition survived. Prior to that, the expedition party had ignored the advice of the Tibetan people not to climb their sacred mountain—an activity which the Tibetan people had disapproved of— but after the disaster they nonetheless held a grand ceremony to pray for the fallen expedition members. This mountaineering story is today one of the myths and fables surrounding Kawagebo mountain. The tragic form it has taken on is testament to the sublime relation the local people have to their sacred natural sites. After a few years, the corpses of the mountaineers washed downstream with the melting of the glacier snow, and the Tibetan people held ceremonies once more to see them off. As we hiked, we saw lush plant life and beautiful mountain scenes, but a Tibetan girl traveling with us told us that, in the short period of time since last year, the glacier had receded significantly. That day, I hiked the whole way with the Buddhist monk, and at the peak he taught me how to bow properly and how to recite the most basic lines of religious text: *nami laji songdi, sangji laji songdi, jia laji songdi, gengdeng laji songdi* . . .

The day I returned to Zhongdian from Deqin, Liangzhong had also rushed back from Chezhu in the Jinsha River valley. That night, he and Ma Jianzhong took me to a small pub to meet and speak with some of their young local Tibetan friends. They were in the midst of carrying out a Tibetan ecological and cultural conservation experiment in a few villages, and although they lacked funds and the ability to carry out tests on a large scale, they had nonetheless managed to mobilize the Tibetan people from two or three different villages to participate. In the course of these experiments, they made special mention of the problems the conservation group sought to control: since the process of marketization was currently eroding the existing forms of community life, if vital community ties could not be established, then declarations of ecological and cultural protection would essentially be futile. After that discussion, I exchanged words with Liangzhong once more, and he said, with the caution of an anthropologist, that we could only garner the results of the experiment once we had made further observations.

The night I left Zhongdian, Liangzhong and I had a long conversation in my room. I thought of what Ma Hua had told me near Benzilan about what was happening with the Jinsha River dam, and made a point of asking Liangzhong about it. He appeared already to have a deep and complex understanding of the situation. Early the next morning Liangzhong sent me off in a car to the airport and headed back to the Jinsha River valley. After only a few days, he called me from Zhongdian, primarily to discuss the Tiger Leaping Gorge Dam and issues of developmentalism, asking if I had any advice. It was on the phone that Liangzhong told me that Ma Hua's car had fallen into the turbulent waters of the Mekong River while he had been driving back to Minyong Village from Deqin the day before, and that no trace of him had been found. Having just returned, I knew what it meant to fall into those waters from the steep ravine—those waters that were bone-chillingly cold even in the summer. On the phone, we talked about his and Ma Hua's life in Deqin, finally returning to the issue of the Tiger Leaping Gorge, which we both cared so much about. I asked Liangzhong how long he would remain in Zhongdian, and he said perhaps another few weeks. I suggested that he settle down and perform some detailed investigative research to improve his understanding of the state of construction, and he specifically brought up the reaction of the Jinsha River valley residents to this issue. We both thought that ecological and environmental preservation movements should not be initiated and driven only by urbanites, but that the voices of the local people were also very important. Ecological issues do not only concern the protection of natural environments, but also of cultural ecologies and social rights. These two areas are closely interlinked, and both pose critical challenges to the developmental model of a society. While he was still in Zhongdian, Liangzhong called me several times to keep me updated on his investigations. On the subject of the construction, among other things, the local authorities concerned were certainly unwilling to allow him to interfere. He mentioned on the phone that he had experienced some difficulties in the course of his investigation, though he never became defeatist. What inspired him were the residents of the Jinsha River valley, who were gradually becoming more concerned and more involved in the resistance movement, and among whom was Liangzhong's father.

A few weeks later, Liangzhong returned from Zhongdian. He made the trip from the city to my house especially to see me, and to give me details concerning what he had discovered regarding the Tiger Leaping Gorge Dam construction in the Jinsha River valley. Liangzhong knew that I had once published a critique of developmentalism, and hoped that I would directly take part in the movement he was organizing against the Tiger Leaping Gorge Dam. I shared Liangzhong's feelings concerning his investigations into the Zhongdian and Deqin situations, which he had introduced me to; but since I did not understand the local conditions and only possessed a layman's knowledge of the dam construction, I could only express my support in principle. I could not publish a critique without having performed any research. Years earlier, some friends of mine—Liu Jianzhi and Xu Baoqiang—had translated a book entitled *Silenced Rivers: The Ecology and Politics of Large Dams* into Chinese (as *Daba Jingjixue*), but could not find a publisher. At that time, I had been working with them to publish a series of books under the general title of *Linglei Shiye* (*Alternative Perspectives*), with the Central Compilation and Translations Press, which included "Fazhan de Youxiang" ("Illusions of Development") and "Fanshichang de Ziben Zhuyi" ("Anti-Market Capitalism"), among others. I passed their book on to the editor responsible for the series, and asked him to arrange for another publisher to take it on. Little did I know that these books would later become significant for this movement. I introduced Liangzhong to *Daba Jingjixue* and *Fazhan de Youxiang*, suggesting that he think through the former alongside the Tiger Leaping Gorge Dam question, and then write an essay on the matter for *Dushu*. *Dushu* is not a mass media publication, and the Tiger Leaping Gorge question could not be discussed in that medium directly; so, as the editor, that was all I could do. After that, Liangzhong began traveling constantly between the Jinsha River, the Nujiang River, and Beijing, and since he was occupied by far more real and urgent issues, the article was never written. But he did buy more than ten copies of *Daba Jingjixue* for friends concerned about the issue, along with his fellow Jinsha River villagers.

Liangzhong started investigating the Tiger Leaping Gorge Dam issue in June, and never ceased to ask for my opinion and advice, though he never asked me to take action. Despite this, however, I could clearly see his hope and his determination. He mentioned repeatedly that things were easier said than done—something he had personally experienced. Returning to Beijing from the river, he asked if I would participate in a conference on the issue, and although I agreed, I didn't know what I would be able to say. But his persistence prevented me from copping out. In mid August I decided to return to Yunnan and visit the Tiger Leaping Gorge, beginning my journey from Lijiang. Because it was the rainy season, the route along the Jinsha was highly susceptible to landslides, and as a result I and two colleagues were forced to go through Haba Snow Mountain on foot to reach the middle section of the Tiger Leaping Gorge. From there we headed to the upper section, where the dam was located. In this final leg of the trip, loose rocks frequently rolled down, which indicated the instability of the geographical structure on both sides of the Tiger Leaping Gorge. Nonetheless, we continued forward, investigating the situation all along the way and coming to understand many things.

While I was in Yunnan, Liangzhong kept in constant phone contact with me, even performing the warm-hearted gesture of introducing his brother and some friends to my two young companions, who were on their first trip to Yunnan and who he had never met before. One of them was the *Oriental Morning Post* reporter Yang Min, who had written the first lengthy report on the Tiger Leaping Gorge question. After I returned from Yunnan, I discovered that Liangzhong had already begun to work with the Green Earth Volunteers (Lujia Yuan), the Friends of Nature (Ziranzi You) and Green Watershed (Luse Liuyu)—all environmental protection groups—and that he had been shuttling between the Jinsha River aboriginal and local environmental protection movement and the green movement in Beijing, establishing a stable network of contacts. Compared with the views he expressed about NGOs during the conference in Zhongdian, his understanding had now become much more concrete, thanks to his having participated in the movement. Social movements involve different outlooks, opportunities, ends, and means in their operations, with the key ingredient being the level of awareness participants have regarding the movements they are engaged in. Yet it was through this process that, entirely because of Liangzhong, I came to have a much deeper and more concrete understanding of the situation of NGOs within the country. Among the movement were many devoted, selfless, and pragmatic people, and for these traits I viewed them with great admiration. The different frameworks and perspectives within these movements, along with the difficulties they faced and the new strength they were gaining bit by bit, make it worth our thinking about and seeking an understanding. Each time I saw Liangzhong during this time, he was extremely travel-worn, but nonetheless in good spirits, filled with pride and deep concern for his fellow villagers and hometown.

In August or September, Liangzhong drafted a proposal resisting the Tiger Leaping Gorge Dam construction project with the environmental conservation group China Rivers (Zhongguo Hewang), and at this point I also became involved. The draft, which Liangzhong spent a lot of energy putting together, specifically opposes the Tiger Leaping Gorge Dam construction along the first turn of the Yangzte River. Because this movement was constituted by participants who inevitably differed in opinion, Liangzhong was unceasingly in the process of coordinating it. We finally agreed upon a division of labor during the course of a meeting, whereby the two of us would revise the declaration together. This declaration was an accumulation of collective wisdom, though no one would have been able to substitute for Liangzhong in all his efforts and accomplishments. During that time, Liangzhong often phoned and wrote letters, diving headlong into the project, and he often experienced distress at the varying opinions expressed. After several setbacks, we finally completed the manuscript for the declaration, which many environmental conservation groups and friends in intellectual circles signed. The Tiger Leaping Gorge issue finally entered public consciousness through the mainstream media.

From October 27 to 29, 2004, the United Nations Symposium on Hydropower and Sustainable Development was held in Beijing. Once Liangzhong got wind of it, he began preparing a paper to present. At the same time, he began mobilizing the residents along the Jinsha River to make the trip to Beijing and make their voices heard. In the course of these actions, Liangzhong's most strikingly unique characteristic was that of always placing the needs, participation and voices of the local people first, and always questioning the way in which actual relations between social movements and members of the community were established. On the afternoon of October 29, I rushed from the editorial department of *Dushu* to the conference site to meet with Liangzhong and Min Yang. We were going to visit Uncle Ge Quanxiao, who had just arrived from the Jinsha River, and the villagers who had come to participate in the event. They had already gone to Tian'anmen, however, so Liangzhong, Min Yang and I first grabbed a quick bite to eat at an inn. As we exchanged some news on the situation, the strength and reason with which Uncle Ge and the numerous other villagers had fought for their cause at the conference was mentioned, and Liangzhong's face filled with pride and excitement. This was the Liangzhong I had known best over the past few months. That night, Uncle Ge Quanxiao's party traveled back from the city to the basement of an inn close to the Beijing Continental Grand Hotel, and after Liangzhong had spoken with them by phone, he accompanied me to this basement inn to visit the villagers. We stayed there chatting for a long time, which gave me a much better understanding of the various local circumstances, attitudes, and possible developments. That night, as we parted ways, we agreed to touch base again. Once you got involved in this process, it then seemed unthinkable to leave it behind. This was a long journey—one which Liangzhong completed in a short time and at great speed, leaving the remainder to his friends.

After he passed away, the media wanted me to give an appraisal of Liangzhong as a scholar and "public intellectual," but I didn't know where to begin. Liangzhong was a rigorous anthropologist, which was the impression I had got throughout our relationship. As an amateur in these matters, I was not in a position to make grand judgments of his work, and in this respect his teacher, Professor Zhuang Kongshao, is the most qualified to speak. I do not possess a deep understanding of the discourse on public intellectuals, and Liangzhong would probably not care too much about this either. Liangzhong was an anthropologist, and his object of study was the Jinsha River that bore him and raised him, along with the various different people who lived in the area. The two reasons he became involved with the resistance against the Tiger Leaping Gorge construction were his critique of theoretical developmentalism, and his strong sensitivity toward the effects of globalization and the developmental strategies of special interest groups and some government departments. Together, these had for him resulted in the disintegration of both cultural and ecological multiplicity. The other reason was his deep affection for his own hometown, and the deep understanding he had of the people and creatures of the Jinsha River region. Liangzhong had a firm grasp on what was happening as the movement progressed, and his enthusiasm did not only stem from feelings of morality or justice. As a scholar, he thought things through diligently, studied the situation earnestly, and read through works related to dams, ecology, and development very carefully. For this reason, Liangzhong's involvement in the movement was not limited to the Jinsha River question. He later became concerned with developmentalism and the social threats plaguing other regions as well. To say that he was the shepherd of the Jinsha River would be accurate, but the scope of his concern was not limited to his own village. The moving thing about Liangzhong was his pure-heartedness, and the motivation to act that arose from it. It was a feeling that enabled him to expand his love for his hometown to the broader world. This concern for the wider world was not only rooted in his love for the Jinsha River, but also gave his love a greater strength and depth.

Last November, two days before I left Beijing for a post as a visiting scholar in Europe, Liangzhong called me to tell me that his reassignment had gone through. He was very happy. Liangzhong was a person who loved his research and cared sincerely about the public affairs of our society, but he would never oppose library research to participation in social movements. In reality, theory and practice are deeply interrelated. The problems we face are not the result of too much reading and too little practical action, nor of too little reading and too much practical action, but rather of the fact that we do too little of either. During times of cataclysmic social change, it is absolutely necessary for scholars to engage in public discussion with the masses; but greater involvement in practical social movements must also be accompanied by greater diligence in studying these issues. We must engage with texts and materials encompassing various theories and experiences—otherwise we run the risk of acting from mere habit and simply drifting along, as if unconsciously. Before Liangzhong passed away, someone wrote a list of the so-called "defenders" of the intellectual world, and included my name. I wrote the person in charge a few times explaining that I really had not done anything, and that the people who had made a truly great effort and contribution to the Jinsha River movement were Liangzhong and his friends. I hoped that the organizer would remove my name from the list, but he ignored my objections. Perhaps his motives were good, but his way of doing things made me suspect a shallow understanding of the matters concerned, and this is why I opposed it. This was partly because of my unease and guilt regarding what normally came from this way of doing things, but also because I fundamentally disapproved of his opposing theoretical research and social practice to one another.

The Liangzhong I knew was always very diligent in fighting such actions, and always saw to it that his social practices and theoretical positions intersected. Viewing the transformations of modern society from below (from the perspective of village communities and their cultural customs), rather than from above; understanding the threats of contemporary development (and developmentalism) from the perspective of cultural multiplicity and the requirements of social equality (rather than that of marketization, globalization, or other contemporary trends); viewing ecological multiplicity and environmental issues from the perspective of peoples' right to subsistence and their cultural rights (rather than from the position of a grand developmental narrative); understanding the obstacles faced by Chinese society, and in particular by the villages of the southwest, by first examining the complex relations between the foundations, the country, and globalization (rather than as single, isolated units or dichotomous relations); viewing the intricate relations that constitute social forces (such as the various levels of government, NGOs and social movements, the media, and the people) from the perspective of the complex relations constituting networks of power: Are these not the priorities of someone who cares deeply about China and the pressing needs of the next generation? Is this not a perspective forged through the continuous interplay between theory and practice? Throughout the twentieth century, practice was not only a question of movements, but also of theory. For intellectuals (and especially academics), the main issue was why practice or reality posed such fundamental problems for theory, while for social movements, the real question was why they and their practices had to be linked to theoretical exploration.

The day before Tomb Sweeping, I went with a few friends to Wuzhu, close to Chezhu Village. We also went to Judian, and by the time we were heading back it was already dark. The road was being rebuilt, and was therefore closed off. We had no choice but to cross the Jinsha River a second time and head back to Liangzhong's village, and by the time we arrived it was already midnight. The river currents flowed in the dark of early spring, and in the boundless dark of night I thought I saw Liangzhong's smiling face. I had finally arrived at Chezhu, where Liangzhong had invited me so many times. I came twice last year, in June and August, to the banks of the Jinsha River, but did not visit his hometown; each time I returned to Beijing, he was unable to conceal his innermost feelings of disappointment. Before he died, Liangzhong never asked anything of me, though he always had hopes for the Jinsha River affair. I was unable to sleep soundly during the days surrounding his death, and perhaps it was for this reason. But now, here along the Jinsha River, my heart was finally opened and, like the flow of the Jinsha River in the spring, was tranquil and serene. I slept soundly through to dawn in the room where Liangzhong used to live. I knew that he still kept watch over the Jinsha River from a small hill behind that room, as he always would.

June 14, 2005

Dead Fire Rekindled
Lu Xun as Revolutionary Intellectual

Sitting by the lamplight, thinking of writing the preface for this book that compiles Lu Xun's debates with his opponents,[1] for a long while I found myself unable to pen a word. I know that Lu Xun, during his lifetime, would have wanted to have such a book edited and published, since only in such battles did he feel alive in the world.

Why would someone be willing to devote his body and soul, his whole life, to such a struggle?

I sat idly, recollecting the literary world constructed by Lu Xun; what appeared before my eyes was surprisingly the "hanging woman." One month before his death, Lu Xun wrote one of his last pieces, "The Hanging Woman," a story about lonely ghosts and avenging spirits in "the home of revenge and redress":

> Of course this too was preceded by mournful trumpeting. The next moment, the curtain was raised and she emerged. She wore a red jacket and a long black sleeveless coat, her long hair was in disorder, two strings of paper coins hung from her neck, and with lowered head and drooping hands, she wound her way across the stage. According to old stagers, she was tracing out the heart sign; why she should do this I do not know. I do know, though, why she wore red . . . When she hanged herself she intended to become an avenging spirit, and red, as one of the more vital colors, would make it easier for her to approach living creatures . . .

In silence, Lu Xun's plain sketch came alive before my eyes. I too seemed to see the hanging woman shaking back her disheveled hair: her round chalk-white face; thick, pitch-black eyebrows; dark eyelids; crimson lips. I saw her shrugging her shoulders slightly; looking around and listening, as if startled, or happy, or angry; and at last uttering a mournful sound. As obsessed as a ghost that died of injustice, she is bound up with revenge, even in death. She wears a bright red jacket, even in hell, and will not let go of her living enemies.

This description is more or less self-referential, since at that time Lu Xun was already fatally ill. Before writing "The Hanging Woman," he had already written a piece titled "Death," in which he quoted from the preface Agnes Smedley wrote for Käthe Kollwitz's collection of woodcuts, and where he also put down his will, the last item of which is, "Never get close to people who deride others when opposing revenge and advocating tolerance." Lu Xun believed that maxims like "Do not take revenge" or "Forgive past injuries" are but the strategies of assassins and their stooges, which is why he said, "I shall not forgive a single one of them!"

And so we know, because Lu Xun considered forgiveness to be a tool for those in power and their stooges, he would never forgive. Still, this cannot fully explain the way he longed for revenge and his relentless curses, which for us today seem morbid.

There have been many discussions in the last decade of Lu Xun's rejection of "fair play," of his harshness and paranoia, of his being unreasonable. For instance: Lu Xun measured his friends and teachers, even those who had passed away, with the above standard. A few days before he died, he wrote at a stretch two essays in commemoration of his former teacher Zhang Taiyan. He passed away before he could finish one of them. He criticized Zhang: "Though he first became known as a revolutionary, he later retired to live as a quiet scholar cut off from the age by means of a wall built by himself and others." Deeply dissatisfied with the omission of the writings that "attack, criticize or even curse others" in Zhang's self-edited *Qiu Shu*, Lu Xun believed those polemical essays to be "the greatest and most lasting monuments" to Zhang's life, for these are the words that make him "live in the heart of the younger generations, in the hearts of those who are fighting" ("Some Recollections of Zhang Taiyan").

That age is far too distant from us. This is a peaceful and nonjudgmental age—one cut off by walls of various kinds; even those like me who study Lu Xun have retired to live as quiet scholars. Behind this illusion of quietness continues a world that is allegedly eternal and has departed from history. If Lu Xun were placed in such an age of peace, he would have been as lost in not knowing what to do as that "fighter," even though he would still raise his javelin. "Under the circumstances of the time, no one hears any battle cry: there is only peace."[2] I am thinking of the image of Lu Xun, were he resurrected today:

> [The] whole body, great as a statue but already wasting, degraded, was shaken by tremors. These tremors, small and distinct at first as fish scales, started seething like water over a blazing fire; and at once the air too was convulsed like waves in the wild, storm-racked ocean ("Tremors of Degradations").

In this "age of the market," this quiet life that is so familiar to me, it is truly unexpected that Lu Xun would still be remembered often, that someone is willing to edit and publish his "combative" writings. Just like my sudden memory of the hanging woman and her singing voice in this night of the hectic, earthly city of noise and excitement—they both are a little bit strange and out of place. For Lu Xun, who hoped that these words "would soon perish along with contemporary social problems,"[3] is this perhaps a misfortune?

I believe that readers will have different thoughts and impressions after reading this collection. Gentlemen of integrity, quiet scholars, cultural celebrities, critics of nationalist literature, moralists showing a face of justice, and of course also friends from the old days and comrades in the past—all have shown their arguments and attitudes, so that we latecomers will also know about the other side of Lu Xun, despite his prejudice, harshness, and paranoia. This is fair to Lu Xun, to his opponents in the debates, and to the society in which they were situated.

Hidden in these debates is the dialectics of the age.

In a preface written for a young writer's work, Lu Xun once regretfully remarked that

> since the Buddha's renunciation of the worldly life, his deeds in past lives, of feeding his flesh to the eagle and the tiger for the respect of all living things, are only of the (lesser) Hinayana school; whereas his vague and elusive lecturing comes to be the greater Mahayana tradition, which has always been prominent. The key, I think, lies exactly in this.

Lu Xun therefore refuses to lecture in any vague or evasive way, or to retire in the end into quietness; he would rather "be a mirror for the present, keep a record for the future."[4] This is Lu Xun's philosophy of life, an outlook on life that believes in the present and disbelieves the future—although he himself was once a passionate admirer of evolutionism, and evolutionists in China in general believe in the future.

One of the writings I cannot forget is the essay entitled "The Evolution of Roughs," written by Lu Xun in the early 1930s. Specialists would probably tell us that it is a piece satirizing the Crescent Moon Society (a literary society that existed between 1923–1931) or other idle troublemakers; yet I remember it serves more than this purpose. This short essay of Lu Xun's, of less than 1,000 words, is a sketch of the history of the evolution of ruffians in China. In this passage, Lu Xun concludes that the men of letters in China are either "scholars" or "swordsmen." To borrow from Sima Qian, "Scholars flout the law by their writings, and gallant men break prohibitions by force of arms"; for Lu Xun, they are merely "usurpers" and "offenders" who "stir up a little trouble"; neither type are "rebels." What is more horrifying is that real swordsmen have already died out; what remains are only wily "swordsmen": Chen Zun of the Han dynasty, for example, had dealings with the nobles "so that [he] could take refuge behind these patrons at critical times." In short, "backed by traditional patrons and faced with opponents neither great nor powerful, he walks sideways across them"—such is the sketch of the "swordsman" in later ages. The crucial point of Lu Xun's commentary on the classic Chinese novels *Water Margin*, *The Cases of Lord Shih*, *The Cases of Lord Peng*, and *The Seven Heroes and Five Gallants* is also that these "gallants" secretly approach and rely on powerful officials, and at the same time "they can lord it over all the others. With a greater degree of security, servility follows suit." They safeguard public morality, educate the ignorant, love law and order, and so become gentlemen of integrity and sages, all quiet and benevolent. To reveal the truth of it, this is but showing off good behavior for the advantages he has taken—these are what Lu Xun calls accomplices and idle troublemakers.

The people rebuked by Lu Xun are countless; many were not only once his companions and friends, but also cultural figures worth studying today. We need not take his words as the only measure by which we evaluate historical figures, for he himself is one of the figures in history who awaits judgment, although I feel that his "scolding" is never without reason. Lu Xun has never liked the principle of reciprocity, and is fond of the straight and narrow path. As he said before, his rebuke, which seems to be about personal grudges, is in fact for a public cause. What is regrettable is that the debates half a century ago have now been seen by many as "disputes on paper" and debased into stories of quarrels among in-laws. Ever ready for private fights, but shying away from public causes—such is Lu Xun's painful summary of the morbidity of the Chinese people. For me, as he rebukes real people, he is also criticizing the history of old China, from Confucius, Laozi, Mencius, and the Buddha in ancient times to sages and philosophers in the modern era. To discuss Lu Xun's stubbornness, then, we must first speak of his stubbornness about Chinese history. The secret of this has been revealed at the outset: "Neither Confucius nor Mencius was satisfied with the status quo. They both wanted reforms. But their first step was to win over their earthly masters, and the tool they used to control their masters was 'Heaven'" ("The Evolution of Roughs").

This type of interpretation is often criticized as radical and anti-traditional by conservatives, and seen by reformists as violating the "politically correct." Since the late Qing period, one of the established conventions of Chinese thinking is cultural representation achieved by contrasting China with the West. Both reformists and conservatives have strived to depict some abstract characteristics of "Chinese culture" and "Western culture" within this comparative structure, and have accordingly set a cultural strategy of their own. Nevertheless, the special characteristic of Lu Xun is precisely that he does not simplistically imagine that description of contrast; the views on culture he conveyed within concrete linguistic contexts should not and could not be simply understood as a general summary about "Chinese culture." His work on literary history, his passion for folk culture, his praise of the atmosphere of the Han and Tang dynasties—all of these illustrate his complex view on tradition. Moreover, while Lu Xun criticizes tradition, he at the same time criticizes radically those "reformists" who uncritically conform to anything new, and those "Westerner's underlings" without backbone. The kernel of his cultural criticism lies in revealing the historical relation between the common beliefs to which people have grown accustomed and morality—this is an historical relation that has never been separated from the social mode of the dominating and the dominated, of the ruler and the ruled. For Lu Xun, no matter how ingenious culture or tradition is, there has not been in history a culture or tradition that could break away from the relations of domination mentioned above; on the contrary, culture and tradition are the basis for legitimizing ruling relations. If we knew well enough Lu Xun's early views on culture, we would discover, too, that this unique vision of his also appears throughout his observations on modern European history: the development of science, the practice of democracy, can likewise lead to the tyranny of "materials" over man, of men (the masses) over man ("On Extremities in Culture"). What he is concerned with is the formation and the regenerating process of the ruling mode.

Dominating Lu Xun's attitude toward culture are, hence, the relationship that historical figures, ideas, and schools of thought have with power (political, economic, cultural, traditional, imported), their attitudes toward power, their positions in a specific relation of domination—and not, as his contemporaries were accustomed to, a simple choice of acceptance or rejection in a comparison between China and the West. The China-West comparative approach has provided a cultural basis for China's social changes, and has constructed for its own culture an historical homogeneity; but this historical homogeneity not only masks the concrete historical relations, but also reconstructs (if not falsely) cultural relations. Lu Xun never renders "power" abstract, nor does he render tradition or culture abstract. In this historical picture, constructed from such categories of thought as tradition and culture, the question Lu Xun continues to pose is: What is hidden behind the veils of tradition or culture? In Lu Xun's view, as modern society continuously produces new forms of oppression and inequality, the forms of accomplices and idle troublemakers become accordingly more varied, too—this applies equally to the political and economic arenas, as well as the cultural arena. And, like their predecessors, the modern men of letters also continuously create "cultural pictures" or knowledge systems that mask this historical relation.

Lu Xun's exposition of this relation not only breaks away from that simplistic China-West comparative representation, but also contains doubts about the common belief of that age—in evolution, or progress. Modern society does not evolve in time; many things have not only long existed, but are all the more entrenched today. Lu Xun's criticism of tradition is indeed intense, but it does not mean that he is a "modernist"—his doubts about modernity are not second to his criticism of the ancient past.

Lu Xun is a figure of paradox, and he is a paradoxical thinker, too

Lu Xun's world is suffused with shadows of darkness; his uncompromising attitude toward the real world is proof of this.

However, our understanding of the theme of darkness in Lu Xun's world is often imbued with our own solitary and dark memories, the memories of "civilized men." Yes, like the hanging woman, he approaches living creatures by wearing red with the sole purpose of revenge; light, for him, is obstructive. But the closer one is to this world, the more one will experience and understand the significance of this world of shadows to Lu Xun: it is at once dark and light. Not only is Lu Xun obsessed with it, he simply sees the world in which he lives with the vision of this world.

This is a world that has not been filtered by the perspectives of the public and of "gentlemen": the man-faced beast; the nine-headed snake; the one-footed ox; the sack-like monster Di Jiang; the headless Xing Tian, who "wielded spear and shield"; the hanging woman, who is like an avenging spirit and yet is unusually beautiful; and that uncouth fellow all in white, Wu Chang, who knits his brows, with white face, red lips, jet-black eyebrows, laughing and crying at the same time . . . love, hatred, life, death, revenge . . . red, black, white . . . the wailing Maudgalyayana trumpet, the dramatic and forceful monolog: "Not though he is surrounded by a wall of bronze or iron, / Not though he is a kinsman of the emperor himself!" ("The Hanging Woman") . . . This is a world of vivid and distinct emotions, a frenzied, absurd world that overturns class and order, a world of folk imagination, primitive and regenerating.

Lu Xun's world possesses the qualities of profound humor and absurdity. It has its origins in that colorful world of "ghosts" on stage during village festivals and in folkloric myths and stories. A theorist once said that "perhaps the greatest humorist is the ghost"; and the humor of this world of "ghosts" is destructive. What the "ghost" avenges itself on, what it ironizes and mocks, are not individual phenomena and individual figures in reality, but the entirety of the world. The real world in the eyes of the "ghost" loses its stability and rationality, its self-control and moral foundation. In the intense, colorful, distinct, humorous atmosphere of the world of "ghosts," our living world reveals its state of ambiguity, terror, otherness—a state of having nothing to rely on. The radicality of the world of "ghosts" illustrates its inherently folkloric, illegitimate, and unofficial nature: all the established rules and accepted opinions, all that is serious and eternal, all of the planned order in life, thinking, and worldviews are a mismatch with it. The relationship between Lu Xun and his opponents in debates is but the relationship between the world of "ghosts" he creates and the real world; this relationship is holistic and does not in any way contain any personal nature.

What we are most likely to forget is nothing other than the atmosphere of folk festivities and folk drama of Lu Xun's world of "ghosts": he rarely depicts problems with the accustomed logic of the real world, but does so rather with methods such as prophesy in reverse, reductio ad absurdum, falsification, pointed mockery and curse, to tear up the given logic of this world and to show it to people in laughter. In the urban newspapers and magazines of the 1920s and 1930s, Lu Xun created a special world like that of the Maudgalyayana drama: that absurd world constructed with humor, irony, comicality, and curse, with only the sense of mystery of the Maudgalyayana drama missing. Nevertheless, as with all folk carnivals, Lu Xun's sardonic laughter takes us temporarily into a world beyond the institution of normal life, onto an alternative world-observing and dramatic stage; yet this world, or this stage, does not exist outside of the real world. On the contrary, it *is* part of this world; it is life itself. Bakhtin discovers, in the carnivals of the Middle Ages and the Renaissance, that

> we find here [in the carnival idiom] the peculiar logic of the "inside out" (*à l'envers*), of the "turnabout," of a continual shifting from top to bottom, from front to rear, of numerous parodies and travesties, humiliations, profanations, comic crownings and un-crownings.

He also discovers that the powerful expression of emotions in folk performances is not a simple negation, but contains within it rebirth and renewal, as well as the wish to place the enemy on dangerous ground by curses, so that he may be reborn; it contains a collective negation of both the world and the self.[5] "I still remember distinctly how in my home town, with those low types, I enjoyed watching this ghostly yet human, just yet merciful, frightening yet lovable Wu Chang. We enjoyed the distress or laughter on his face, the bravado and jokes that fell from his lips" ("Wu Chang, or Life-Is-Transient").

As we attribute Lu Xun's curse to his personal radicalism and morbidity, we belong to the world he curses, obeying the rules of this world. As we are deeply shocked by his resoluteness, we have long forgotten that world of the hanging woman and Wu Chang hidden behind him, the human sympathy and happiness of that world. As we feel defeated by his heartfelt despair, we too have lost our proximity with the festive atmosphere that carries in it a sense of rebirth and renewal. We cannot shed our identity to enter that carnivalesque world: we are scholars, citizens, moralists, gentlemen. We cannot understand the language of that folkloric world, and, ultimately, we have lost, too, the ability to understand hatred and love, happiness and absurdity.

Lu Xun's world connotes also what is absent in the folkloric world of the hanging woman and Wu Chang, which is the understanding of the interiority, the complexity, and the depth of the human. In this understanding grows a culture of self-reflection. The pain and guilt he experiences bring a profoundly melancholic and desperate essence into the folkloric world of his creation.

Lu Xun compulsively experiences things repressed in memory as things that are happening before his eyes, to the extent that there are no longer any clear boundaries between reality and history. People and events before his eyes seem to be no more than a past that should have been gone long ago, but nonetheless refuses to be gone. He does not trust any outward, superficial form of things or events, but must look into the reality hidden beneath the façade; the humor, wit, and satirical laughs adrift among his stray thoughts and clear insights tear off the mask in life. Lu Xun rejects any form or sphere of power relations and oppression: oppression of the nation, oppression of classes, men's oppression of women, elders' oppression of the young, oppression by intellect, the strong's oppression of the weak, society's oppression of individuals, and so on. Perhaps what this book tells the reader is, moreover, that Lu Xun detests all the knowledge, indoctrination, and lies that legitimize these unequal relations; his lifelong vocation is to tear apart the veils forged by words that are "proper and fair." Nevertheless, Lu Xun is not an idealist, unlike poets such as S. A. Yesenin or A. Soboly, who retain unrealistic fantasies about revolutions and changes. His critique of his opponents and their thoughts and opinions encompasses the cross-examination and analysis of the conditions in which these opponents and their thoughts are produced. Lu Xun's tireless revelation of unequal relations and their social conditions implied in the "natural order" not only unsettles those who place themselves in the ruling position, but also illustrates, to those who strive for a vocation of criticism, a not-so-wonderful prospect for future society.

And yet that sense of distrust caused by wounds of spiritual slavery and dark memories, that psychological schema which always sees reality as the tragic recurrence of past experiences, often leads to the split of Lu Xun's psyche as well. The historical methodology of "digging ancestral graves" and "settling old scores" endows him with a profound sense of history; but his unique and exceptional sensitivity to dark experiences also prevents him from steeping unreservedly into one particular value or ideal, as many of his contemporaries did. Rather, Lu Xun always makes use of his independent thinking and devotes his life, though never without doubts, to the movements of his time. "What gave me love and life, hope and happiness, before has vanished. There is nothing but emptiness, the emptiness of existence I exchanged for the truth" ("Regret for the Past"). Lu Xun is a passionate propagator of evolutionist history, but as I have pointed out elsewhere, what is truly terrifying and disturbing is precisely his tragic sense of the repetitive and cyclical nature of historical experience: historical development is but constituted by one repetition after another, by one cycle after another; and reality—including the movements in which one is personally involved—does not seem to have marked the progress of history but rather has fallen into a ridiculous transmigration. "In short, whether classicists or refugees, wise men or fools, worthy men or rascals, all seem to be longing for the peaceful days of three centuries ago, when the Chinese had succeeded in becoming slaves for a time" ("Some Notions Jotted Down by Lamplight").

> I'm afraid that I behave like this: If I received a charity from somebody, then I would need to hover around like the eagle that catches sight of a corpse, longing for her death and hoping to see it myself. Or I curse all other people but her and pray that they may perish, including myself, for I deserve to be cursed ("The Passer-by").

This partly explains, too, his stubbornness in debates: he sees that what is at stake in these debates are not only the people he faces, but the history that he needs to face and shoulder—that famous "gate of darkness."[6]

Yoshimi Takeuchi, in Japan, is the outstanding thinker who first raised the thesis of "overcoming modernity" (*kindai no chokoku*); he sees Lu Xun as the great pioneer representing Asia's effort to overtake modernity. In analyzing the relationship between Lu Xun and politics, he thinks that appearing throughout Lu Xun's series of essays is the idea that "true revolution is 'permanent revolution.'" Takeuchi expands Lu Xun's view and argues that "only those who are self-conscious about 'permanent revolution' are true revolutionaries. Conversely, those who cry 'my revolution succeeded' are not true revolutionaries but people who are like flies hovering around the corpses of fighters."[7] For Lu Xun, only "permanent revolution" can break away from the never-ending repetition and cycle of history, and the one who maintains from beginning to end his "revolutionary" spirit will inevitably become the critic of his own comrades in the past, because the moment his comrades become satisfied with their "success" is the moment they will become mired in that historical cycle—it is this cycle that is the real revolutionary's ultimate target of revolution.

This is Lu Xun's disappointment, at every remembrance of which I would feel the shock and grief that penetrate to the marrow of the bones: "So China has had very few heroes who refuse to admit defeat, very few who resist to the last, very few who dare fight on alone, very few who dare mourn for dead rebels" ("This and That"). This regretful sigh has the same effect, albeit from a different approach, as his praising of "the backbone of China": they "have firm convictions and do not deceive themselves"; on the one hand, they are "trampled on, kept out of news, smothered in darkness," and on the other, "when one in front falls others behind him fight on" ("Have the Chinese Lost Their Self-Confidence?"). What Lu Xun promotes has been, all along, that permanent revolutionist who is unafraid of failure or loneliness and who is forever progressive. For these eternal revolutionists, the only way to break away from the strange circle of "reform—preservation—revivalism" is ceaseless struggle, or perhaps desperate resistance.

However, the motivation for "permanent revolution" is not a heroic dream of the superhuman, but rather a pessimism and sense of hopelessness toward the self. Lu Xun's heart is ultimately still entangled with that almost fatalist sense of sin; he has never seen himself as an innocent and decent member of this world, but believes that he is set in the order of history, an accomplice of this world that he detests. "How can a man like myself, after four thousand years of man-eating history—even though I knew nothing about it at first—ever hope to face real men?" ("A Madman's Diary"). Compulsively, he "raises his javelin," not for achieving heroic feats but because otherwise he would sink into being the master of "the lines of nothingness":

Above their heads hang all sorts of flags and banners, embroidered with all manners of titles: philanthropist, scholar, writer, elder, youth, dilettante, gentleman . . . Beneath are all sorts of surcoats, embroidered with all the fine names: scholarship, morality, national culture, public opinion, logic, justice, Asian civilization . . . ("Such a Fighter").

"Ah, no! I don't want to. I would rather wander in nothingness" ("The Shadow's Leave-Taking").

Lu Xun's cultural practice creates the image of a real revolutionist; this image is suffused with the weight of history and a hopeless expectation at heart. The basic characteristic of this revolutionist image is that he never places himself outside of the target he satirizes, criticizes, and attacks, never locates himself as opposed to it, but ultimately includes himself as part of this target. And for that, what is negated is not a partial phenomenon in this world, but is holistic and subsumes even his critics. This is a transient world, and the revolutionist is also an organic part of this transient world—so, contained in the nature of the revolutionist's attack, satire, and critique of the world is a self-reflective quality.

The revolutionist image has also constructed the standard by which Lu Xun judges the world. In an essay, Lu Xun talks about the advice given to latecomers by gentlemen of great vision: if one cannot give birth to a sage, or a hero, or a genius, then it is better not to give birth at all; if one cannot write immortal works, then it is better not to write at all. "Is he, then, a conservative? No, we are told, he is not. In point of fact he is a true revolutionist. He is the only one with a reform program which is fair, proper, solid, thorough, measured, and absolutely foolproof. [The program] is at the moment being studied in the research lab—the only trouble is it is not yet ready" ("This and That"). Lu Xun pointedly discovers that such attitudes and methods of the intellectuals are but part of the "rational" operation of this world. In this ever-changing world, such attitudes and methods express the understanding of the permanence of this world.

Lu Xun's criticism of the intellectual mostly has its origin in this.

Lu Xun is not a revolutionary who makes revolution his profession; he has always remained cautious of those who take revolution as their "rice bowl." Nor is he the spokesperson for any clique or party. He seems always to be deeply suspicious of collective movements. But real revolution is what he truly looks forward to. In the period between the

May Fourth era and the 1930s, he has great expectations for the Russian Revolution and its culture, not out of fanaticism but because the revolution he longs for overturned the unequal but eternal order. On the other hand, having been through the 1911 Revolution, the Second Revolution, Zhang Xun's attempt to restore the Qing Empire, Yuan Shikai's proclamation as emperor, up to the rise and fall of the May Fourth movement, Lu Xun not only expresses profound skepticism over the fruition of large-scale revolutionary movements, but also believes that revolution is accompanied by filth and blood.

> So desolate is the new garden of letters,
> and the old battlefront is a scene of peace.
> There remains one fighter between two fronts
> still wandering alone shouldering his arms.[8]

This is his self-description, but it is also a realistic portrayal of the age. What he doubts is not whether revolution can ever succeed, but whether the new world created by revolution is merely old China in a new guise—whether what is changed is only the dramatic actor on stage, with the order of the old days remaining unchanged. This is Ah Q's style of revolution, in which "New peach-wood boards replace the old charms on the door."[9]

Lu Xun's experience with revolutions exerts an immense influence on his social strategy. He no longer works for large-scale revolutions, nor for tightly organized political activities; instead, he begins "guerrilla warfare" in the modern city jungle: founding periodical publications, organizing social groups, opening up special columns, changing his pseudonyms, commencing small-scale assaults in various aspects of social life. He calls this "social criticism" and "cultural criticism"; the essays collected in this book are precisely examples of his "guerrilla warfare." To borrow from Gramsci, "in politics the 'war of position,' once won, is decisive definitively. In politics, in other words, the war of manoeuvre subsists so long as it is a question of winning positions which are not decisive, so that all the resources of the State hegemony cannot be mobilized."[10] The stray thoughts of Lu Xun, including the many essays collected in this book, are also precisely a kind of "war of position": not all of the figures and areas he touches upon are political per se, but without exception these struggles are political in nature—the resistance to all unequal relations, both old and new, as well as to their reproduction mechanisms.

Nor does Lu Xun give up the non-mainstream social force, or even the non-mainstream social collective, created by cultural criticism. Throughout his life he continues to cultivate a newborn cultural force, "believing that the battlefront should be broadened," "anxious to create a large group of new fighters."[11] From *Threads of Talk*, *The Wilderness*, and *The Torrent*, to the Woodcut Movement, the League of Left-Wing Writers—all these publications, movements, and social groups connected with the name of Lu Xun join to mark such an effort. In the ruling order constructed by politicians, agents of capital, warlords, men of letters playing the roles of accomplices and idle troublemakers, he continuously looks for opportunities for breakthroughs, and finally makes the non-mainstream culture a commanding or leading culture in the world of the rulers.

It is through practical experiences rather than preaching that Lu Xun establishes his understanding of the intellectual.

Lu Xun sees himself as a member of the intelligentsia, but a rebellious one. He does not think of himself as belonging to the future or to the class representing the future—not because he believes that intellectuals are a "crystallised social bloc," a "continuous and uninterrupted existence in the course of history," "thus independent of group struggle" (as Gramsci notes critically),[12] but because he guiltily considers himself too steeped and ingrained in the old ways to be the representative and embodiment of the "new" intellectual of the future. Yet read his "Thoughts on the League of Left-Wing Writers," and it becomes clear that he believes that the movements in which he participated represented a new social collective, that they were the products of a new stage in historical development, and absolutely not the traditionalist remnants of an obsolete social group, nor of the "distilled intellectual" who has long existed in history and who transcends all new social relations. The crucial point of Lu Xun's discussion of class, especially of class in literature, does not lie in the question of whether human nature exists, or of the relation between human nature and class. What finally still concerns Lu Xun is the relation between rulers and the ruled, as well as the reproductive mechanism of this relation; what he is anxious to ask, therefore, is this: Within unequal social relations, what does the concept of human nature mask?

Perhaps what should not be forgotten is that, even in such a social collective as the League of Left-Wing Writers, he still struggles tirelessly against unequal power relations. Inside those "new" collective organizations and among those "socialists in the salon," the spirit of the old era is still being reproduced in the same way as before. What divides the "leftist" and the "rightist" is less than a sheet of paper.

Lu Xun is an outstanding scholar, an excellent novelist. And yet his literary career cannot be generalized by the term *scholar*, nor by *novelist* or *writer*. Speaking of Lu Xun's academic achievement, scholars cannot help but feel excited; sometimes I also behave like that. Consider, for example, *A Brief History of Chinese Fiction, An Outline of Chinese Literary History*, and the more acclaimed "On the Behavior and Writing of Writers of the Wei and Jin Periods and Their Relationship with Drugs and Alcohol": Lu Xun's contribution to the study of Chinese literary history is beyond doubt. In Cao Cao's execution of Kong Rong in the name of the latter's disregard for filial piety, Lu Xun sees the relationship between men of letters and politics. While many believe that the habit of wearing loose garments and light clothes in the Jin Dynasty is a sign of elegance and refinement, Lu Xun relates this to He Yan's drug use. While many believe that Ji Kang and Ruan Ji challenged and destroyed Confucianism, Lu Xun attributes their behavior to their over-reliance on Confucianism. While Tao Qian has been considered the model of the recluse for scholars over the centuries, Lu Xun argues that in fact he could neither disentangle himself from the secular world nor, "still concerned with the state of government, forget 'death.'" Such sensitivity and insightful understanding of the secluded scholar derives from Lu Xun's awareness that "the superior men of China understand ceremony and righteousness, but are deplorably ignorant of the minds of men."[13] Moreover, "those who understand ceremony and righteousness are, inevitably, deplorably ignorant of the minds of men, and thus many had suffered from great injustice in ancient times."[14] Lu Xun, who has this historical insight, has been a lecturer and professor, but he chooses to leave the university in the end. He does not want himself and his work to be weaved into the increasingly narrow cage of modern society; he does not want his social criticism and cultural criticism to be absorbed, or even bound, by the university institution. Nor does he want his work—which is not only clear in an academic sense but also perceptive about human nature—to fall into the trap of norms and regulations.

He would rather be a fighter against what Gramsci calls the "organic intellectual."

Fighter is a favorite word of Lu Xun's: a simpler, more direct concept.

Discussions on ending the era of Ah Q had already been circulating during Lu Xun's lifetime. When comparing today's society to the age in which Lu Xun lived, the change is evidently profound. What sort of change, then, is taking place?

The age in which Lu Xun was situated was one of revolution and change, and also of dramatic turbulence; today, the progress of modernization has already disintegrated the revolutionary class of that age, and consequently the possibility for any radical revolution. The characteristic of the modernization movement is the organization of different social aspects, through a gradual means of legitimation, into what Weber calls a "rationalized" order. This "rationalized" order has now crossed national boundaries and become part of the process of globalization.

In Lu Xun's age—despite the close relationship between knowledge and cultural activities, on the one hand, and the university institution, on the other—intellectual activities shared with social life a close, organic connection. One of the important marks of contemporary cultural life is the disintegration and retreat of the Lu Xun style of "organic intellectual," reforming in the end the intellectual's cultural activity into a professional activity. The process of professionalization in practice destroyed or reformed the intelligentsia.

Another matter related to this is that the media, especially newspapers and magazines, used to enjoy a special status in intellectual and cultural activities in Lu Xun's age, while in contemporary society this phenomenon has undergone profound changes. Besides fulfilling their specific political function, the media have also become, and increasingly so, a major site of consumerist culture. The critical intellectuals of Lu Xun's age used to establish a direct organic relationship with society, politics, and the public through media activities; their cultural practice, especially their criticism and self-reflection on the various social inequalities in their age, became an important force of effective social and cultural change. In contemporary media, the image of "scholar" or "intellectual" appears constantly, too, but this image and characterization of the "intellectual" is often a kind of cultural construction and illusion, since the major force of the media activities that propel the "intellectual" is not the self-reflective function of criticism, but the rules of the market that regulate and control. Thus, when we discuss the tradition of the "organic intellectual," it is not simply to demand that the intellectual return to the media, but to point out that this change is itself only part of the structural change in society.

The changes mentioned above have clearly transformed the way in which contemporary intellectuals engage in cultural activities. This transformation was once considered as a certain change in the intellectual's attitude and values ("the loss of humanism," for example); this view, however, shows an incomplete awareness of the fact that the retreat of the "organic intellectual" is the historical outcome of the modernization movement. Along with the progress of modernization, Chinese society is ushered into a process of social development wherein particularization, professionalization, and departmentalization increase by the day; accordingly, knowledge-production incorporates more and more of its corresponding features. The fundamental task of the university, as the most important institution responsible for the production of professionalized knowledge, is thus the training of professionals who will coordinate with the above process of social development. Since the university institution has as its premise precisely this particularization of the disintegration of knowledge, it has not reflected—and cannot possibly be reflecting—on this social process in general, and on the problem of increasingly disintegrated knowledge in particular. Not only is the institutionalization of knowledge-production the organic part of the entire process of social modernization; its task is to provide for this process the training of professionals and the preparation of knowledge, as well as the apology for the task itself. The cultural activities of intellectuals, being part of the institutionalization process, must therefore also abide by the norms and regulations of institutionalization. Whether in terms of educational institution, or of the system of scientific research, they both require that the intellectuals' thinking about society and culture increasingly carry characteristics of academia. We can perhaps argue that "self-reflection" has always been an important feature of the academic activities of sensitive scholars and intellectuals; yet we cannot but admit that this is not a feature of institutionalized knowledge-production.

The structure of the academy implies in itself the severance between academic study as a professional act and socio-cultural activities in general.

The result of this severance is evidently double-edged. On the one hand, due to the institutionalized nature of academic activities, there is no direct connection between a scholar's work and the social process; education and research institutions thus provide for professional intellectual activity the conditions for its reproduction. In this sense, academia provides a unique space and opportunity for self-reflective activities, substantially reinforcing the autonomy of intellectual activities. On the other hand, however, since the structure of the academy implies at the same time an institutionalized production of knowledge, this activity not only contains no self-reflectiveness in itself, but reproduces the social relations of domination by separating itself from society. Only those intellectuals with a special sensitivity, therefore, would make academic space a site of self-reflection and engage in self-reflective intellectual activities.

More importantly, through the professionalization of knowledge, the increasingly meticulous division of subjects separates intellectuals into professionals of different domains, and turns them into specialists who find it difficult to exchange ideas. In the face of a public that can neither understand nor interrogate the knowledge produced by the specialists, the organic connection between intellectuals and the masses henceforth disappears. The professionalization of knowledge-production not only suppresses the critical faculty of intellectuals, but also completely marginalizes folk culture. Thus, while the effects of the intellectuals' self-reflective culture on contemporary life are weakened day by day, the public's interactive relationship with intellectuals cannot be established. The enlightening posture of intellectuals in the past has, perhaps, been rightly criticized as an excessive inclination toward elitism; nonetheless, the real force leading to the "elitization" of intellectuals is a matter not of "mindset" but of the process of institutionalization—the process of transforming an intellectual identity into a professional identity. The culture of the specialist has accelerated the process of intellectual elitization, turning it into a class remote from the public and occupying certain positions of control. As specialists become legislators of various kinds of laws, systems, regulations, and even values, they cease to be intellectuals—and in this transformation their knowledge has become the power of social control. At the advent of fundamental changes in society, the few intellectuals remaining can only become the passive receivers of these changes, unable to raise their own critical voice—and even if they could, this voice remains incomprehensible to others.

*   *   *

This is the contemporary scene in which we review the legacy of Lu Xun. We live in an age when the degree of "rationalization" has become greater; and for this reason, it is also the age of the marginalization of self-reflective culture and folk culture. The university and the media are effectively producing cultural products that can adapt to the prevailing politico-economic relations, successfully organizing themselves into this large, reproductive mechanical movement. No one would deny that there still exists in modern society severe social inequality; more and more people discover, too, that the new social relations are intervening and restraining human life in an unprecedented form—the form of this intervention and restraint often seems to be "a natural event," to the extent that anyone who suspects its legitimacy would be deemed irrational. Lu Xun's legacy of thinking retains its significance today because he reveals the secret connection between the legitimation of knowledge and unequal relations—a connection that recurs in history and society. His legacy of thinking should become an important source of critical thinking for contemporary intellectuals.

Lu Xun's cultural practice provides a system of reference for intellectuals situated in the process of professionalized knowledge-production, and prompts us to think about the limit and social implication of the way in which knowledge is produced in the contemporary moment. I do not oppose the institutionalization and professionalization of knowledge-production in a general sense: in the logic of modernization, no single person or society can simply oppose this process, as such opposition would be equal to self-destruction. However, Lu Xun reveals that all the explanations about the singular, eternal, and indisputable nature of the world are but deceitful illusions, hence implying all kinds of possibilities for the modern world. The task of this essay is not to discuss in detail the academic institution as the site of cultural reproduction; what I investigate with force here is the relationship between this mode of knowledge-production and critical thinking—and, with this relationship as our axis, the self-reflection of intellectual activities within which we are situated. The object of my inquiry is only this: given the fact that the disciplinary model and its knowledge-production in contemporary education and systems of scientific research have obvious connections with professionalized education and professionalized knowledge, critical intellectuals find it difficult to reflect on their premises of knowledge, as well as on the complex relations between intellectual activities and contemporary social progress. It is in this mode of knowledge-production, in an age when increasing marginalization of the "organic intellectual" is a cultural phenomenon, that the glorious achievements of Lu Xun are worth our consideration. In an increasingly specialized state of knowledge, in a cultural condition that has become increasingly controlled by the rules of the market and consumerist culture, Lu Xun's acute sensitivity to social injustice, his profound criticism of the relations between knowledge and society, his continual concern with the relationship between culture and the public, his flexible cultural practice—all re-create in these new historical conditions the possibility for the intellectual's "organicity."

This is the great tradition of the Chinese intellectual.

Reading the critical writings of Lu Xun and those of his opponents, I am often like a researcher on war history, conjecturing the strategies and tactics of both sides of the front. After reading, I am more like a psychoanalyst, imagining the inner world of Lu Xun. Perhaps this piece of writing should have been more like a preface—should not, at least, have digressed so much from its main subject. I should indeed apologize for this. But I believe the intelligent reader would not be bewitched by my words, for the words of both Lu Xun and his opponents are here, as yesterday's "arrow whistling through the forest." For the sages in the world of peace, those are but the rigmarole of scholars scorning each other, talking nonsense without any idea of right or wrong, and are not worth the concern. "Under the circumstances of the time, no one hears any battle cry: there is only peace."

As for myself, I am a bit weary, in such a deep night. Looking through the window at the high-rise buildings outside, I, nonetheless, somehow miss the two date trees in Lu Xun's backyard: the bare boughs rigid as iron piercing the strange high sky.

For some unknown reason, I begin to miss the fierce night bird; or perhaps is the hanging woman more familiar still?

Beijing
September 11, 1996

Notes

Foreword

1   Liu Zaifu and Li Zehou, *Gaobie geming: Hui wang ershi shiji zhongguo*
    [Farewell to Revolution: Looking back at Twentieth Century China],
    Hong Kong, 1995.
2   See Chapter 2, p. 19.
3   See Chapter 1, p. 17.

Preface to the English Edition

1   Giovanni Arrighi, *Adam Smith in Beijing*, New York: Verso Books, 2008. 321.
2   Ibid., 351.
3   "Three Represents" signifies the threefold representation of the
    developmental needs of China's advanced production capacity, the
    progressive direction of China's advanced culture, and the fundamental
    interests of the broad majority. The "Harmonious Society" was a socio-
    economic vision forged under Hu Jintao that advocated a shift in focus
    from economic growth to social balance and harmony. The "Scientific
    Outlook on Development" is a socio-economic ideology that is prioritizes
    the interests of the people and aims for sustainable modes of development.

1

1   Alessandro Russo, "How to Translate 'Cultural Revolution'," *Inter-Asia
    Cultural Studies*, vol. 7, no. 4.
2   See Carl Schmitt, "The Age of Neutralizations and Depoliticizations"
    [1929], *Telos*, Summer 1993, issue 96.
3   Louis Althusser, "Ideology and Ideological State Apparatuses (Notes
    Toward an Investigation)" in *Lenin and Philosophy and Other Essays*,
    trans. Ben Brewster, London 1971, p. 135.

2

1   According to sociological studies, the five major expressions of this "urban-rural divide" are: (1) gaps in political power, where rural populations are the recipients of complete government leadership in political, economic, cultural, and other aspects, and where the representatives of this government power—officials and implementers alike—are non-rural people; (2) gaps in economic position, where industrial and rural product prices are set according to a "scissors differential," in order to develop the accumulation of capital in industry while monopolizing economic resources and opportunities that limit the establishment and growth of rural industry; (3) gaps in income, where the difference between urban and rural incomes is between 3:1 and 6:1; (4) gaps in social benefits and services, where residents of cities and towns (state and collective-enterprise workers as well as state cadres) receive free medical care, are eligible for pensions, and receive stable amounts of grain, oil, and meat rations, while peasants receive none of these benefits and services; (5) gaps in social position, where city dwellers' social positions are far above those of rural people. See Wang Hansheng and Zhang Xinxiang, "Jiefang yilai Zhongguo de shehui cengci fenhua" ("Social Stratifications in China since Liberation"), *Shehuixue yanjiu* (*Research in Sociology*) 6, 1993; Li Qiang, "Dangdai Zhongguo shehui fenceng jiegou bianqian baogao" ("A Report on the Structures of Social Division in Contemporary China"), in Li Peilin, ed., *Zhongguo xinshiqi jieji jieceng baogao* (*A Report on Class and Status in China's New Era*), Shenyang: Liaoning Renmin Chubanshe, 1995, 65–7; and Zhang Wanli's summary and commentary, "Zhongguo shehui jieji jieceng yanjiu ershi nian" ("Twenty Years of Research on Social Class and Strata in China"), *Shehuixue yanjiu* 1, 2000: 26.

2   Lu Xueyi divides the rural population into eight strata. See "Congxin renshi nongmin wenti" ("Reconceptualizing the Peasant Problem"), *Shehuixue yanjiu* 6, 1999.

3   Zhang Wanli has divided this process into two components: the appearance of new groupings from outside the old structural system, and the great increase in the proportion of resources they commanded; the transformation in position of groupings from within the old structural system, and the incipient polarization among these groupings. See Zhang Wanli, "Twenty Years," 28–9.

4   Wang Shaoguang, "Jianli yige qiang youli de minzhu guojia—taolun 'zhengquan xingshi' yu 'guojia nengli' de qubie" ("Building a Powerful Democratic State—On 'Regime Type' and 'State Capacity'"), *Dangdai Zhongguo Yanjiu Zhongxin Lunwen* (*Essays from the Center for Research on Contemporary China*) 4, 1991: 15–17.

5   The conclusions reached by Wang Shaoguang are:

> The reform policy of decentralizing power and interests did not in any way reduce the power of public entities (governments of all levels and their organs) in the distribution of people's revenue; it merely reduced the power of the central government over this … Accompanying the expansion over the power of finance by local governments was their ability to use administrative means to interfere in economic life, which was not in any way weakened, but rather strengthened: moreover, this type of interference was even more direct than that of the central government. The decentralization of power and interests in no way led to the disappearance of the traditional command economy; it merely led to the miniaturization of this traditional structure. (Ibid. p. 20)

6   The gap in income was first expressed in a comparison between the income of individual entrepreneurs and that of state-owned-enterprise workers, where the latter lost in relation to the former. Zhao Renwei, "Zhongguo zhuanxingqi zhong shouru fenpei de yixie teshu xianxiang" ("Some Special Aspects in Income Distribution during China's Transition Period"), in Zhao, ed., *Zhongguo jumin shouru fenpei yanjiu* (*Research on Income Distribution among the Chinese People*), Beijing: Shehui Kexue Chubanshe, 1994. Internal polarization was first expressed in the increase in the gap between managers, technologists, and workers. Feng Tongqing et al., *Zhongguo zhigong zhuangkuang, neibu jiegou ji xianghu guanxi* (*The Situation of Chinese Laborers, Internal Structure, and Their Mutual Relationship*), Beijing: Zhongguo Shehui Chubanshe, 1993. Laborers with experience are not guaranteed labor time, labor security or labor bonuses; the weakest strata of laborers lack support for entry work. Zhang Wanli, "Twenty Years," 29–30.

7   Wu Jinglian has generally been seen as the main spokesperson for the coordination of price reform and industrial reform, while most also know of Li Yining's advocacy through the 1980s of divided stocks. In 1988 Wu Jinglian presided over the report on the middle period of reform planning. *Zhongguo gaige da silu* (*Major Outlines of China's Reform*), Shenyang: Shenyang

Chubanshe, 1988. For other related documents, see *Zhongguo jingji gaige zongti guihua ji* (*Collection on Overall Outline of China's Economic Reforms*), Zhongyang: Zhongyang Dangxiao Chubanshe, 1987; *Zhongguo jingji gaige de zhengti sheji* (*The Overall Design of China's Economic Reforms*), Beijing: Zhongguo Zhanwang Chubanshe, 1990; "Jiage gaige he tizhi zhuangui de chenggong baozheng" ("Guarantees for the Success of Price Reform and the Changed Path of the Economic System"), *Gaige zazhi* (*Journal of Reform*) 6, 1988.

8　　Guo Shuqing, *Jingji tizhi zhuangui yu hongguan tiaokong* (*Transformation in the Economic System and Macro Adjustments and Controls*), Tianjin: Renmin Chubanshe, 1992: 181.

9　　On the main goals of the policy of "consolidation of control" (*zhili zhengdun*), see "Zhonggong zhongyang guanyu jin yi bu zhili zhengdun he shenhua gaige de jueding" ("Chinese Communist Party Central Committee Decision on the Continuation of Consolidation and Control and the Deepening of Reform") (published on November 9, 1988), in *Zhongguo jinrong nianbiao 1990* (*Yearbook of Chinese Banking and Finance 1990*), Beijing: Zhongguo Jihua Chubanshe, 1989.

10　　Hu Heyuan, "1988 nian Zhongguo zujin jiazhi de gusuan" ("An Estimate of the Value of Rent in China in 1988"), *Jingji tizhi bijiao* (*Comparative Economic Systems*) 7, 1989.

11　　On the changes in the cadre stratum before and after the reforms, see Li Qiang, *Dangdai Zhongguo shehui fenceng yu liudong* (*Stratification and Movement in Contemporary Chinese Society*), Beijing: Zhongguo Jingji Chubanshe, 1993.

12　　Of the people who played important roles during the historical period generally labeled "the new era" (1978–88), the majority were older intellectuals (including economists, political scientists, philosophers, historians, and literary critics) who were university and research institute leaders. For example, some of the disputes among economists had their origins in intrastate policy debates. In this era, the labels of "left" and "right" in the intellectual arena actually arose from intrastate debates and factions. Because of the importance of their positions, the "left"/"right" splits among them were often mistaken for "left"/"right" splits among intellectuals in general. Even these days, some people use the model of intra-party struggles to understand China's social polarization in terms of "left" and "right."

13　　The political system established by the Chinese government and the party after 1949 was the premise of its own legitimacy; for this reason, people are accustomed to viewing the relationship between the Maoist and Dengist eras in terms of continuities. The dual legitimacy of the organs of state ideology and of the party-state (the Marxist party-state and the party-state that promotes market-based economic reform) lends the critique of the state some confused characteristics: in the name of opposing the old system, it often launches a critique of current state policies. As for 1989, the use of the slogans of opposition to "official malfeasance," "corruption," and "princeling parties" to mobilize a critical movement cannot simply be incorporated into or understood through a critique of the traditional socialist state, for it was a critique of the reform-state; or, more accurately, it was a critique of both.

14 For example, after the signing of the Sino-US WTO treaty, practically all the media reported it in exactly the same way. However, regular people—and even intellectuals—had not a clue about the content of this treaty, so what was it that they were rejoicing about? In the absence of market and development ideology, it would be impossible to understand this phenomenon. After 1989, we can say that state ideology includes marketism and developmentalism, along with some traditional aspects of socialist ideology. The latter factor no longer has any persuasive power, and has become mere propagandistic puppetry.

15 See the sobering summaries of income differentials carried out by the "income distribution" group for economic research at the Chinese Academy of Social Sciences. Zhao Renwei et al., *Zhongguo jumin shouru fenpei yanjiu* (*Research on Income Distribution in China*), Beijing: Zhongguo Shehui Kexue Chubanshe, 1994). In addition, Zhang Yuanli's "Zhongguo shehui jieji jieceng yanjiu ershi nian" ("Twenty Years of Research on Chinese Social Classes and Strata") has a summary of these figures; see *Shehuixue yanjiu* (*Sociology Research*) 1, 2000: 36.

16 Strong on both the ideological and economic fronts.

17 Lu Mai, "Shizhong bu neng wangji nongcun de fazhan" ("We Should Never Forget Rural Development"); also see Luo Suping's interview in *Sanlian shenghuo zhoukan* (*Sanlian Life Weekly*), July 31, 1998: 26.

18 In the last few years, more and more scholars have paid attention to the problems of "urbanization" and "de-ruralization"; one reason for this is that the economic downturn has turned the surplus of rural labor power into a huge social problem. Fei Xiaotong's 1980s discussion of "the big problem of small townships" is being replaced by discussions of urbanization. See Wang Ying, "Chengshi fazhan yanjiu de huigu yu qianzhan" ("A Review of Urban Development and Its Precursors"), *Shehuixue yanjiu* 1 (2000): 65–75.

19 Lu Xueyi, "Zouchu 'chengxian fenzhi, yi guo liang ci' de kunjing" ("Getting Out of 'Diverging Rule for Urban and Rural Areas under the System of One Country, Two Policies'"), *Dushu (Readings)* 5, 2000: 3–9.

20 China's rural reforms and its crises had not been noticed much by economists and reform implementers; but in the aftermath of the 1997 financial crisis, when the rate of China's economic growth slowed and deflationary pressures emerged, the rural crisis began to receive wider attention. However, a good proportion of those who do study the rural question do so from the perspective of stimulating economic growth, and begin from the perspective of solving the economic pressures on urban areas; they do not study the question from the perspective of peasants' right to freedom, or of equitable social relations. In other words, the freedom of peasant labor contracts and social equity taken seriously merely as aspects of investigations into obstacles to economic growth.

21 In September 1988, Yu Yingshih gave a talk at Hong Kong University entitled "Zhongguo jindai sixiang shi zhong de jijin yu baoshou" ("Radicalism and Conservativism in Modern Chinese Thought"). His thesis became an important point of departure for the subsequent debate on radicalism and conservatism. Another influential essay was Gan Yang, "Yangqi 'minzhu yu kexue,' dianding 'ziyou' yu 'zhixu'" ("Sublating 'Democracy and Science,' Establishing 'Freedom' and 'Order'"), *Ershiyi shiji (Twenty-First Century)* 3, 1991: 7–10. The main early-1990s discussions on radicalism can be found in the following essays, in the identified issues of *Ershiyi shiji*: Lin Gang, "Jijin zhuyi zai Zhongguo" ("Radicalism in China"), 3 1991: 17–27; Yu Yingshih, "Zhongguo zhishifenzi de bianyuanhua" ("The Marginalization of Chinese Intellectuals"), 6, 1991: 15–25; Jiang Yihua, "Jijin yu baoshou: yu Yu Yingshi shangque" ("Radicalism and Conservatism: A Discussion with Mr. Yu Yingshih"), 10, 1992: 134–42; Yu Yingshih, "Zilun Zhongguo jindai sixiang shi zhong de jijin yu baoshou: da Jiang Yihua xiansheng" ("Another Discussion of Radicalism and Conservatism in Modern Chinese Intellectual History: A Reply to Mr. Jiang Yihua"), 10, 1992: 143–9; Wang Rongzu, "Jijin yu baoshou zhuyan" ("Superfluous Words on Radicalism and Conservatism"), 11, 1992: 133–6; Xu Jilin, "Jijin yu baoshou de mihuo" ("Radical and Conservative Puzzles"), 11, 1992: 137–40; Li Liangyu, "Jijin, baoshou yu zhishifenzi de zeren" ("Radicalism, Conservatism, and the Responsibility of Intellectuals"),

12, 1992: 132–4; Wang Shaoguang, "'Baoshou' yu 'baoshou zhuyi'" ("'Conservatives' and 'Conservatism'"), 12, 1992: 135–8; Hu Cheng, "Jijin zhuyi yihuo baoli zhuyi?" ("Radicalism or an Ideology of Violence?"), 13, 1992: 139–45; and Liu Shuxian, "Duiyu jijin zhuyi de fansi" ("Thinking about Radicalism"), 31, 1995: 40–2.

22 Cited from Wang Yan's 1998 speech given at the conference to commemorate the hundredth anniversary of the *wuxu* reform period cosponsored by *Dushu* and Tian Ze's *Economic Research*. The traditional emphasis in *wuxu* reform studies centers on Kang, Liang, and the reformists; comparatively few studies pay attention to local reforms or to the changes in relations between the center and localities. For this reason, it is entirely necessary to pay attention to the significance of changes at the local level to the Qing Dynasty's social reforms. Such studies undertaken in the 1990s were not by any means limited to the *wuxu* reforms, but rather were informed by a much broader political view.

23 See the various essays by Liu Junning included in *Report on China's Reforms*, published in 1998 by the Institutional Reform Group of the State Council.

24 Even as the three markets identified here were opened, the financial system was not completely opened, and rural society was not systemically altered. For this reason, social polarization did not immediately lead to large-scale social unrest and conflict. This partly explains why China was able to ride out the 1997 financial crisis (which nevertheless exposed the serious crisis in China's financial system). The issue here is not opposition to opening markets or the promotion of state protectionism; rather, the question is how to open markets and under which conditions, to what extent state regulation is required, and how to formulate democratic structures under open-market conditions. The decentralization of power and interests could lead to the loss of the state's ability to regulate, which would lead to the decline of the fundamental conditions for a system of social benefits. If there is insufficient tax revenue, the state not only has no way to regulate the market efficiently—it also has no possibility of inventing new forms of social guarantees in the context of the complete undermining of the older systems of social guarantees. This would also make it impossible for any re-establishment of the system of social guarantees to become the basis for reforming the state-owned industrial sector (since one of the major obstacles to the reform of state-owned industries is the social burdens shouldered by them).

25 In 1991 the inaugural issue of *Xueren* (*The Scholar*) announced the beginning of this process of reconsideration and research. Its appearance represented the aspirations of a group of young scholars to undertake scholarly work and to maintain a serious and strict attitude toward scholarly inquiry. Arriving upon the heels of social crisis, the debates of the late 1990s were re-engaged; yet there was still a significant group of intellectuals who, though they remained concerned with social questions, refused to have their personal research linked to a response to any actually existing social situation. In my view, it will be a long time before the significance of the existence of this tiny group is completely understood. (I do not mean here to assimilate this type of research into the category of "conservatism.")

26 The issue does not end here, for we must then ask the following questions. First, if the student movement and its intellectuals were unable to propose clear reform goals and to adopt the basic motivations from which this spontaneous and broad-based social movement derived, then exactly what type of intellectual forces and/or ideological predispositions constrained them from doing so? Second, if there was no resonance between, on the one hand, the student movement and its demands for democracy and, on the other, the internal contradictions within the 1980s reform process, and if there was no way to establish an internal link between, on the one hand, the broad-based social movement along with its demands and, on the other, the immediate goals of the movement, then what could have been the motivating force behind the student movement itself? In the process of writing and thinking, I began to discover that not only were the internal limitations of the intellectual liberation movement of the 1980s directly linked to the failure of the movement, but also that these limitations explain the intellectual reasons behind the lack of any critique on the part of 1990s Chinese intellectuals of—and the inability to fashion a creative response to—market expansion, systemic monopolization, and the process of globalization.

27 Samuel Huntington, "Wenming de congtu?" ("The Clash of Civilizations?"), *Ershiyi shiji* 19, 1993: 5–21. Also, in the same issue: Jin Guantao, "Xifang zhongxinlun de pomie: ping quanqiuhua de chongtu lun" ("The Destruction of Eurocentrism: A Critique of the Theory of Global Culture Clash"): 22–5; Liu Xiaofeng, "Liyi zhongyu wenhua" ("Interest Trumps Culture"): 26–7; Chen Fangzheng, "Lun Zhongguo minzuzhuyi yu shijie yishi" ("On Chinese Nationalism and Cosmopolitanism"): 28–35.

28 Translator's note: The English version of this essay can be found in *Social Text*, 55, 1998, trans. Rebecca E. Karl; it is reprinted in Xudong Zhang,

ed., *Whither China? Intellectual Politics in Contemporary China*, Durham, NC: Duke University Press, 2001.

29   Mostly found in *Chinese Social Sciences Quarterly* (*Zhongguo shehui kexue jikan*) and related journals. See related discussion and analysis in Wang Hui, "Dangdai Zhongguo de sixiang zhuangkuang yu xiandaixing wenti" ("Contemporary China's Intellectuals and the Question of Modernity"), *Tianya* (*Horizons*) 5, 1997.

30   It is hard to believe that there was not a certain amount of silent complicity and indulgence here on the part of the central state for the privatizations carried out by local governments and interest groups to enable them to proceed to such an extraordinary point, since these systemic privatization activities seriously harmed the domestic market—particularly the transformation of state-owned industries, which indirectly destroyed the broader interests of the working class.

31   In this sense, it is important to place the relationship between the central state, local elites, and the broad masses of people, and the possibility of their dynamic interaction in a "mixed constitution" and "mixed system," at the center of any consideration of democracy. In his September 1996 essay published in *Dushu* 9 titled "'Eryuan lianbang zhuyi' de xiaowang" ("The Destruction of 'Dual Federalism'"), and in his essay published in *Zhanlue yu guanli* (*Strategies and Management*) 3, 1998, titled "'Hunhe xianfa' yu dui Zhongguo zhengzhi de sanceng fenxi" ("'Mixed Constitution' and a Tripartite Analysis of Chinese Politics"), Cui Zhiyuan mapped out, from a political analysis of superstructures, a type of mixed constitution and system, and built a conscientiously circular dynamic tripartite system with a "top" (the central state), "middle" (local governments and big capitalists), and "bottom" (regular citizens). He emphasized how to turn mass demands into state will, thereby forestalling a new aristocratic system. This political ideal was the exact counterpart to civil society. Of course, this is not a radical ideal; however, if we locate this suggestion in the context of the social stratification of Chinese society since 1989, it clearly has an active critical significance.

32   See the related explorations of this topic in the essays by Charles Taylor, "Gongmin yu guojia zhijian de juli" ("The Distance between the Citizen and the State"), and by Wang Hui, "Daolun 'wenhua yu gonggongxing'" (*Discussing 'Culture and the Public'*), in Wang Hui and Chen Yangu, eds., *Wenhua yu gonggongxing* (*Culture and the Public*), Beijing: Sanlian Shudian, 1998: 199–220, 38–47.

33 Gan Yang, "Xiangtu Zhongguo congjian yu Zhongguo wenhua qianjing" ("Reconstructing Rural China and the Future of Chinese Culture"), *Ershiyi shiji* 16, 1993: 4; Gan Yang, "Fan minzhu de ziyou zhuyi haishi minzhu de ziyou zhuyi?" ("Antidemocratic Liberalism or Democratic Liberalism?"), *Ershiyi shiji* 39, 1997: 4–17; Cui Zhiyuan, "Zhidu chuangxin yu dierci sixiang jiefang" ("Systemic Innovation and the Second Liberation of Thought"), *Ershiyi shiji* 24, 1994: 5–16; Wang Shaoguang, "Xiaolu, gongping, minzhu" ("Efficiency, Equality, Democracy"), *Ershiyi shiji* 26, 1994: 21–33; Qin Hui, "Li tu bu li xiang? Ye tan xiangtu Zhongguo congjian wenti" ("Leaving the Soil But Not the Village? Continuing the Discussion of Reconstructing Rural China"), *Dongfang* 1, 1994; Su Wen, "Shan zhong shui fu ying you lu" ("In the Weight of Mountains and Flow of Streams There Should Be a Path"), *Dongfang* 1, 1996. The theories and perspectives of Qin Hui and Cui Zhiyuan are very different; nevertheless, both pay attention to the importance of the extension of considerations of justice and equality into Chinese social life and the economy.

34 The problem of "state capacity" was first raised in 1991—see Wang Shaoguang, "Building a Powerful Democratic State." See also Wang Shaoguang and Hu Angang, "Zhongguo zhengfu jiqu nengli de xiajiang ji qi houguo" ("The Decline in the Derivative Capacity of the Chinese Government and Its Consequences"), *Ershiyi shiji* 21, 1994: 5–14; Cui Zhiyuan, "'Guojia nengli' bianzheng guan" ("On the Dialectics of 'State Capacity'"), *Ershiyi shiji* 21: 19–21. The 1990s discussions on the Chinese economy and Southeast Asia also touched on the issue: see Zhang Shuguang, "Jingji zengzhang he guojia xingshuai" ("Economic Growth and the Rise and Fall of the State"), *Dushu* 9 (1996); in his critical review of Lin Yifu and foreign economic theory, Zhang referred to the problem of the relationship between the state and special interest factions.

35 Wang Jing, "'Guojia' san yi" ("Three Meanings of 'State'"), *Dushu* 4, 2000. (When this essay was published it was abridged; I read the complete manuscript.) The most comprehensive exposition of this topic is that of Chu Wanwen, who clearly notes that, in the context of globalization,

> in order for late-developing countries to catch up to already developed countries, they must, based on the nation-state unit, use production policies and tools to draw up strategies for developing production; use subsidies and bonuses to assist nascent industries and support domestic enterprises; and quickly learn technology from the advanced countries. Only in this

way will it be possible in the contexts of daily increasing competition and the widening gap between advanced and late-developing countries, not only to avoid being wiped out in the global marketplace but also, as the hierarchy of the international division of labor gradually becomes more widespread, to transform and raise the relative national interests. Only in this way, then, will it be possible for the economy to continue to grow and for productivity to continue to progress.

Chu Wanwen, "Quanchouhua yu houjinguo zhi jingji fazhan" ("Globalization and Development Strategy in Less-Developed Countries"), *Taiwan shehui yanjiu jikan* (*Journal of Research on Taiwanese Society*) 37, 2000: 91–117.

36 Roberto Unger and Cui Zhiyuan, "Yi E wei jin kan Zhongguo" ("A Close Look at China through the Lens of Russia"), *Ershiyi shiji* 24 (1994): 17–25. For explorations of the Chinese reformist path, it is also possible to consult later essays, such as Lin Chun's "Shehui zhuyi yu xiaomie pinkun" ("Socialism and the Eradication of Poverty"), *Dushu* 9, 1999, and "Jiaotiao yanjiu yu zhidu chuangxin" ("Dogmatic Research and Systemic Innovation"), *Dushu* 11, 1999.

37 Wang Hui, "Dangdai Zhongguo de sixiang zhuangkuang yu xiandaixing wenti" ("Contemporary Chinese Intellectuals and the Question of Modernity"), *Tianya* (*Horizons*) 5, 1997; P. Anderson, "Wenming ji qi neihan" ("Civilization and Its Connotations"), *Dushu* 11–12, 1997; Chen Yangu, "Lishi zongjie haishi quanmian minzhu?" ("The End of History, or Complete Democracy?"), *Dushu* 12, 1998.

38 *Jindai* denotes the period from the 1840 Opium War to the birth of the May Fourth movement in 1919, and *xiandai* denotes the period from 1919 to the establishment of the PRC in 1949.

39 For example, He Qinglian's *Xiandaihua de xianjing* (*Modernization's Abyss*), Beijing: Jinri Zhongguo Chubanshe, 1998; and Qin Hui's numerous essays. See also He Qinglian, "Jingjixue lilun he 'tulong shu'" ("Economic Theory and 'The Strategy of Killing the Dragon'"), *Dushu* 3, 1997; "Jinrong weiji tiaozhan jingji qiyi" ("On the Strange Tracks of the Challenge Posed by the Financial Crisis to the Economy"), *Dushu* 12, 1997; "'Shizhe shengcun' yu 'youxian jieji'" ("'Survival of the Fittest' and the 'Leisure Classes'"), *Dushu* 10, 1998; Bian Wu (Qin Hui), "Jujue yuanshi jilei" ("Repudiate Primitive Accumulation"), *Dushu* 1, 1998; "Youle zhen wenti cai you zhen xuewen" ("Only with Real Questions Is There True Scholarship"), *Dushu* 6, 1998.

40 On the discussions of liberalism within conservatism, see Liu Junning, "Dang minzhu fang'ai ziyou de shihou" ("When Democracy Hinders Freedom"), *Dushu* 11, 1993; "Baoshou de Boke ziyou de Boke" ("The Burke of Conservatives' Burkean Freedom"), *Dushu* 3, 1995; "Wu wang wo" ("Don't Forget Me"), *Dushu* 11, 1995; "Shan'e: Liangzhong zhengzhiguan yu guojia nengli" ("Good and Evil: Two Types of Vision of the State and State Capacity"), *Dushu* 5, 1994, etc. In the latter half of the 1990s, Xiao Gongqin, one of the main voices of neo-authoritarianism, publicly declared that his views were close to those of contemporary China's "liberals," that China's greatest threat was embodied in "new leftism," and so on. With the commodification of power, and with reference to China's concrete situation, it is truly a grand discovery that democracy "obstructs" freedom, although the author never pauses to ask: Whose freedom? Which democracy?

41 Gan Yang, "Fanminzhu de ziyou zhuyi haishi minzhu de ziyou zhuyi?" ("Antidemocratic Liberalism or Democratic Liberalism?"), *Ershiyi shiji* 39, 1997: 4–17; Gan Yang, "Bolin yu hou ziyou zhuyi" ("Berlin and Post-liberalism"), *Dushu* 4, 1998, and "Ziyou zhuyi: guizu de haishi pingmin de?" ("Liberalism: Aristocratic or Popular?"), *Dushu* 1, 1999; Wang Hui, "Wenhua yu gonggongxing daolun" ("On Culture and the Public"); Qian Yongxian, "Wo zongshi huo zai biaoceng shang" ("I Am All the While Living on the Surface"), *Dushu* 4, 1999; Kang Chao, "Duwei dui ziyou zhuyi de pipan yu chongjian" ("Dewey's Critique and Reconstruction of Liberalism"), *Xueshu sixiang pinglun* (*A Critical Review of Academic Thought*) 3, Shenyang: Liaoning Daxue Chubanshe, 1998; Luo Yongsheng, "Jingjixue hai shi ziyou zhuyi?" ("Economics or Liberalism?"), *Dushu* 9, 1998; Wang Junren, "Quanchouhua de ling yimian" ("The Other Side of Globalization"), *Dushu* 1, 2000. Hayek became a fashionable topic in the 1990s; however, neoliberals seem never to have paused to consider the contradictions between their advocacy of radical marketization and Hayek's historicized attitude, nor the internal contradictions between their conservative political stance—combined with their radical plans for a free market—and Hayek's critique of "planning." In this sense, my critique of neoliberalism is not a simple rejection of further investigations into liberal theory; on the contrary, the more systematic and profound our explorations into these theories, the more possible it might be to expose definitive weaknesses in neoliberal theory.

42 Fan Gang, "'Bu daode' de jingjixue" ("'Immoral' Economics"), *Dushu* 6, 1998; Zhang Shuguang, "Piping guizi, jiaowang lixing, he ziyou jingshen"

("Critical Guides, Communicative Rationality, and the Liberal Spirit"), parts 1 and 2, *Dushu* 10, 1999, and 3, 2000.

43 Wallerstein, "Jintui liangnan de shehui kexue" ("The Two Difficulties of an Advancing and Retreating Social Science"), *Dushu* 2–3, 1998; Xu Baoqiang, "Weizhong zhi ji" ("Opportunity amid Crisis"), *Dushu* 4, 1998; B. Anderson, "'Qiji' beihou de youling" ("The Spirit behind 'Miracles'"), *Dushu* 8–9, 1998; Wang Hui, "Kexue zhuyi yu shehui lilun de jige wenti" ("Some Questions about Scientism and Social Theory"), *Tianya* 6, 1998; Lu Di, "Dongyajingnian yu lishi ziben zhuyi" ("The East Asian Experience and Historical Capitalism"), *Dushu* 9, 1998; Han Yuhai, "Zai 'ziyou zhuyi' zitai de beihou" ("Behind Liberalism's Posturing"), *Tianya* 9, 1998; Lu Di, "Chongdu Sun Yefang's *Diguo zhuyi lun*" ("Rereading Sun Yefang's *On Imperialism*"), *Dushu* 6, 1999.

44 On November 16, 1999, China and the United States came to agreement on the provisions for China's entry into the WTO; on that day, *Duowei xinwen* (*Multidimensional News*) published Liu Junning's "Zhongguo jiaru WTO de zhengzhi yiyi" ("The Political Significance of China's Entry into the WTO"), which expressed support for the agreement. In addition, the *Financial Times* published a report titled "China to Enter WTO after Signing US Deal," by James Kynge and Mark Suzman, in which they cited a Chinese scholar who said that this was the second big phase of China's post-1978 opening policies. The next day, the *Washington Post* published a report by John Pomfret and Michael Laris titled "WTO Deal Welcomed by China's Reformers"; it cited the enthusiasm for the WTO deal shown by Wang Shan, Li Ke, Mao Yushi, Xu Youyu, and others, who maintained that the deal would be beneficial to China's democracy and legal system. There is absolutely no difference between these views and those of the state and its media, and they were all enthusiastically welcomed by the United States media. On this type of issue, moreover, there is no way to differentiate between "economic liberalism" and "humanistic liberalism."

45 Cui Zhiyuan, "Zhongguo jiaru shijie maoyi zuzhi de wojian" ("My Views on China's Entry into Global Trade Organizations"), *Lianhe zaobao* (*United Morning News*), July 4, 1999; Wen Tiejun, "'Sannong wenti': Shijimo de fansi" ("'The Three Rural Issues': Reflections at the End of the Century"), *Dushu* 12, 1999. *Guoji jingji pinglun* (*A Critical Review of International Economy*) published a special issue (issue 7–8, 1999) on "WTO and China," which discussed the concrete conditions surrounding China's entry into the WTO. Essays included Song Hong, "Gongye youshi, bijiao youshi, he jingzheng youshi: Zhongguo jiaru shijie maoyi zuzhi de shouyi yu daijia" ("Industrial

Advantage, Comparative Advantage, and Competitive Advantage: The Benefits and Costs of China's Entry into Global Trade Organizations"); Sun Zengyuan, "Jiaru shijie maoyi zuzhi de Zhongguo nongye ji duici sikao" ("Considerations on China's Agricultural Industry and Its Policies after Entry into Global Trade Organizations"); Wang Songqi, "Jiaru shijie maoyi zuzhi hui yingxiang Zhongguo de jinrong anchuan ma?" ("Will Entry into Global Trade Organizations Impact China's Financial Security?"); He Liping, "Yinhangye de jingzheng zhuyao shifei jiage jingzheng: Jiaru shijie maoyi zuzhi yu wanshan Zhongguo yinghang jigou de zhifu fuwu tixi" ("Is Bank Competition Primarily Price Competition? Entry into Global Trade Organizations and the Perfection of the Payment Services Sector of China's Banking System"); Zhang Yansheng, "Zhongguo ying ruhu zoujin shijie maoyi zuzhi" ("On How China Should Join Global Trade Organizations"); Wang Xiaoya and Xu Guoping, "Jinru shijie maoyi zuzhi dui Zhongguo yinhangye de yingxiang" ("The Impact on China's Banking System of Entry into Global Trade Organizations").

46 Wang Hui, "Xiandaixing wenti dawen" ("Answers to Questions on Modernity"), *Tianya* 1, 1999; Xu Baoqiang, "Zhishi, quanli, yu 'xiandaixing' fazhan lunshu" ("On Knowledge, Power, and the Development of 'Modernity'"), *Dushu* 2, 1999; Xu Baoqiang, "Fazhan zhuyi de misi" ("The Mystificatory Idea of Developmentalism"), *Dushu* 7, 1999; Huang Ping, "'Fazhan zhuyi' de biji" ("Notes on 'Developmentalism'"), *Tianya* 1, 2000. In the latter half of October 1999, an international scholarly conference on "Ecology and Literature" was held in Hainan Province, sponsored by the Hainan Provincial Writers' Association and the Hainan Province subsidiary of Southern Airlines. In the course of the conference, some of its participants held a roundtable on the problems of the environment, ecology, and development. In its first issue of 2000, *Tianya* published edited excerpts from the records of this roundtable under the title "Nanshan jiyao" ("Recorded Notes from the Southern Mountain"), which provided a systematic critique of developmentalism from the perspective of ecology. Participants included Huang Ping, Li Tuo, Chen Yangu, Dai Jinhua, Wang Xiaoming, Chen Sihe, Nan Fan, Wang Hongsheng, Geng Zhanxiang, and Han Shaogong, among others. It is included in *positions*, 12:1 (Spring 2004).

47 The expansion of public social space is not necessarily directly expressed in an advocacy of freedom of speech; rather, it is a demand that active discussion be fostered around every important arena and every sort of social problem. In this sense, with years of effort, discussions have

succeeded in incorporating many aspects of social problems and have opened a certain discursive space under very challenging conditions. There is a tendency in much intellectual discussion to blame external conditions for the limits placed on the capacity for thought (I am by no means denying here that external conditions are important); however, in my opinion, this is in reality merely an abdication of responsibility. For a direct discussion of freedom of speech and the problem of news, see Lu Xinyu, "Dangdai Zhongguo de dianshi jilupian yundong" ("The Contemporary Chinese TV Documentary Movement"), *Dushu* 5, 1999; Lin Xudong and Chen Meng, "'Shenghuo kongjian': Yizhong jilu/meiti shijian" ("'Life Space': A Sort of Record/Media Experience"), *Dushu* 5, 1999; Bu Wei, "V-Chip yu Meiguo de yanlun ziyou" ("The V-Chip and American Freedom of Speech"), *Dushu* 5, 1999; Wang Huazhi, "Meiti yu jinri zhi xianshi" ("The Media and Today's Reality"), *Dushu* 8, 1999.

48   Chen Yangu, "Chao diguo zhuyi shidai de shengzhan" ("Holy War in the Era of Hyper-Imperialism"), *Tianya* 4, 1999; Yue Gang, "Jiegou Kesewo" ("Deconstructing Kosovo"), *Dushu* 11, 1999; Zhang Rulun, "Habeimasi he diguo zhuyi" ("Habermas and Imperialism"), *Dushu* 9, 1999; Wang Xi, "Minzhu de feiminzhuhua" ("The De-Democratization of Democracy"), *Dushu* 10, 1999.

49   Cui Zhiyuan, "Minzhu zijuequan, renquan, yu zhuquan" ("The Right to National Self-Determination, Human Rights, and Sovereignty"), *Dushu* 8, 1999.

50   Many scholars are now taking on the question of nationalism and its relationship to internationalism, gender, and Asia in important ways. On nationalism and internationalism, see Wang Hui, *Sihuo chongwen: Zi xu* (*To Rekindle a Dead Flame: Preface*), Beijing: Renmin Wenxue Chubanshe, 2000; Han Shaogong, "Guojing de jeibian he neibian" ("On This or That Side of National Boundaries"), *Tianya* 6 (1999). On gender, see Xia Shaohong, "Cong fumu zhuanhun dao fumu zhuhun" ("From Parent-Arranged Marriage to Parent-Initiated Marriage"), *Dushu* 1, 1999; and, in *Dushu*'s third issue of 1999 (devoted to "feminism and nationalism"), see Liu Jianzhi, "Kongju, baoli, guojia, nuren" ("Terror, Violence, the State, and Women"); Dai Jinhua, "Jianzheng yu jianzhengren" ("Witnessing and Witnesses"); Chen Shunxin, "Qiangbao, zhanzheng yu minzu zhuyi" ("Rape, War, and Nationalism"); and Sun Ge, "Lixiangjia de huanghun" ("The Jaundiced Spirit of an Idealist"). On Asia, see Sun Ge, "Yazhou yiweizhe shenma?" ("What does Asia mean?"); and "Xueshu sixiang pinglun" ("A Critical Review of Academic Thought"), both in *Xueshu sixiang pinglun* (*Review of Academic Thought*), 5, Shonyang:

Liaoning Daxue Chubanshe, 1999; Paek Young Suh, "Shiji zhi jiao zaisi Dongya" ("Rethinking East Asia at the Turn of the Century"), 8, 1999; Kojima Kiyoshi, "Sikao de qianti" ("Premises of Thinking"), 3, 2000; Mizoguchi Yuz, "'Zhanzheng yu geming' zhi yu ribenren" ("'War and Revolutionaries' and the Japanese"), 3, 2000; Choi Won-Sik, "Disanzhong da'an" ("The Third Case"), *Tianya* 3 (1999); Kuang Xinnian, "Zai Yazhou de tiankongxia sikao" ("Thinking under the Asian Heavens"), *Tianya* 3 (1999).

51 Social contradictions and crises have forced people to notice actual social questions, while also leading many theorists to participate directly in society and in intellectual debate. This process is well coordinated with the current trend toward media commodification, which could just as easily lead to the exclusion of theoretical work itself. However, the more urgent social issues become, the more urgent it is to conduct theoretical investigations in as wide a perspective and scope as possible, so as to reconstruct our perspectives on history and current reality. If there is no serious dialogue and research at the level of theory, then it will be impossible to come to any deeper an engagement with current reality. For scholars, the hot topic of freedom of thought must be located within the seriousness of theoretical work itself. In this sense, we must reject both wishy-washy condemnations of theoretical work and those who claim that the urgency of current problems overrides the necessity for any theoretical innovation at all.

3

1 Available at <www.hartford-hwp.com/archives/25/116.html>.

4

1 The Neo-Confucianism of Cheng Yi, Cheng Hao and Zhu Xi.
2 A Chinese system of land-distribution in which square fields are divided into nine blocks with the center block being communal and the surrounding blocks private. The entire field is aristocrat-owned, but the yield from the private fields belong entirely to the family farming the block, with only the yield from the communal block (that all eight farming families work on) going to the aristocrat. This system dates to the ninth century, though it is debatable whether it ever existed at all.
3 Nickname of Hu Han, sometimes known as Hu Shi.

4   Five state rites performed in ancient times, which include ancestral worship rites; royal wedding and other congratulatory rites; military rites; rites regarding foreign envoys; and funeral rites.

5   The character for *li* in *tianli* is identical to that for *li* ("reason"); *tian* implies heaven or nature.

6   The *li* of *libeng* being "rites" and the *yue* of *yuehuai* being music. *Li* and *yue* together are the *liyue* mentioned above, and translated as "rites and music."

7   A school of Neo-Confucianism commonly associated with Wang Anshi (1021–86).

8   A Chinese system of land distribution in which all land was government-owned and assigned to individual families. It was introduced around 485 AD and fell into disuse during the mid-eighth century.

9   Chen Yingque has also done a lot of research on the General Officer (*jiangguan*) and Fubing military systems.

10 The *tusi* system was a political and administrative system under which leaders and chiefs in regions incorporated into China were allowed to maintain their status and hereditary rights.

11 The leading school of New Text Confucianism Studies. "New text Confucianism" consists of oral traditions offering different interpretations of Confucius's *Spring and Autumn Annals*. The Gongyang Commentary was recorded during the Han Dynasty (206 BCE–220 CE).

12 "Preface for the Revised Zhuang Lineage Genealogy," in *Jiapu yu difang wenhua* (*Genealogies and Local Culture*), edited by Zhu Bingguo, Beijing: Zhongguo wenhui chubanshe, 2007, pp. 11-19.

5

1   Whether the truth of fact and the truth of value can be distinguished clearly is another question that needs further exploration. The generalization of this dichotomy is closely related to the development of modern Western thought.

2   The Foreign Affairs Movement (*yangwu yundong*, dating to the late Qing and meant to strengthen the empire's internal and external power through Western techniques) led to the establishment of a few Westernized schools. Centered on military business, they were excluded from the civil exam system. In other words, despite the fact that the Qing government had been exposed to Western scientific, technological, and military knowledge during a crisis, the distinction between *ti* ("substance") and *yong* ("function") was further consolidated through the educational system. During the reform movement

of 1898, a Guizhou official, Yan Xiu, suggested to Emperor Guangxu that a special civil exam be designed to include economics, in addition to the regular subjects on the *bagu* ("eight-legged essays") examination. Furthermore, those who were good at domestic affairs, foreign affairs, finance, military affairs, and engineering, regardless of whether or not they had any official positions, should be recommended by higher officials according to the same routine established for *bo xue hong* poems. All recommended persons should be able to take the exam and experience the same treatment as the regular scholars after being enrolled. He also suggested that this kind of exam should be held immediately, and "held every ten years or twenty years by order of the emperor," but that it should not replace the regular exam. Guangxu accepted this suggestion in February 1898, but was unable to carry it out due to failure of the reform. See *Qing dezong shilu* (*Records of Qing Dezong*), vol. 414: 4–5; quoted from *Wuxu bianfa* (*Wuxu reform*), vol. 2 ("Shenzhou guoguang she"): 9.

3   On the relation between local dialects, the modern language movement, and nationalism, see my article, "Local Forms, Dialects, and the Debate on National Form During the Anti-Japanese War" (in Chinese), in *Xueren* (*The Scholar*), vol. 10, Nanjing: Jiangsu Weyi Chubanshe, 1999: 271–312.

4   Foucault argues that there is no human being in classical knowledge. What actually exists in the place where we find human beings is the discursive or verbal power that can represent the order of things. This acute observation is very inspiring. See David Macey, *The Lives of Michel Foucault*, London: Hutchinson, 1993: 170.

5   In the late Qing period, the introduction of categories such as community, society, and state led to the redefinition of people—people as national subject. In the 1930s, the understanding of people came to be associated with the concept of class. If the design of the modern system and the understanding of people are closely related, then the moral base of the modern revolution was based upon the reconstruction of the people.

6   Alexandre Koyre, *From the Closed World to the Infinite Universe*, Baltimore, MD: Johns Hopkins University Press, 1957: 276.

7   Hannah Arendt, *The Human Condition: A Study of the Central Dilemmas Facing Modern Man*, Garden City, NJ, and New York: Doubleday Anchor Books, 1959: 38–9.

8   Michel Foucault, *Discipline and Punish: The Birth of the Prison*, trans. Alan Sheridan, New York: Vintage Books, 1977: 194.

9   Zhang Taiyan, "Guixin shiji" ("To regulate the new century"), *Minbao*, 24.

7

1 Unless otherwise indicated, all references to Lu Xun's works are taken from *Selected Works of Lu Hsun*, vols. 1–4, trans. Yang Hsien-Yi and Gladys Yang, Peking: Foreign Languages Press, 1956–1960, and are cited parenthetically by title.

2 Lu Xun, "Such a Fighter" (in Chinese), in *Lu Xun Quan Ji (Complete Works of Lu Xun)*, Beijing: Renmin Wenxue Chubanshe, 1982, vol. 2: 215.

3 Lu Xun, "Preface to Hot Wind" (in Chinese), in *Lu Xun Quan Ji*, vol. 1: 292.

4 Lu Xun, "Preface for Ye Yongzhen's *Only Ten Years*" (in Chinese), in *Lu Xun Quan Ji*, vol. 4: 146–7.

5 M. Bakhtin, *Rabelais and His World*, trans. Helene Iswolsky, Cambridge, MA: MIT Press, 1968: 11.

6 Ysi-an Hsia, *The Gate of Darkness: Studies on the Leftist Literary Movement in China*, Seattle: University of Washington Press, 1968.

7 Takeuchi Yoshimi, *Lu Xun*, ed. and trans. Xinfeng Li, Yihang Li, and Ruizhi Liu, Hangzhou: Zhejiang wen yi chu ban she, 1986 (translation modified).

8 The poem appears as an inscription in *Wandering*. Translation taken from Lu Xun, *Lu Hsun: Complete Poems*, trans. David Y. Ch'en, Tempe: Center for Asian Studies, Arizona State University, 1988: 31.

9 "The Story of Ah Q." The quotation comes from a poem by An-shih Wang, "New Year's Day," in *One Hundred and One Chinese Poems*, trans. Shih Shun Liu, Hong Kong: Hong Kong University Press, 1967: 114.

10 Antonio Gramsci, *Selections from the Prison Notebooks*, ed. and trans. Quintin Hoare and Geoffrey Nowell Smith, London: Lawrence & Wishart, 1971: 495–6.

11 Lu Xun, "Thoughts on the League of Left-Wing Writers" (in Chinese), in *Lu Xun Quan Ji*, vol. 4: 236.

12 Gramsci, *Selections from the Prison Notebooks*: 817.

13 Translation taken from Laozi and Chuangzi, *Dao de jing ji Zhuangzi quan ji* ("The Complete *Book of the Way and Its Virtue* and *The Book of Zhuangzi*"), trans. James Legge, Taipei: Wen xing shu ju, 1963, book 21.

14 Lu Xun, "On the Behavior and Writing of Writers of the Wei and Jin Periods and Their Relationship with Drugs and Alcohol" (in Chinese), in *Lu Xun Quan Ji*, vol. 3: 501–29, esp. 513–15, 516.

Acknowledgments

The "Preface to the Chinese Edition" was translated by Audrea Lim.

Chapter 1, "Depoliticized Politics, from East to West," appeared in *New Left Review* 41, September–October 2006 and was translated by Christopher Connery. The text was published in a fuller version as "Depoliticized Politics, Multiple Components of Hegemony and the Eclipse of the Sixties" in *Inter-Asia Cultural Studies*, vol. 7, no. 4, a special issue on the Asian Sixties edited by Christopher Connery.

Chapter 2, "The Year 1989 and the Historical Roots of Neoliberalism in China," appeared in *positions*, vol. 12, no. 1, pp. 7–69. Copyright © 2004, Duke University Press. Used by permission of the publisher. Text translated by Rebecca E. Karl.

Chapter 3, "An Interview on Modernity: A Conversation with Ke Kaijun," was translated by Audrea Lim.

Chapter 4, "Rethinking *The Rise of Modern Chinese Thought*," was translated by Audrea Lim. The text was based upon a lecture given in Chinese at the Minzu University of China on September 28, 2006, entitled "Translating 'China' into 'Modernity.'"

Chapter 5, "Scientific Worldview, Culture Debates, and the Reclassification of Knowledge in Twentieth-Century China," originally appeared in *boundary 2*, vol. 35, no. 2, pp. 125–155. Copyright © 2008, Duke University Press. All rights reserved. Used by permission of the publisher. Text translated by Hongmei Yu.

Chapter 6, "Son of Jinsha River: In Memory of Xiao Liangzhong," was translated by Audrea Lim.

Index